ASIAN
ECONOMIC
SYSTEMS

ASIAN
ECONOMIC
SYSTEMS

STEVEN ROSEFIELDE
University of North Carolina at Chapel Hill, USA

World Scientific

NEW JERSEY · LONDON · SINGAPORE · BEIJING · SHANGHAI · HONG KONG · TAIPEI · CHENNAI

Published by

World Scientific Publishing Co. Pte. Ltd.

5 Toh Tuck Link, Singapore 596224

USA office: 27 Warren Street, Suite 401-402, Hackensack, NJ 07601

UK office: 57 Shelton Street, Covent Garden, London WC2H 9HE

British Library Cataloguing-in-Publication Data
A catalogue record for this book is available from the British Library.

ISBN 978-981-4425-38-4

In-house Editor: Zheng Danjun

Typeset by Stallion Press
Email: enquiries@stallionpress.com

Printed in Singapore by World Scientific Printers.

About the Author

 Steven Rosefielde is a Professor of Economics at the University of North Carolina, Chapel Hill and a co-director of the Japan Foundation's Center For Global Partnership project on Two Asias: The Emerging Postcrisis Divide. He received his Ph.D. in Economics from Harvard University, and is a member of the Russian Academy of Natural Sciences (RAEN). He has taught in Russia, China, Japan, and Thailand. Most recently, he published *Russia in the 21st Century: The Prodigal Superpower*, Cambridge University Press, 2005, *Masters of Illusion*, Cambridge University Press, 2007 (with Quinn Mills), *Russia Since 1980*, Cambridge University Press, 2008 (with Stefan Hedlund), *Rising Nations*, Amazon, 2009 (with Quinn Mills), *Red Holocaust*, Routledge, 2010, *Democracy and its Elected Enemies: American Political Culture and Economic Decline*, Cambridge University Press, 2013, and *Prevention and Crisis Management: Lessons for Asia from the 2008 Crisis*, World Scientific Publishing, 2012.

Preface

The origins of this Asian economic systems text can be traced to the mid 1970s when the author trained in Soviet economics and comparative economic systems began to wonder how Japan would fit into an economic universe that appeared divided between communist planning and capitalist markets. However, serious research on Japan and Asia was deferred until 1990 when I first traveled extensively in Japan and China. During the nineties I returned to Japan every year teaching and researching on various projects, mostly connected with Russo–Japanese relations.

Thereafter, I gradually expanded the scope of my knowledge by teaching and researching for extended periods of time in Japan, China, Taiwan, South Korea, Thailand, Myanmar, Cambodia, Laos, and Sri Lanka, and deepened my grasp of the integrated region as co-director of a Japan Foundation funded project on the global economic crisis's impact on Asia.

I studied conventional applied micro, macro, financial, development and regional trade issues, but also made a considerable effort to understand the cultures of Japan, China, South Korea, and Southeast Asia, which ultimately led me back to my original point of departure, interpreting the Asian moment from a coherent systems perspective.

The task proved difficult because Asia could not be narrowly forced into established systems frameworks centered on market and plans, and the factors that made Asia distinctive involved humanistic and religious issues that largely fall beyond the purview of neoclassical economic theory. However, eventually synthesis was achieved by remembering that the autonomous, individualist premise of neoclassical theory is not the only viable approach to rational utility seeking. Self-seeking outcomes are not always best from humanistic, cultural and social perspectives, despite the positive influence of Adam Smith's invisible hand, and consequently Asia's economic systems could be modeled as potentially viable alternatives to democratic free enterprise that sacrifice some aspects of competitive individual utility maximizing for other benefits.

The result presented in this text is a set of five Asian alternatives to the neoclassical paradigm that crystallize Asia's distinctive potentials and serve as a framework for interpreting a vast array of applied economic issues.

No attempt is made to definitively judge these system's comparative merit, or future possibilities either on free standing, or supranational, regional or World Governmental bases. Further, readers are encouraged to make their own normative judgments.

Acknowledgments

Asian Economic Systems is a complex reflection of diverse lifetime professional interests. My teachers: Alec Nove, Leonard Shapiro, Abram Bergson, Alexander Gerschenkron, Wassily Leontief, Evsei Domar, Simon Kuznets, and Kenneth Arrow shaped my early attitudes. Their influence was enhanced over the decades by Emil Ershov, Vitaly Shlykov, Jan Rylander, Quinn Mills, Bruno Dallago, Robert Levy and many others. The collapse of the Soviet Union, and the abandonment of command communism everywhere (except North Korea) deepened my understanding and led me to abandon the neoclassical individualist notion that ideal governments everywhere should and could be consumer sovereign, maximizing individual welfare either through perfect markets or perfect planning.

Robert Levy, George Kleiner, Stefan Hedlund, Yoji Koyama, Masumi Hakogi and Ken Morita sensitized me to the importance of culture and neoinstitutional economics. Their insights helped crystallize my experiences in Japan, China, South Korea, Thailand, Cambodia, Laos, and Myanmar during the past 25 years. Innumerable scholars contributed to my understanding of Japan, China, and Thailand including Masaaki Kuboniwa, Haruki Niwa, Yasushi Toda, Martin Bronfenbrenner, Kumiko Haba, Philippe Debroux, Edith Terry, Dwight Perkins, Jonathan Leightner, Teerana Bhongmakapat, Kaemthong Indaratna, and Peter Pham. Mark Peterson tutored me on South Korea. Richard Shek illuminated Confucianism.

Various Asian institutions facilitated the development of this text by hosting my research including: Ryukoku University (1992–1993), Hiroshima University (1994), Australian National Univerity (1994),

Hitotsubashi University (1997, 2008–2012), John Hopkins Nanjing Center (2003), UNC Study Abroad/Xiamen University (2006), Chulalongkorn University (2007–2012), Kyoto University (2008–2012). This and other pertinent research were funded by Fulbright Foundation (Japan Today Program 1992), Abe Foundation (Japan 1993), Japan Foundation for the Promotion of Science (1994), Social Science Research Council 1994), Australian National University Peace Institute and the Institute for Economies in Transition (1994), Japanese Ministry of Foreign Affairs and Monbusho (1997), International Arts and Humanities Center (2000), Grier Woods Presbyterian China Initiative (2006), K.I. Asia (Indochina 2007), UNC Asian Studies Southeast Asia course development grant (2009), Center for Global Partnership, Japan Foundation (2009), Center for Global Partnership, Japan Foundation 2010–2012), and the Korean Studies division of the Korean Society, especially Vice President Jong Jin Choi.

Zhou Huan acquired the data and processed all the tables and figures for Chapter 4 (together with Zhou Teresa), and Yu Tianying provided similar assistance for the Hong Kong and Singapore section of Chapter 7, the graphics in Chapter 1, and insightfully commented on other parts of the text. Olga Belskaya compiled the bibliography.

Nancy Kocher graciously typed the text and seemingly endless revisions. My wife, Susan was an invaluable support.
All deserve immense credit and my profound gratitude.

Contents

Instructional Guidance

This text has been classroom tested for a decade. The volume is structured to alert students from the outset to the fact that the economic behavior and potential of Asia cannot be adequately grasped without an appreciation of the region's systemic diversity. This is accomplished in Chapters 2 and 3. Instructors can then directly proceed to the core systems chapters clustered by countries and groups, weaving the theoretical foundations (Chapter 1) into the narrative. The statistical material assembled in Chapter 4 can be handled the same way. After the students have mastered these basics, they will be fully prepared to enter into an informed and lively debate on Asia's future.

The text is designed to be fully self-contained. However, if instructors have expertise on neighboring countries like India, they can easily incorporate an additional section using the basic systems framework elaborated in Chapter 1. Also, some may desire to exclude North Korea, but I suggest retaining it because the hermit kingdom provides a convenient way to inform students about Asian Communism before Deng Xiaoping, and allows instructors to help students appreciate why economic systems matter by contrasting North Korea's and South Korea's disparate economic performance.

The course can be taught in two alternative ways. First, instructors can focus on helping students to understand how deeply felt and laudable cultural goals (or isms) cause regional economic behavior to deviate from the neoclassical ideal. The emphasis here is on inculcating students with an appreciation of Asian cultural priorities and their economic consequences. Second, instructors can concentrate on formal theoretical aspects of Asian systems by using analytic geometry to show precisely how cultural or ideological factors impair Pareto efficiency. The basic subject matter is the same in both approaches, but instructors should note that stressing one approach necessarily crowds out the other.

The exercises at the end of each systems chapter provide a third option. Instructors can focus on the cultural and ideological issues in class, and assign students to drill themselves on the micro theory at home using analytic geometry.

Figures and Tables

Introduction

The Asian Moment

Asia today is center stage in the debate over the new global order.[1] During the last two decades both East Asia and South Asia significantly closed the per capita income gap with the west. Living standards in Singapore and Hong Kong now exceed the American standard,[2] and many forecast continued catch up that could culminate in Asia becoming the world's economic, political and military leader.

The drama, supported by a vast literature on country specific economic development captures headlines, but analyses tend to be incomplete and one-sidedly focused on power.[3] They are incomplete because relatively little attention is paid to the special characteristics of Asian economic systems other than sporadic applause for state management (the Beijing Consensus).[4] The literature mostly lauds liberalization as a device for transitioning to free enterprise (the Washington Consensus),[5] without considering whether there is any reason to believe that Asian

---

[1] see Tselichtchev (2012) and Mahbubani (2008).

[2] CIA Factbook, 2012. The living standard of indigenous Singaporeans however is far below America's. See Chapter 7.

[3] World Bank (2012).

[4] see Ramo (2004), Huang (2011). "Based on a careful analysis of data going beyond GDP performance, this essay shows that when measured by factors that directly track the living standards of the average Chinese person, China has performed the best when it pursued liberalizing, market-oriented economic reforms, as well as conducted modest political reform, and moved away from statist policies." (see Williamson, 2012; Yang, 2010; Breslin, 2011; Breslin, 2011; McNally, 2008; Paus *et al.*, 2009).

[5] see Williamson (1993).

1

systems might be intrinsically superior to western democratic market competition.

The analyses are one-sided because they treat global power in its various aspects as the *summum bonum* (highest good) rather than considering other plausible alternatives like wellbeing, fulfillment and contentment. It is easy to understand why many find it useful to equate power with bountiful and serene existences, but scholars concerned with the good society always have known that there is more to virtuous societies than money, politics, and military might.

This text offers a humanistic alternative that encompasses conventional concerns for economic, political and military power as elements in a larger process of fashioning economic systems that provide nations with high levels of material wellbeing together with psychological and spiritual fulfillment. Affluence does not necessarily make people happy, and happiness does not necessarily make them rich. Good economic systems do both, and superior ones strike the optimal balance.

Neoclassical theorists have long taken it for granted that the best economic system in all regards is an inclusive individual utility-seeking model where competitive markets supply private wants, and democratic governments satisfy the people's public needs (democratic free enterprise). The fundamental premise in both the private and public sectors is that individual preferences take precedence over the claims of groups seeking to impose their demands on others, subject to constitutionally mandated minority protections (the inclusive democratic competitive standard).[6]

This premise although appealing has been vigorously contested for more than two centuries on humanistic, cultural and social grounds. Secular thinkers of diverse persuasions argue that individual utility-seeking often is harmful to others, communities, societies and the nation, and must be restricted for the greater good. Some contend that it makes people mercenary and shallow, and religious authorities for millennia have gone a step further insisting that divine commandments supersede both individual and group desires.

---

[6]This model does not require markets because it has been shown that perfect planning in principle can simulate competitive outcomes. After the collapse of the Soviet Union the consensus view is that markets are really best (see Dorfman *et al.*, 1958; Rosefielde and Pfouts, 1988).

During the 19th century and most of the 20th century socialists descried individualism and applauded social and communitarian consciousness. Their normative premises were not any sounder than the individualist alternative, but the controversy makes it clear in accordance with neoclassical welfare theory that assessments of comparative merit cannot be disposed of solely on positive grounds (productivity and distributive efficiency) (See Chapter 1). Values are just as important, and therefore there is nothing inherently irrational in the decision of any nation to choose a secular communitarian, or divinely inspired economic system over the inclusive universal competitive ideal. The preponderance of the literature on globalism steadfastly affirms that the Washington Consensus is best, but few analysts seriously consider the humanist, cultural and ideological dimensions from a rigorous welfare theoretic perspective.

The analytic foundations for dispassionate modeling and appraisal were elaborated by Abram Bergson, Paul Samuelson and Kenneth Arrow between 1938 and 1951.[7] They were expanded thereafter to the (1) welfare state, (2) self-regulating, egalitarian labor managed economies, (3) Japan's economy of trust, and (4) socially just economic systems by leading theoreticians including James Meade, Evsei Domar, Masahiko Aoki, and Amartyr Sen.[8]

This text continues the tradition, applying the accumulated experience to model and evaluate the performance potentials of East and Southeast Asia's economic systems. This requires grouping Asia's economies into a few categories governed by common "sovereigns" (isms) rather than treating each country's economy as unique. For example, systems theorists in Joseph Schumpeter's era divided economies into two categories: capitalism and socialism.[9] In this scheme "capitalists" and "socialists" are the "sovereigns" (isms) and markets and planning their signature institutions. Bergson altered the terminology dubbing "capitalists" as "consumers" (consumers' sovereignty) and "socialists" as "systems directors" (planners' sovereignty) implying that it was the demands of consumers

---

[7] see Bergson, (1954); Bergson (1966); Bergson (1967); Samuelson (1977); Samuelson (1966); Arrow (1981); Bergson (1976); Arrow (1963).
[8] see Meade (1978), Sen (1977), Domar (1966), Rosefielde and Pfouts (1986).
[9] see Schumpeter (1942).

in market economies, and systems directors in planned economies that governed supply. Consumers and planners were in command in market and planned economies.

This emphasis on sovereignty (isms) proved to be robust. Toward the end of the Soviet age, planning's merit was called into question and there was a resurgence of interest in market socialism.[10] Planning was no longer synonymous with socialism (or communism), but sovereignty had not changed. Communist Party systems directors in the Soviet Union and China circa 1990 were still the economic sovereigns despite the introduction of markets.

The same principle applies in contemporary Asia. Both North Korea and China are ruled by Communist Party systems directors, but Pyongyang's supply system is centrally planned, whereas Beijing relies primarily on the market. It is sovereignty (ism), not the supply mechanism (institutions) that is decisive.

This point is critical in Asia because many continue to anachronistically associate all markets with capitalism or in Bergson's sense with consumer sovereignty and democratic free enterprise. They believe that the market is more powerful than the Chinese, Vietnamese and Laotian communist parties, if not at the moment then soon. In the same way many take it for granted that Japan's, Taiwan's and Thailand's economic potentials are more or less the same because they all employ markets without pondering where economic sovereignty lies in these systems.

Close analysis reveals that it is not only erroneous to assume that all market systems are essentially the same, or in Andrei Schleifer's terminology "normal",[11] but the presumption prevents analysts from adequately grasping the positivist and humanist potentials of East and Southeast Asia's diverse economic systems.

Specifically, this volume will demonstrate that there are four rival market systems in contemporary Asia each with its own distinctive performance characteristics, potentials and humanist properties:[12] (1) communist

---

[10]There was considerable interest in market socialism during the 1930s (see Lange and Taylor, 1938; Bergson, 1967).

[11]see Shleifer (2005), Shleifer and Treisman (2004), Rosefielde (2005).

[12]see Rosefielde *et al.* (2012).

(China, Vietnam, Laos and Cambodia), (2) Confucian (Taiwan, Singapore, Hong Kong, and South Korea), (3) communal (Japan), and (4) Theravada Buddhist (Thailand). Their comparative merit is partly obscured by differences in stages of economic development, epochal, and conjunctural factors, but their special positive and negative attributes are unmistakable, and easily compared with North Korea's communist command system; the region's fifth core alternative to democratic free enterprise.

It will also become apparent that these systems cannot be merged into a pan-Asian entity like an ASEAN Union (counterpart of the European Union) without violating fundamental principles of one or more core Asian system. There can be federations, but not a pan-Asian Union that preserves basic mutually incompatible cultural values. This has deep implications for the larger debate over supranationality and globalization broached in Chapter 10.

The five core Asian systems investigated in the text are not comprehensive. There are other East and Southeast Asian nations like the Philippines and Myanmar that fall between the cracks and have been excluded from the volume. Likewise, Muslim Southeast Asia (Malaysia and Indonesia) and Hindu South Asia (India) have been omitted because they lie outside the Confucian, Buddhist, Taoist, Shinto and communalist shame cultural zone. Thus, the term Asia in this volume is used as a shorthand for the cultural region dominated historically by Confucian kinship networks, Japanese communalism and Theravada Buddhism, and more recently by Marxist–Leninist communism. It excludes the Middle East, Central Asia, the Himalayan states, South Asia, Islamic Southeast Asia, Indonesia, the Philippines, Russia and America's Asia Pacific possessions.

Contemporary Asia as will become apparent cannot be disconnected from the region's multi-millennial history. The text provides the requisite background where essential, but narratives are necessarily selective and incomplete. Likewise, there are many applied micro, macro and financial economic issues that are better treated in policy and development treatises. They too are only touched upon lightly to showcase systemic essentials.

The foundations of pure systems theory are elaborated in Chapter 1, and applied sequentially in chapters on the core communist, Confucian, communalist and Theravada Buddhist paradigms. The pure theory chapter provides a thorough review of the microeconomic and welfare theory needed for the Asian systems chapters. Reviews, questions and exercises at the end of each chapter offer readers and instructors the opportunity to crystallize their understanding by matching narratives with analytic geometry.

Most of the economic terms used in the volume are drawn from the standard neoclassical lexicon. They should be familiar, although there may be some exemptions. For example, Herbert Simon's concept of "satisficing" (incomplete utility maximizing caused by impulse or obligation to accommodate others) is commonplace in the professional literature, but seldom finds its way into undergraduate microeconomics.[13] A glossary therefore is provided to bridge this gap, and assist readers with esoteric acronyms. A brief biography of key historical figures also is included.

---

[13] see Simon (1956).

PART I

UNIVERSAL ECONOMY

Chapter 1

Economics and Economic Systems

Synopsis: Economics is a process of rational choice making. This makes it universal because people everywhere make rational choices. However, systems of rational choice making are not all alike. Neoclassical theorists tend to believe that one economic system, democratic free enterprise is best, and often suggest that it should be taken as the universal standard. They are probably right, if the criterion is maximizing the utility of autonomous individuals, but the merit of this criterion has been challenged by humanists for centuries and by religious thinkers from time immemorial. They have crafted rival constructs, often associated with distinct philosophies of economic governance, classified as "isms". The best known of these rivals is socialism, a system where "society" serves as the "sovereign" whose demand governs supplies in both the private and public sectors. Sovereignty in democratic free enterprise regimes by contrast rests with the majority of the people (the demos) rather than the ill-defined abstraction called "society". There are four core market systems (isms) in contemporary Asia, each with its own distinctive performance characteristics, potentials and humanist properties: (1) communist (China, Vietnam, Laos, and Cambodia), (2) Confucian (Taiwan, Singapore, Hong Kong, and South Korea), (3) communal (Japan), and (4) Theravada Buddhist (Thailand and Sri Lanka). North Korea's communist command system is the region's fifth alternative to democratic free enterprise. All systems are defined by their "sovereigns", that is, the primary source of demand governing national supply and distribution. The communist party guided by Marxist–Leninist ideology (culture) is the sovereign in China, Vietnam, Laos, Cambodia, and North Korea. Confucian kinship is sovereign in Taiwan, Singapore, Hong Kong, and South Korea. Communalism rules in Japan, and Theravada Buddhist religion (culture) in Thailand and Sri Lanka. All five Asian systems claim to be better than democratic free enterprise in some ways, and therefore in Asian eyes are legitimate rivals to the inclusive neoclassical paradigm.

Economic Behavior

Most people seek to better themselves through a process of rationally guided self-discovery, enlightenment, consumer choice, and investment.[1] They learn by means of trial and error how best to script their lives, what activities to undertake, and how to efficiently work, produce, market, consume, finance, and invest. If choices are rational, that is, if people conserve scarce resources, sell on favorable terms, and cost effectively purchase preferred goods, then their behavior is economic. Economic behavior may be imperfect. People may fail to cost minimize, profit maximize, optimally consume, and fully realize their human potential (wellbeing and fulfillment),[2] yet still improve their utility. Actions are economic if people merely undertake a rational utility search, but all people do not economize

---

[1]Humans do not need preprogrammed preferences to undertake utility enhancing searches. This is fortunate because no one is born with well formed preference sets, or the complete knowledge required for constructing them. Utility searching is more complicated than information retrieval (acquiring stored data) and accession (obtaining new intelligence). Shopping is only one aspect of the process. From the standpoint of artificial intelligence, learning understood as preference formation and adjustment is integral, beyond information retrieval and acquisition. It involves discovering anticipated and unexpected possibilities, exploring their emotional content through our sensory systems, reconciling them with prior emotional structures, and in many instances modifying values and attitudes. Rationality, defined as utility enhancing choice making, requires people not just to match prices and marginal utilities, but additionally to ceaselessly discover better states, and attitude adjust. These behaviors are only consistent with individual and collective equilibrium to a restricted extent because of the inherent ambiguity between "true" attitude adjustment and wishful thinking. Individual utility in economic theory is said to be maximized based on people's subjective assessment. They are required to be sober, but no consideration is given to the internal manipulation of psychological states. As a consequence, there exists no objective basis for faulting anyone's sunny temperament, or harmless daydreaming. People's proclivity (including public policymakers) for believing what they want, is a reflection of this deep indeterminism clouding economic science. Pervasive paradox, physical and metaphysical alike obfuscates matters further, lending support to those who prefer euphoria to dry-eyed utility maximization.

[2]Wellbeing and fulfillment involves a judgment about the composite effect of diverse utilitarian experiences.

to the same degree. Thorough profit and utility seekers will come close to realizing their potential; those who are less thorough because they prejudge prospects without adequate justification (satisficers) and therefore incompletely search utility possibilities will do less well.[3]

Economic behavior conceived in this way need not be moral. A devil that delights in torturing can maximize his utility by cost effectively harming others. While such behavior is repugnant, it is still economic as long as the devil torments sinners as effectively as he can.[4]

Economic behavior may be self-deceptive. A recovering alcoholic, who takes just one drink, may feel that she is making a sound decision at the moment of choice, but her judgment may be wishful thinking.

Behavior however cannot be economic when rationality is seriously impaired. Decisions made in the heat of passion (love or hate), under the influence of intoxicants or in a psychotic state cannot be expected to be utility improving, judged by the decision maker's own sober assessment.[5] Choices must be rationally calibrated given the information at hand (bounded rationality) by individuals in "normal" states of mind to qualify as economic.

---

[3] Incomplete utility (wellbeing) searching without evaluating the likely costs and benefits of additional exploration.

[4] It can be counter-argued that people are better off being good than bad and therefore that being bad is irrational (non-economic) because bad people knowingly chose inferior options. This counter-argument is sound, if one grants that virtuous conduct is intrinsically beneficial, but the claim is disputable and rejected by those who contend that if it feels good, it is good for you. The devil's behavior is rational and therefore economic, given the devil's own premises, but not the premises of those who reject sin.

[5] Economizing requires people to be conscious, mindful, and calculating. They must be aware that it could be beneficial to change activities, calibrate switching points, and monitor their feelings as decision time approaches. This cannot occur if people are unconscious of utilitarian alternatives, an insight that clarifies why passion, intoxicants, addictions and psycho-dramas preclude rational economic behavior. The same principle holds when people passively coast through life or shut down. Although, sometimes it is made to seem that people are perpetually economizing, their actions are mostly governed by subconscious (a-rational) forces. Also, some contend that people's personalities and personas are distinct, raising the possibility that utility enhancing choices are not consciously made by people's real selves (personalities), but by the requirements of the psychological masks they wear (personas).

Economic Systems[6]

Economic men and women, sinners and saints alike should advantageously exchange services, taking into account search and behavioral

---

[6]The field of comparative economic systems has been a magnet for scholars attracted by ideological claims about the merits of capitalism, fascism, socialism and communism. During much of the 19th and 20th centuries, laissez-faire advocates contended that socialism and communism were utopian follies, while socialists and communists insisted that capitalism was on its death bed. The dispute mesmerized the profession for almost a century.

The emergence of the Soviet Union, its empire and communist Asia reversed the polarity. Attention shifted from the theoretical potential of ideal systems to the assessments of comparative performance. This was accomplished in two steps. First, it was proven that both planned and market communism theoretically could maximize individual consumer welfare like their capitalist twins, while achieving additional benefits such as fair distributions of income, superior growth and permanent full employment. Therefore, and second, it was asserted that the only outstanding issue was the practical merit of capitalism, communism and socialism, judged in terms of conventional micro and macroeconomic indicators. The consensus until 1989, when the Soviet Union began to founder, was that socialist and communist economic systems performed surprisingly well. They were less micro-economically efficient than capitalist markets, but had compensating virtues, particularly full employment, stability and equitable income distributions. This was Abram Bergson's position, the leading western specialist on Soviet economics, qualified by the observation that communist economies seemed to be vulnerable to diminishing factor productivity growth.

Many liberals, socialists and communists painted an even brighter picture of Soviet, east European and Chinese economic performance, while Ludwig von Mises challenged both outlooks. He contended not only that planning was *chaos*, but that Stalin's and Mao's systems were designed to yoke people on the party's behalf rather than empowering them. Mises doubted the validity of communist statistics, but even if they were accurate, he and Fredrich von Hayek insisted they gave a false humanistic gloss to despotism. Comparative economic systems as they saw it was not about formalisms like plans and markets, or statistical indicators that swept everything important under the rug. What counted were the ways in which culture, institutions, ideology and political power shaped rational individual utility seeking, wellbeing, fulfillment, and contentment.

The Soviet Union's implosion and China's liberalization have relegated much of the older comparative economic systems literature obsolete, and/or absorbed it into a new field called transition economics, concerned with the euthanasia of planning, and the rapid adoption of competitive markets. Transition economics is ebbing because most former Soviet satellite states have acceded to the European Union.

adjustment costs. Theory teaches that this can be accomplished best through open, unfettered competition which makes individual consumers economically sovereign in accordance with their competitively acquired income and wealth. However, individuals, groups and cultures may reject open unfettered competition choosing instead to impose their will on others in the market place and through various forms of governance (including the mafia). If they succeed in exerting power and become predominant forces in the market and/or the state they can dethrone consumers making themselves the economy's principal "sovereigns" (isms).[7] Bad sovereigns who usurp the people's (consumers' power) rule solely in their own interests; their virtuous counterparts (Plato's philosopher kings),[8] govern for the people, or deserving elements of society.

Sovereigns of diverse persuasions can employ existing political and economic institutions, or modify them. If the system is a true democracy, then the sovereign is the people, and consumers rule.[9] If it is not, others are in control. Every system has its own sovereign(s) [dominant policymaker(s) /terms-setter(s)] who strives to preserve power and orchestrate the nation's utility seeking, behind an idealistic facade.

Economic systems can be divided broadly into two categories: coercive and voluntary. Coercive systems thwart self-discovery, enlightenment, free utility seeking and the empowerment of individuals, minorities, majorities and rivals. The coercers may be individuals (authoritarians), groups (classes, castes, parties, etc.), religions (theocracies), and even cultures (Confucianism, communalism, etc.)

Voluntary systems foster self-discovery, enlightenment, free utility seeking and the harmonious empowerment of individuals, minorities, majorities and rivals. This paradigm is epitomized by democracies committed to free enterprise and the protection of minority rights, but all democracies are not the same.[10] Social democracies like the European

---

[7] An "ism" here is a philosophy of economic governance as in capitalism, socialism, Confucianism, Buddhism, etc.

[8] The utopian republic of Kallipolis in Plato's narrative was ruled by philosopher kings. See Plato (1991).

[9] Rosefielde and Mills (2013).

[10] Rosefielde and Mills (2013).

Union infringe individual property rights in order to transfer wealth to social groups its sovereigns consider deserving.[11]

American democratic sovereigns are elected on the principle of restricted majority rule, where all minority rights are constitutionally protected. EU democracy also upholds the concept of electoral majority rule, but with exceedingly weak property rights protections enabling officials to transfer more of the nation's purchasing power from individual consumers to the state than in America.

Economic systems are heterogeneous, and the criteria for appraising them are correspondingly diverse. Systems analysis requires an open mind, and careful scrutiny of outcomes from internal and external perspectives to appreciate various economies' strengths and weaknesses.

This liberal approach is particularly important in Asia where all systems have some coercive aspects. North Korea's communist regime is the most despotic. Communist China, Laos, Vietnam and Cambodia are more permissive in the household and civic spheres, but remain politically repressive, while Japan, South Korea, Taiwan, and Thailand are maturing democracies with elements of market competition, and civil liberties. The restrictive dimension of Japan's, South Korea's, Taiwan's, and Thailand's systems judged from the standpoint of the American democratic free enterprise model mostly reflect consensus cultural values (isms) and are voluntary from this perspective. They are approved by the vast majority even though they violate individualist neoclassical textbook principles of economic efficiency and national welfare maximizing. The restrictive dimensions of China's, Laos's, Vietnam's and Cambodia's regimes by contrast are involuntary because they are imposed by their communist parties.

Modernization

The wealth of nations is not determined solely by systems. Endowments, the vicissitudes of time, war, taste, market size and scope generate windfall gains and losses that influence relative international prosperity.

---

[11]Coercive systems including theocracies can be transformed into voluntary ones if the oppressed gradually embrace their oppressors' values.

Wealth, income and power are continuously being reconfigured. The United States was a primitive wilderness in 1776, but a century later it had become affluent despite the civil war. For a time it seemed that America's standing in the global order might be surpassed by Soviet Russia, Nazi Germany and Japan. Perhaps someday it will be eclipsed by China and India, but the important point to appreciate is that nations which surge ahead create opportunities for those left behind, a phenomenon described in the literature as the advantage of relative economic backwardness. Laggards not only find themselves in a position to copy, and borrow advanced technologies, but businessmen in leading countries are lured by the prospect of huge profits to bring superior techniques to less developed nations. Low factor costs created by the low value-added characteristic of developing economies draw outsourcers and other direct foreign investors, transferring superior technologies to the poor at no or little recipient cost. The process may modify their cultures, but this is not necessary. Nations can modernize; adopting advanced technologies that narrow the gap between rich and poor countries without discarding their systems. During much of the catch up, inferior economic systems may shine, exhibiting impressive rates of sustained GDP growth despite embedded inefficiencies. However, the miracle seldom lasts. Japan once seemed to possess a superlative economic system, but when the advantages of relative economic backwardness vanished, the underlying shortcomings became apparent.[12]

Inclusive Systems

Economic systems provide citizens with private and public goods.[13] It is important therefore to avoid making a false dichotomy between government

---

[12]Rosefielde *et al.* (2012).

[13] The Paretian principles that apply in the competitive private sector cannot be fully employed in the public sector because states typically use administrative methods (requisitioning and rationing) to determine which public goods should be provided and who should receive them. Nonetheless, the spirit of the universal individual utility optimizing model can be invoked by requiring governments to only supply goods desired by the majority of the people, where the state sector has a clear cost advantage. This rule provides a bridge connecting individual utility maximizing in the market place with

administration and economics. The term "inclusive" emphasizes this unity. Democratic free enterprise system provides a familiar example. In true democracies public goods are supplied by elected officials in accordance with the individual preferences of the majority,[14] and private goods are supplied by competitive markets. The two mechanisms do not have to be homogeneous. Free enterprise in the private sector can be paired with authoritarian state provision of public goods.

Democratic Competitive Ideal

Neoclassical economic theory teaches that every individual can actualize his or her full human potential within limits imposed by bounded rationality,[15] under the rule of law, through market competition in the private sector and democratic governance in the public domain. The competitive and democratic assumptions exclude the possibility of monopolistic distortions and insider governance although this condition can be softened by invoking the concept of workable competition.[16] All individuals in the

---

individual utility maximizing accomplished through government agency (people's agent). The concept is compatible with principle of majority rule, and also with the Enlightenment democracy if minority constitutional rights are protected. This bridge illuminates why most theorists consider democracy to an inextricable aspect of complete individual utility maximizing.

[14]In Enlightenment democracies of the American type (henceforth referred to as true democracies where minority rights protections trump majority rule), majorities cannot tax and transfer sums in amounts that violate minority property rights. This restriction does not hold in electoral systems that govern solely on the basis of majority rule without minority protections. The distinction between majority rule and minority rights is fundamental, but also may be elusive in practice because the "social contract" that creates minority rights itself is subject to evolutionary change.

[15]The term bounded rationality limits the scope of rational action to individual's capacity to know, given reasoned expectations of the costs and benefits of further informal search and processing. The nuance is important for some purposes, but is not essential for the purposes of this text.

[16]The term workable competition implies a high, but imperfect degree of competition. Systems that are less than workably competitive can be described as anticompetitive. The concept covers both the private and public sectors (Rosefielde and Mills, 2013). Rulers craft economic systems to serve their purposes, constrained by culture and established institutions. They adorn their actions with noble concepts like free enterprise, democratic

perfectly competitive paradigm are assumed to have equal political, civil and business opportunity. They advance their wellbeing by utility seeking in the private sector, and availing themselves of democratic government services whenever the state is a least cost provider. The primary functions of democratic government are providing public services, administering the law, and regulating the economy as the majority desires, subject to various constitutional protections.

The characteristics of this best can be illustrated in the factor, production, distribution and income transfer spaces with standard geometry, assuming that utility seekers offer their labor to the point where the value of leisure and additional work at the margin are equal, and employers hire workers until the value of their marginal products equal the competitive wage. Employers profit maximize, given competitively determined product prices, and employees utility maximize, earning incomes and enjoying leisure given equilibrium wages. As a consequence, consumers are sovereign; that is, the supplies produced competitively maximize their utility.

---

socialism, communism and ummah to garner support, without unduly constraining themselves. All systems regardless of ideology are compatible with a wide range of policies across the political spectrum from radical to ultra conservative, as long as fundamentals are not infringed. Communist societies, whether market or planned, must suppress non-communist influences in pursuing party objectives. The corporatist organization of European Union societies can be employed for progressive or Nazi purposes. American free enterprise has accommodated both slavery and minority empowerment without violating its constitution.

As a consequence, although politics everywhere is important, culture and institutions play a more enduring role in determining how systems are organized. Even in extreme cases where communists have seized power and criminalized the market, prior regimes always have been autocratic and undeveloped with feeble market penetration. Communist ideology was less potent in determining the choice of directive methods than commonly supposed.

Culture as employed in this text therefore always means the written and unwritten rules that govern individual and collective utility seeking. If society is acculturated to providing equal opportunity, then politics will be correspondingly restrained. However, in most instances entrenched patterns of privilege and deference, codified formally and informally in institutions empower some at the expense of others. The patterns of privilege, including the mechanisms of enforcement determine each system's signature.

Most consumer goods are bought in retail outlets, where once again profit maximizing and utility maximizing govern product distribution to final buyers. If people are uncharitable, this constitutes the social welfare maximum otherwise, the analysis proceeds to the goods transfer space, where each individual decides how much of his or her income should be bestowed upon others.

Each phase of the competitive maximization process in the private sector is governed by a logic known as Pareto optimality,[17] where transactions continue until it is impossible to voluntarily improve one person's utility without diminishing the utility of another. The composite maximization is often described as Pareto ideal, or a Pareto general equilibrium, and applies to all business and civic activities. Public programs operate according to similar principles, but differ in important details because balloting provides officials with less information about people's preferences than direct face-to-face discussion and negotiation.

Pareto Efficiency

These concepts can be expressed graphically with the aid of analytic geometry. The exercise provides a useful benchmark for pinpointing, assessing and evaluating the inefficiencies of Asia's diverse systems. There are four spaces that require close consideration: factor, production, distribution and welfare.

Factor supply and allocation in the private sector are connected with production in the Edgeworth–Bowley box displayed in Fig. 1.1. The coordinate axes forming the sides of the box indicate voluntary equilibrium supplies of capital (k) and labor (l). The sides end where the derived utility in consumption of each factor is just equal to the foregone value of leisure. Their dimensions can change with the credit supply and workers attitudes toward leisure. Tightened credit and increased leisure reduce GDP, but this will be optimal if it maximizes utility even though it might superficially seem like a depression.

The box's interior contains all possible allocations of labor and capital in the production of the two goods (q_1) and (q_2) shown at the lower and upper

---

[17]Pareto (1906).

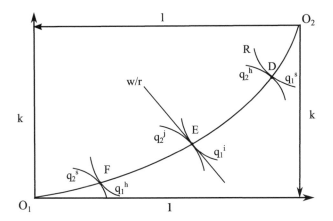

Figure 1.1. Pareto Factor Allocation.

intersection of coordinate axes (their origins). The space also contains two nested, convex, radial sets of isoquants (production functions: $q = F(k, 1)$), one for each good. These are the best technologies in the sense that they maximize profits and individual utilities. The value of the superscripts on every isoquant is the highest competitively attainable. The further any isoquant lies from its respective origin, the higher the output level designated by the isoquant superscripts.

If an economy is in a state of total utility maximizing equilibrium, there must be one corresponding point inside the Edgeworth–Bowley box. This point represents the utility optimizing supply assortment, and the maximum volumes consistent with it. If they did not, the utility maximizing process would be incomplete. The condition can be geometrically expressed as an isoquant double tangency (point E) because production at other points along either isoquant would mean that more of q_1 or q_2 could be generated without lowering the output of the other, again implying that optimization was incomplete. The price line at all double tangencies is the wage-rental ratio. The only factual equilibrium is at point E.

It is also possible to imagine a set of Pareto equilibria for alternative configurations of factor and product demand (caused by a change of individuals' taste). These entail minor adjustments of the sides of the Edgeworth–Bowley box (not shown), and correspond with other isoquant double tangencies. The set of all efficient factor supply, input allocation and production points, actual or counterfactual is called the contract curve, and represents a menu of actual and potential Pareto optimal outputs (GDPs). The locus is useful because it allows us to visualize the characteristics of inferior economies. Any point other than E along the contract curve like D or F, is inferior because the goods supplied do not maximize consumer utility. The outputs at D and F could be efficiently produced, if the actual demand patterns were different, but it is not. And of course, if the economy operated at point R, off the contract curve, it would be even more inferior because factor mis-allocation means that society could have done better by sliding down the isoquant to point D, increasing the production of one good, while holding the supply of the other fixed. All counterfactual outcomes on the contract curve are classified as technically efficient because even though consumers disprefer them, they could be counterfactually ideal. All other points in the Edgeworth–Bowley box are technically and economically inefficient because they fail to maximize utility and minimize system wide cost. E and only E is the true Pareto equilibrium.

These principles are depicted in an alternative way in the private sector production space (Fig. 1.2). The coordinate axes represent outputs q_1 and q_2 instead of the factors k and l, which have been suppressed. The space inside the coordinate axes contains the equilibrium production point

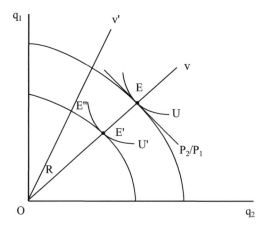

Figure 1.2. Pareto Production Possibilities.

E, and all counterfactual Pareto equilibria like D and F forming the contract curve in Fig. 1.1. This locus remapped in the production space (Fig. 1.2) is called the production possibility frontier (PPF), and like its Edgeworth–Bowley box twin serves as a Paretian supply ideal for two products jointly. As before, point E and only point E is a true Paretian equilibrium. Other points on the PPF are technically, but not economically efficient, and all points off the frontier are inefficient, although it can be said that points along the ray from the origin through E other than E, are right assortments in the wrong volumes, and economically efficient in an inferior technical sense.

The merit of any nation's economic performance is easily evaluated with this conceptual apparatus. Insofar as incomplete profit-seeking and authoritarian public programs supersede consumer and popular preferences, a country cannot operate at the Pareto ideal point E. Nor can it be technically efficient with respect to counterfactual individual demand for the same reasons. It necessarily operates below (E' or E"), on a constrained production feasibility frontier (PFF), due to the intrinsic deficiencies of its imperfectly competitive authoritarianism.

Distributional merit can also be illustrated geometrically with reference to the Pareto standard. The Edgeworth–Bowley box employed for this purpose, and displayed in Fig. 1.3 takes the equilibrium private sector outputs q_1 and q_2, (points E in Figs. 1.1 and 1.2), and arrays them unit by unit along the coordinate axes without regard to how they are distributed to income earning claimants A and B. The end points represent the total amount of each good available for distribution between individuals A and B in a two participant economy. Points at the southwest and northeast vertices, and in the box's interior represent feasible distributions of the goods between the parties, who are guided by their convex, nested ordinal indifference curves (iso-utility) radiating from the lower and upper origins. [$U_A = G(q_1, q_2)$; $U_B = H(q_1, q_2)$].

If an economy is in a state of total utility maximizing equilibrium, there must be one corresponding corner or inside point in the Edgeworth–Bowley distribution space. This point represents the utility optimizing retail allocation of the Pareto ideal output supply because otherwise the utility maximizing process would be incomplete. It is achieved through unfettered negotiation, given the wages and rents earned by claimants

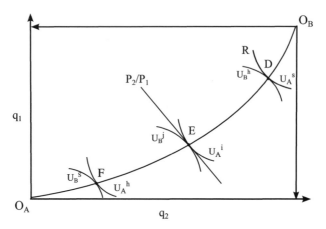

Figure 1.3. Pareto Retail Distribution.

A and B in Fig. 1.1. The condition is expressed geometrically as an indifference curve double tangency (point E) because distribution at any other point along either iso-utility curve would mean that one participant could attain greater utility without reducing the other's utility, given the equilibrium income distribution. The price line P_2/P_1 at the double tangency E is the only true price equilibrium.

Point E is the only Pareto efficient distribution in the Edgeworth–Bowley box, but if tastes were different (given the same retail supplies), or there were post-production tax-transfers altering the distribution of purchasing power, a locus of counterfactual Pareto ideal distributions would be generated represented by the contract curve in Fig. 1.3. Just as in the production case, contract curve points other than E can be viewed as technically efficient in the sense that the distribution would be ideal, if purchasing power were allocated in some alternative Pareto efficient way. Points off the contract curve however are always technically and economically inefficient because better outcomes are possible for one participant without reducing the utility of the other, given the prevailing after tax income distribution.

The distributional inefficiency of any retail sector is easily visualized with the aid of Fig. 1.3. Consumption cannot occur at E, or any other point on the contract curve if the underlying supply produced in Fig. 1.2 lies on a production feasibility frontier because technologies chosen are inferior, or factors are misallocated given the factual or counterfactual state of demand. And, even if the country operates on its production possibilities frontier, retail distribution can only be factually or counterfactually efficient if there were no barriers to competitive wholesale and retail shopping access. Wherever some individuals have preferential shopping access or, distribution networks are inefficient, social welfare cannot be optimal, even if the incomes shoppers earn precisely equal the values they add.

The Paretian standard is also helpful in evaluating the utility possibilities of economic systems. This is accomplished by mapping the Pareto ideal retail distribution point E in Fig. 1.3 into utilities in the utility space shown in Fig. 1.4. The coordinate axes array ordinal iso-utilities in increasing order from the origin, and points within the space identify the iso-utility level attained by each participant consuming his or her respective share of the retail distribution. The Pareto optimal utilities are those at point E, and can be complemented with a set of counterfactual utility optima derived variously by assuming different states of appreciation, or by redistributing equilibrium retail allotments. This set which takes account of compassionate welfare transfers is called the utility possibilities frontier (UPF) and can be compared with alternative utility feasibility frontiers (UFF) generated from points like E" in Fig. 1.2 and corresponding points like R in Fig. 1.3. A grand utility possibility frontier (GUPF) can also be computed that explores the impact of changes in the initial

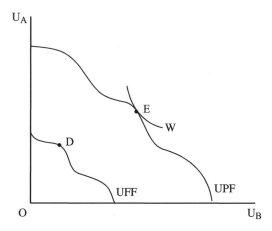

Figure 1.4. Pareto Utility Possibilities.

wealth distribution on factor allocation, production, distribution and redistribution.

It should be obvious that ordinal utility states in inefficient systems are inferior to the Paretian ideal in every instance because they under-produce, manufacture dispreferred items with inferior characteristics, fail to optimally distribute supplies in the retail sector, and cannot efficiently redistribute given authoritarian priorities, and prevailing institutions. Instead of generating Pareto ideal utility at E, non-Pareto systems only allow citizens to achieve the iso-utilities shown at D.

Although point E is indisputably superior to D as both participants perceive their utility, there are other factors to be considered in appraising merit. Altruism or envy (inter-dependent utilities) which violates Pareto assumptions, if taken into account could modify utilitarian outcomes and welfare judgments. This could be important for communalist societies like Japan, where utilities often are strongly inter-dependent. The complication can be expressed by redrawing the utility frontiers, or by constructing a separate welfare space where external observers evaluate the social merit of utilitarian outcomes given their own scale of values.[18] Alternatively, if analysts are solely interested in making judgments about the merit of inter-participant utility distributions, this can be illustrated with a nested set of Bergsonian social welfare contours shaped like community indifference curves, convex to the origin.[19] If the judge prefers the competitive outcome, then the Bergsonian W will be tangent at point E (see Appendix 1.1).[20]

---

[18] The value space can be a single vector, which assigns a scalar value to the Pareto optimal point E, and all counterfactual points along the utility possibilities frontier. The highest value of W will be best, even it is associated with a utility score other than E.

[19] Bergson (1938).

[20] The Bergsonian welfare score at point E is indicated by the superscript value placed on the welfare curve tangent at E. If the judge, disprefers E, then there will be another Bergsonian welfare contour with a higher superscript value tangent at some point E' along the utility possibilities frontier. Although the example given stresses the utility distribution, Bergsonian welfare functions can include much finer judgments including the moral worth of every individual's consumption bundle, as well as welfare interdependencies. Judges also are free to consider other counterfactuals such as wealth reallocations, and the spiritual environment.

This conclusion also can be extended to the public sector. Elected government officials in principle can use markets where appropriate, and simulate ideal Paretian outcomes with optimal quantitative methods. Kenneth Arrow however has shown that democratic provision of public services is intrinsically inefficient because elected officials cannot completely ascertain individual desires through majority rule balloting;[21] a deficiency compounded whenever governments distribute services with administrative methods instead of through competitive markets.

Inclusive democratic competitive outcomes thus are not necessarily superior. The Pareto standard is helpful, but seldom is the final word.[22]

Disequilibrium Adjustment Mechanism

Figures 1.1–1.4 illustrate the characteristics of general equilibria where market participants exhaustively optimize their utility in work, production, distribution, transfers and other pursuits. These results are attained through extensive, rational negotiations with other transactors influenced by prices (terms of exchange) and the requirements of profit maximization.

The search takes two basic forms depending on whether transactors negotiate the exchange of stocks (including inventories and labor), or the production of new manufactures. Both may involve profit seeking, but in the first case price adjustment is primary, and in the second output adjustment dominates.

The price negotiation processes is called the Walrasian excess demand, price adjustment mechanism in honor of Leon Walras (1834–1910), an eminent 19th century French general equilibrium theorist. It hypothesizes

---

[21]This is called the "Arrow Paradox". (Arrow, 1951; Bergson, 1938).

[22]There are a variety of practical indicators available for appraising systems merit, including Gini coefficients, the United Nation's Human Development Index, and Legatum index (see Gini, 1921; Kuan, 2004; United Nations, *The State of Human Development*, 2006; *The 2009 Legatum Prosperity Index: An Inquiry into Global Wealth and Wellbeing*). Nicolas Sarkozy created the Commission on the Measurement of Economic and Social Progress in 2008. The Commission issued an inaugural report September 14, 2009, with some useful aspects, diminished by thinly veiled advocacy of Sarkozy's political agenda (see Bate, 2009).

that if at any moment sellers perceive that their offer prices exceed buyers' willingness to pay (excess supply) leaving suppliers with excess inventories, they will respond by reducing their offer price. If the discount proves to be insufficient, they will continue cutting prices until their inventory holdings are optimal. Should they over-discount, they will swiftly discover that their inventories are too low. At this point, they will probe buyers' willingness to bid by raising prices, continuing to do so until supply and demand are equal.

The decision rules are simple. The market price (p) at any instant (t) is specified to be a function (F) of the difference between the quantity (q) demanded (d) and the quantity supplied (s).

$$dp/dt = F(q^d - q^s) \tag{1.1}$$

If $q^d > q^s$, then

$dp/dt > 0$; and prices will rise.

If $q^d < q^s$, then

$dp/dt < 0$; and prices will fall.

Both processes will continue until $dp/dt = 0$, which will be a stable equilibrium because the adjustment mechanism is symmetric. Both excess demand and excess supply are automatically reduced to zero through a competitive utility search.

Figure 1.5 provides a geometric version of the Walrasian process in the retail market. Price is arrayed on the ordinate, quantity along the abscissa. The demand curve is downward sloping in accordance with the principle of diminishing marginal utility. The supply curve slopes upward because the cost of stocking inventories increases with congestion. Consider the case where the retailer is overstocked at point A'. The corresponding offer price is p_1, which intersects the demand curve at A. Supply exceeds demand, which according to the Walrasian rule causes the retailer to discount to p_2. Excess supply here diminishes, but the process is not complete. Discounting continues to E, where demand and supply are equal. If the retailer overshoots the mark, and over-discounts, the Walrasian process will work in reverse, with prices rising until E is attained.

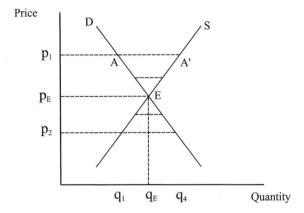

Figure 1.5. Walrasian Price Adjustment.

The Walrasian excess demand price adjustment mechanism causes capital and labor to be reallocated from R in Fig. 1.1 to D. The wage rate at R is too low compared with the rental rate on capital. This creates excess demand for labor, which raises the wage making it the same for both employers. D is a counterfactual, not a true competitive equilibrium so the process is incomplete, and will be modified further as profit seeking causes the first output activity to contract, and the second to expand.

The Walrasian excess demand price adjustment mechanism also applies in Fig. 1.3. Here bidding causes the price of good to rise, redistributing the assortment of retail supplies from R to D, which again is a counterfactual equilibrium point. Then the ability of individuals A and B to pay, given their budget constraints derived from earned income in Fig. 1.1, brings about the full equilibrium at E. There is no new production in the retail diagram. All goods sold were created at E in Fig. 1.2.

Clearly, Walrasian price adjustment has broad scope, but it does not govern production. Prices also may vary in determining optimal supplies, but the driving force in the competitive model is profit maximization. As before, transactors are ultimately striving to augment their utility, but do so indirectly by increasing income (profit) and wealth. This process is called the Marshallian excess price, quantity adjustment mechanism after the British economist Alfred Marshall (1840–1924). In the most general case, manufacturers are assumed to know the buyers' demand curve. This allows them to compare the demand price they face for every level of production with the firm's corresponding unit cost. The difference is the excess price, that is, unit profit computed as the difference between unit revenue and cost.

The firm's decision rule is elementary. The quantity supplied (q) at any instant (t) is specified to be a function (G) of the difference between the demand price (p^d) and the unit production cost (p^s).

$$dq/dt = G(p^d - p^s) \tag{1.2}$$

If $p^d > p^s$, then

$dq/dt > 0$, and firms will expand production.

If $p^d < p^s$, then

$dq/dt < 0$, and managers will curtail production.

Both process will continue until, $dq/dt = 0$, which will be a stable equilibrium because the adjustment mechanism is symmetric. Both excess quantities demanded, and excess quantities supplied are automatically reduced to zero through a competitive utility/profit maximization search.

Figure 1.6 provides a geometric version of the Marshallian process in manufacturing. Price is arrayed on the ordinate, quantity along the abscissa. The demand curve is downward sloping reflecting buyers' diminishing marginal utility. The supply curve slopes upward because the marginal physical productivity of inputs (valued at fixed prices) is an diminishing function of output. Consider the case where the firm discovers that for the achieved production level q_1, the demand price p_1 at A exceeds the supply price (marginal cost) p_2 at A'. The vertical difference means that the firm makes a unit profit, and according to the Marshallian rule expands production to q_2. A recalculation of the demand price and supply cost reveals that unit profit remains positive, and the search proceeds to q_E, where unit revenue (price) exactly equals unit supply cost. If the manager overshoots the mark, expanding production beyond E, the Marshallian process will work in reverse. The firm will discover that it is losing money on the production of each unit beyond q_E, and will return to E.

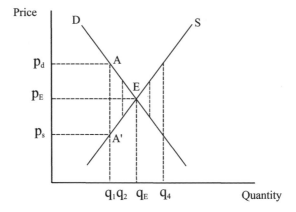

Figure 1.6. Marshallian Production Adjustment.

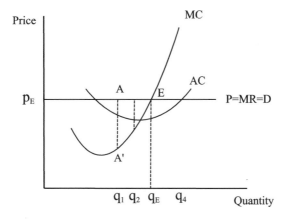

Figure 1.7. Profit Maximizing.

The soundness of the Marshallian principle can be confirmed with the conventional geometry of profit maximization illustrated in Fig. 1.7. The variables on the ordinate and abscissa are the same, but the downward sloping demand curve has been replaced with an infinitely elastic marginal revenue curve in accordance with the perfectly competitive assumption that small firms cannot influence market prices. A marginal cost curve substitutes for the Marshallian supply curve, and an average variable cost curve is added for completeness. Suppose as before that at q_1, marginal revenue (A) exceeds marginal cost (A'). The difference between MR and MC is a unit profit that will encourage the firm to expand q_2. Once again, unit profit is positive, and the manager will continue probing until equilibrium (profit maximization) is achieved at E. If there is a miscalculation, and the enterprise expands output to q_4, a loss will be incurred, prompting a return to E. The Marshallian principle and profit maximization thus come to the same thing, yielding the familiar conclusion that profit seeking governs managerial action in competitive economies.

Specifically, the Marshallian excess price, quantity adjustment mechanism causes both firms in Fig. 1.1 to produce the optimal assortment and volumes of their respective goods. If, for example, the economy were operating at the counterfactual optimum D, profit seeking would cause firm 1 to expand, and firm 2 to contract production until the true equilibrium was achieved at E. Likewise, in Fig. 1.2, firms operating on production feasibility frontiers will be driven to expand output along any vector until they reach the production possibility frontier, and then will be guided to E by a combination of Walrasian and Marshallian processes.

The invisible hand is the combination of both automatic adjustment mechanisms, or equilibration can be thought of as a two handed process, one Walrasian, the other Marshallian, often operating interactively.

The power of economic theory lies in its existence theorems which demonstrate the possibility of attaining E in all figures under planned, competitive and mixed regimes, and further in the efficacy of the invisible hand. It is often claimed that planning and mixed methods are as good as, or even better than the invisible hand, but this is false. Planning and administrative methods are informationally and computationally inferior.

It should also be observed that the core competitive model not only is capable of achieving a global utility maximizing equilibrium at any instant, but can be extended to encompass the future. The same logic invoked to demonstrate the existence and competitive feasibility of static general equilibrium can be applied to investment, technology choice and hence long term growth. The analysis reveals that the fastest growth rate is not necessarily best. As Irving Fisher (1867–1947) taught, investment is a device by which people can trade with the future. They do not simply invest. When people choose to save, they necessarily forego an equivalent amount of current consumption, in effect determining their preferred lifetime pattern of consumption. They can borrow to consume today, repaying out of future income, or can save to enjoy an augmented consumption stream. Either way, not only will a rational best economic outcome exist in the present, but in all futures too.

Paternalist Sovereignty

Many governments, both elected and self-appointed choose to disregard the will of the majority, and selectively infringe minority rights claiming to act paternalistically in the name of this or that social entity. Communist leaders for example, contend that they are duty bound to violate the democratic competitive standard in the interest of the working class, even if the proletariat is a minority. Other sovereigns adopt affirmative action programs for groups they contend are disadvantaged or particularly deserving. Systems of these kinds cannot be comprehensively efficient from a Paretian perspective, but they can employ automatic Walrasian and Marshallian equilibrium adjustment mechanisms subject to constraints imposed by privileging favorites. Those who share the rulers' paternalistic assessment may find these anti-democratic systems superior to democratic competitive alternatives,[23] but judgments are apt to be harsher if rulers are merely paying lip service to what they claim are paternalist ideals, serving themselves instead.

Authoritarian Sovereignty

The word authoritarian refers to a relationship where an entity subjugates others to its will. Authoritarians may be paternalistic, but they can also intentionally rule on their own behalf. Authoritarianism of both stripes overrides the people's wishes, and therefore is intrinsically anti-democratic. There are many kinds of authorities running the gamut from fathers, bosses, gurus to tyrants. Most are viewed negatively from a contemporary liberal

---

[23] Paternalist systems are anti-democratic because their preferences supersede the people's will.

viewpoint because they repress free individual choice in the market place and the provision of public services.

Authoritarians are inclined to compel subjects to do their bidding through edicts, commands, plan directives, mandates, requisitions and regulations. They usually prefer administrative controls to markets, and some scholars continue to believe that they are justified.[24]

Cultural Sovereignty

Some sovereigns are neither paternalists nor self-serving authoritarians. They are cultures or ideologies like socialism,[25] which consider individualist democratic competitive systems harmful to the wellbeing, fulfillment and contentment.[26] Both restrict market scope and democracy for what members deem the greater national good, trading efficiency for equity, social justice or enlightenment. They recognize that in limiting the scope of market competition and democratic public services, they necessarily diminish national productive and distributive potential from an individual point of view, but believe benefits outweigh the costs.[27]

---

[24]This preference is sometimes defended by advocates of planning who contend that optimal programming can be as efficient as market competition (see Dorfman *et al.*, 1958; Ramo, 2004; Huang, 2011; Williamson, 2012).

[25]This distinction however often becomes blurred because yesterday's ideology tends to become tomorrow's culture.

[26]The inclusive democratic competitive universal model permits individuals to choose their own concept of self-realization. They can be renaissance humanists or clods according to their temperament.

[27]It is easy to assume that an inter-temporally competitive equilibrium supplemented with a true democratic provision of public goods will maximize national welfare and provide people with a high, or even the highest quality of life. Quality of life however is like beauty. It is the eye of the beholder. The existence chosen by rational men and women at any moment in time will be a matter of taste, and anyone is free to deprecate the life style competitively and voluntarily chosen by others. Economics is a science of rational choice, not of taste, and cannot settle age old disputes about beauty, truth, justice and the good life. Careful analysis may provide a presumption that some types of systems broadly provide better life quality than others, but there will always be grounds for dissent.

Culturally sovereign systems and regimes operating on universal competitive principles are mutually exclusive to the extent that cultural and ideological systems sidestep or rig markets, and suppress popular control over public services.

Review

*People can better themselves through rationally guided self-discovery, enlightenment, investment and consumption.

*If their search for improved wellbeing is judicious, the process is economic.

*Economically rational men and women should cost minimize and profit maximize to generate income and wealth that allows them to maximize consumer utility.

*People may be inefficient, but their behavior will still be economic if utility searches are governed by rational choice-making.

*Not all utility enhancing/diminishing experiences are the result of economic behavior. People may rely on "animal cunning", or be driven by addiction, passion, dementia, or psychodrama.

*Sovereign is a term designating the person or persons whose demands govern supply. When consumers' preferences determine the characteristics, production and distribution of goods, they are sovereign. Other possibilities are autocratic, systems directors, planners, and various isms including Confucianism, Buddhism and socialism.

*Systems which violate popular sovereignty are unjust and inefficient from a democratic perspective, and often serve the narrow interests of the few.

*Different systems violate popular sovereignty in different degrees. Communist command economies ration, whereas monopolists merely impose unfavorable terms of exchange. Command forced substitution is harsher than monopoly terms of exchange.

*Some economic systems are coercive. Coercion is defined with respect to popular will. Democratically approved laws compel compliance, but are not coercive. They are just popular rules.

*Some economic systems are voluntary. They may be either electoral democracies, or alternative forms of popular rule, like communalism.

*Voluntarism is not an absolute standard of merit. The holocaust might have been approved in Nazi Germany, if Hitler had put the question on the ballot.

*All economic outcomes, even perfectly competitive ones are still subject to external worthiness tests.

*Systems reflect diverse values that are not reducible to western competitive norms. They must be judged on a case by case basis.

*All Asian economic systems have coercive aspects, but their restrictiveness and welfare consequences vary.

*Economic modernization and development are not one way streets.

*The success of some nations creates opportunities for others, and some successful systems are subject to decay.

*The factors that foster catch up by lagging nations are called the "advantages of backwardness".

*Modernization and westernization are not synonymous. Asian nations can borrow western technologies and practices without surrendering features that define their systems.

*Neoclassical theorists discovered that there exists an exact correspondence between perfectly planned and perfect market economies, raising hopes that socialism could be as good or better than laissez-faire, but the practice proved inferior.

*Perfect competition assures optimal outcomes in the factor, production, finance, distribution and transfer markets.

*Optimality requires that every transactor exploit his or her utility possibilities to the point where it is impossible to voluntarily improve one person's utility without diminishing the utility of another. This is called the Pareto ideal.

*Voters cannot control the micro-choices of their representatives with the same precision because agents have only a limited understanding of the popular will.

*Pareto efficient negotiation has been reformulated by economists as two disequilibrium adjustment mechanisms: the Walrasian excess price, and Marshallian excess quantity mechanism.

*The Pareto idea can be extended to cover transfers.

*Government programs, including tax transfers cannot be Pareto efficient, due to "Arrow's Paradox", but they can approximate the standard.

*The Pareto ideal can be illustrated in the factor-production space by employing a geometric tool called the Edgeworth–Bowley Box.

*The isoquants in the factor-production space represent best technologies.

*The set of all potential competitive equilibrium points is called the contract curve.

*Only equilibrium point E is based on prevailing preferences. The other points along the contract curve are counterfactual; that is, hypothetical assuming alternative preferences.

*The sum of each output point valued at corresponding equilibrium prices can be interpreted as the value of aggregate production, that is, GDP.

*All points other than E in the Edgeworth–Bowley box are points of disequilibrium, whether or not they are on the contract curve.

*All points along the contract curve are technically efficient. Only point E is both technically and economically efficient.

*E and only E is the true Pareto equilibrium.

*The contract curve can be remapped in the production space.

*The remapping clarifies the distinction between technical and economic efficiency, by showing how goods can be underproduced in the right assortment.

*Scitovsky community indifference curves can be utilized to gauge the social welfare content of all points other than the true equilibrium E.

*Authoritarian and paternalistic economies are economically and technically inefficient, lying beneath the production possibilities frontier, on a wrong ray from the origin. The same holds true for most culturally and ideologically governed systems.

*After goods are produced, they are sold in retail outlets. Distribution possibilities are geometrically illustrated in the Edgeworth–Bowley retail box. Product supplies and income distributions are fixed (people earn the value of their marginal products), but tastes are treated as variable.

*There is only one truly efficient point, a set of technically efficient, counterfactual equilibrium points reflecting alternative tastes, and a universe of technically and economically inefficient outcomes.

*The utilitarian impact of consumption can be illustrated in the utility possibilities space. The exercise assumes that individuals can rank utility states, without requiring that rankings be interpersonally consistent.

*The utility ranks at point E are set by the equilibrium distribution of retail goods. As before, there are many technically efficient counterfactual possibilities, and other inferior points.

*Bergsonian welfare functions cannot be reliably computed, but Gini coefficients, the United Nations Development Index and the Legatum Index provide some insight into economies' comparative merit.

*Adam Smith's invisible hand is the combination of both the Walrasian and Marshallian automatic adjustment mechanisms, or equilibration can be thought of as a two handed process, one Walrasian, the other Marshallian, often operating interactively.

*E and only E is factually Pareto efficient.

*Pareto optimality can be expanded to include the future through investment, growth and trading with the future.

Questions

1. Suppose someone is demented, but still cost minimizes, profit seeks, and utility maximizes. Explain why such behavior only seems economic, but is not.
2. Can immoral behavior be economic? Explain.
3. Why did Adam Smith argue that "true" economic behavior must be virtuous? Explain.
4. What is a summum bonum (See Aristotle, St. Augustine and Emanuel Kant)? Why is the concept essential for distinguishing worthwhile from profane economic processes? Explain.
5. Is the summum bonum necessary divine, or can it be given a secular interpretation?
6. Why does command economy forced substitution impair consumer wellbeing more than monopoly terms of trade? Ponder the problem, and explain.
7. How does forced substitution lead to the overstatement of value-added, and value-added growth? Explain.
8. How can an economic system be voluntary, if it substitutes communal consensus building for electoral balloting? Ponder and explain.
9. Why is the merit of diverse systems better judged from a multiculturalist than a single universal standard? Explain.
10. All Asian economic systems have coercive aspects, but differ in character and intensity. Why should this diversity be interesting to systems theorists?
11. What is the difference between modernization and westernization? Does the distinction matter?
12. What is Pareto optimality, and why does it ensure the achievement of the competitive market ideal?
13. Why does not the Pareto ideal apply to public programs? Does this make state programs intrinsically inferior? Explain.
14. What are the Walrasian and Marshallian adjustment mechanisms, and how are they related to Pareto optimality? Explain.
15. In what sense can Pareto efficient systems be considered universalist, and compatible with Kant's categorical imperative? Hint: The categorical

imperative stresses fairness, and equal opportunity for all participants. It is similar to the Christian golden rule.

16. What is Samuel Huntington's idea of the west, and how is it related to The Pareto standard?

17. Construct and explain the derivation of all Edgeworth–Bowley box elements in the factor production space.

18. What is the economic meaning of point E in the Edgeworth–Bowley factor-production box? How does it differ from other points along the contract curve?

19. Is it valid to interpret the sum of every enterprise's output valued at equilibrium prices as GDP? Explain.

20. Why is point E Pareto ideal?

21. Map the contract curve in the Edgeworth–Bowley factor-production space into a production possibilities frontier. Explain your mapping and the meaning of the production possibilities frontier.

22. How can an economy be technically inefficient, and still economically efficient in a limited sense? Illustrate in the production space.

23. Where do authoritarian economies lie in the production space, compared with the Pareto ideal? Illustrate and explain.

24. Construct the Edgeworth–Bowley retail space. Elaborate the meaning of all its components. Distinguish points that are technically efficient, from the rest. Explain why point E is the only true equilibrium.

25. Is point E Pareto optimal? Does it mean that supply and demand are equal?

26. If some individuals have privileged retail access, can the retail sector be in a competitive equilibrium? Explain.

27. Can the utility consequences of consumption be illustrated geometrically? Demonstrate how this can be done. Elaborate the nuances.

28. If individuals themselves, or through faithful state agents choose to transfer part of their equilibrium incomes to others (charity), can this be expressed by redefining E, and the rest of the points in the utility possibilities set?

29. Suppose that transfers are involuntary (forced substitution), how does this affect the Pareto interpretation?

30. Can external observers validly conclude that E is inferior? Hint: distinguish utility from wellbeing, fulfillment and contentment.

31. What is the difference between the Marshallian and Walrasian disequilibrium adjustment models? Do they apply to the same markets? If not, why not?
32. Illustrate and explain the operation of the Walrasian excess demand adjustment mechanism.
33. Illustrate and explain the operation of the Marshallian excess price adjustment mechanism.
34. How can investment, and the concept of trading with the future (choosing an optimal time profile of consumption) lead to a Pareto intertemporal ideal equilibrium? Explain.
35. Does the diversity of economic systems belie the universalist assumptions that make GDP seem to be a reliable measure of comparative social wellbeing? Explain.

Appendix 1.1 Bergsonian Social Welfare Functions

Abram Bergson demonstrated more than a half century ago that the virtue of any system can be calibrated with social welfare functions,[28] given the appraiser's scale of value. Algebraically,

$$W = F(U_1, U_2, U_3, U_n; x,y,z), \qquad (A1.1)$$

where

U_i = the utility of the ith individual derived from consumption and savings;

x, y, z = relational determinants of utility such as civil liberties and equality;

F = a value forming function aggregating individual utilities generated directly from consumption and indirectly from the relational variables.

The Bergsonian W can be a point estimate, or interpreted as a set of social welfare curves (iso-welfare), analogous to consumer iso-utility curves. They are illustrated in Fig. 1.4, and drawn convex to the origin. If the highest attainable iso-welfare curve is tangent at E, then the competitive outcome is best not only from the standpoint of underlying Pareto

---

[28] (see Bergson, 1938, pp. 310–334; Bergson, 1954; Bergson, 1976).

optimizing axioms, but in terms of the judge's norms. The relational variable (x) in Fig. 1.4 is the distribution of utilities between the two participants.

The judge's notion of the best however need not coincide with point E. The highest tangency can lie at any point E* along a utility possibilities frontier (UPF), derived from alternative retail distributions (including transfers) in Fig. 1.3. Moreover, once the game is begun, constants like the initial wealth distribution can be transformed into variables, generating new sets of utility possibilities (the envelop of which is a grand utility possibilities frontier), so that point E which once provisionally seemed best becomes quite inferior from the judge's point of view. For example, a welfare forming function F may assign a very low weight to men's utility. This will make point E in Fig. 1.4 immediately inferior (assuming one participant is male, the other female), and trigger a series of interactive adjustments of many complex kinds that in the end yield a solution where men receive a bare minimum, while women consume the rest. This can be illustrated in the utility possibility space as an E point close to the axis of the female participant, and above a level attainable merely by redistributing the Pareto retail supply of goods in Fig. 1.3.

Judges can compute Bergsonian Ws from ordinal or cardinal utility indicators. Cardinal measures are better because they yield exact interpersonally consistent magnitudes that can facilitate rational debate among rival judges. Alas, despite the probabilistic cardinal utility measurement techniques devised by John von Neumann and Oskar Morgenstern,[29] experience has shown that it is impossible to calculate credible Bergsonian Ws fixing a unique and supreme social welfare optimum. Women may justifiably feel that men deserve little, but they cannot prove it with utility calculus.

---

[29]Neumann and Morgenstern (2007).

PART II

ASIAN ECONOMY

Chapter 2

Contemporary Asia

Synopsis: The economies of contemporary Asia are dominated by three cultures ("isms"): Confucianism (Taiwan, South Korea, Singapore and Hong Kong), communalism (Japan), Theravada Buddhism (Thailand), and one ideology, communism (China, Vietnam, Laos, and Cambodia). All have evolved over the course of history, and continued to adapt to ever changing environments. The rapidity of Asian communist evolution is distinctive, but otherwise consistent with the broad pattern. Communism began in Maoist China as an Asian version of Stalin's coercive command planning, and then morphed in stages to reformist command planning in the late seventies, and market communism thereafter. North Korea has remained Stalinist, but the coercive aspect has gradually declined. For the sake of simplicity, it is convenient to think of Asia having three core cultural types (Confucian, communal, Theravada Buddhist), and one ideologically driven economic system with two important subtypes (North Korean command communism, and Chinese, Vietnamese, Laotian and Cambodian market communism/socialism).

The influence of Asian cultures on people's lives is pervasive. However, what counts from an economic standpoint is the diverse ways that Asian cultures compel people to modify neoclassical utility searching for diverse humanistic and social purposes. Satisficing, duty and forced substitution reduce neoclassical efficiency in pursuit of non-individualistic ends.

Yesterday's Asia

East and Southeast Asia share a common heritage of animist (Taoist, Shinto), Buddhist, Confucian and imperial influences. A little more than hundred years ago in the waning days of the Ching Dynasty, and just before Japan's annexation of Korea and Taiwan, Asia was ruled by absolutist emperors.[1] This imperial order was shattered by the collapse of Manchu rule in 1911. Sun Yatsen's erstwhile democratic revolution, which toppled China's emperor soon degenerated into Chiang Kaishek's Kuomintang party rule, complicated by civil war with Mao Tsetung's communist insurgents, muddied further by expanding Japanese colonial occupation in Manchuria and coastal China 1931–1945. Thailand was transformed into a democratic constitutional monarchy in 1932, but the popular sovereignty movement declined everywhere else as a result of Japanese repression at home and conquests abroad.

America's victory in the Pacific resuscitated and deepened Japan's fledgling Meiji and Taisho era democratic institutions. This momentarily raised hopes throughout the region, but they were dashed by North Korea's Stalinization, and Mao's victory. Suddenly East and Southeast Asia were mostly communist. North Korea, China, Vietnam, Cambodia and Laos became dictatorships. They criminalized private property, business and entrepreneurship, replacing them with command planning. Chiang, after retreating to Taiwan installed a Kuomintang dictatorship that was cloned in South Korea and Singapore, but private property, business and entrepreneurship remained legal.

Communist Asia's economic system began evolving in the late 1970s. Freehold private property remained prohibited, but leasehold property, business and entrepreneurship were gradually legalized. After a brief interlude occasioned by the Tiananmen Square massacre, China, Vietnam, Laos, and Cambodia resumed and then accelerated market reforms and business liberalization right up to the present. This was accompanied by some increase in civil liberties, but no genuine electoral democratization.

Taiwan's, South Korea's, and Singapore's relatively advanced markets were liberalized further and opened after 1970, and some significant

---

[1]Japan became a constitutional monarchy with limited male suffrage in 1889 (Meiji constitution).

progress was made toward democratization and civic empowerment. North Korea alone has made virtually no progress toward legalizing any form of private property, private business and entrepreneurship, fostering civil liberties, or tinkering with electoral democracy.

Today's Asia

The nations of contemporary East and Southeast Asia are all market economies, with the exception of North Korea. Japan, Taiwan, South Korea, and Thailand have imperfect electoral democracies that are capable of evolving into textbook democratic free enterprise systems with constitutionally guaranteed minority property and civil rights. Cambodia, Hong Kong, and Singapore are authoritarian regimes trending toward electoral democracy, and China, Vietnam, Laos, and North Korea are communist dictatorships.

No East or Southeast Asian country has fully westernized judged by the democratic free enterprise standard (inclusive democratic competitive norm) (see Chapter 1). All are governed by cultural and ideological sovereigns who determine the supply of public and/or private goods, and violate Paretian individualist efficiency norms.

There are three core cultures (isms) shaping Asian economic behavior (see Chapter 3):

1. Taiwanese, Hong Kong, Singaporean and South Korean Confucian kinship networks (Confucianism);
2. Japanese communalism;
3. Thai Theravada Buddhism.

Their systems are inclusive, governing both private and public sector economic behavior.

Ideology rules the region's other major system:

4. North Korean (command communism);
5. Chinese, Vietnamese, Laotian and Cambodian (market communism).

These regimes are inclusively authoritarian.

We will investigate later why Asia's various sovereigns behave as they do, and evaluate their options, but for the moment the key point to understand is that Asia's systems are not western in the democratic, individualist American and European sense.[2]

Tomorrow's Asia

Will Confucian kinship networks, communalism, Theravada Buddhism and communism continue to matter?[3] The answer to this question depends squarely on whether the systems directors and people in each East and Southeast Asian economic system judge net benefits to be equal or superior to those offered by democratic free enterprise, or more realistically, the west's prevailing second best systems. This judgment should take account of living standards, sustainable growth rates, income inequalities, empowerment, diversity, life styles, various humanistic factors, wellbeing, and contentment. The decision is Asia's, not the west's.

Nonetheless, no one should be surprised if some or all of Asia's contemporary economic systems fail to surpass the west in the long run at the west's own game. The inclusive democratic universal competitive standard maximizes the utility of autonomous individuals without making concessions to families, communities, religious mandates and systems directors' preferences. Accommodating Confucian kinship networks, community norms, religious imperatives and communist party directives necessarily impair individual wellbeing as individuals themselves perceive it, and for this reason Asian systems will always look inferior from an individualistic perspective.

---

[2]The contemporary west has a dominant persona. It is individualistic, self-reliant and democratic with liberal markets and civic societies that support minority empowerment (Huntington, 1996). Both America and the European Union claim that their systems maximize wellbeing, a term commonly used in philosophy to describe what is ultimately good for a person. It has become standard to distinguish hedonist, desire, and objective list theories of wellbeing. According to the view known as welfarism, wellbeing is the only value, a position Theravada Buddhists contest. (Griffin, 1986; Crisp, 2006; Haybron, 2008; Kraut, 2007; Nozick, 1974; Nussbaum and Sen, 1993).

[3](see Landes, 1999; Landes, 2000; North, 1990; North and Thomas, 1973; Gerschenkron, 1962).

The issue therefore for Asians is whether the gains from preserving their systems judged in terms of their own values outweigh the sacrifices in Paretian efficiency.

A good case can be made for questioning the sustainability of command and market communism. The Soviet Union voluntarily rejected both forms of communism in 1991.

Confucianism, Japanese communalism and Theravada Buddhism however seem durable. They have evolved and successfully adapted for more than two millennia, and there are no compelling reasons for supposing that their days are numbered.

Review

*Asia's diverse economic systems evolved rapidly after 1950.

*Contemporary Asia has three mature cultural (isms) economic systems: Confucianism, Japanese communalism, and Theravada Buddhism.

*All are inclusive market systems with some form of elected public governance.

*Contemporary Asia also features one ideological system expressed in two different forms: North Korean command communism and Chinese, Vietnamese, Laotian and Cambodian market communism.

*All of Asia's economic system are likely to evolve further. Changes in communist systems are apt to be the most drastic.

*Asian and western systems differ profoundly because the American and European systems are built to promote individualism, while Asian cultures and Marxist ideology seeks to subordinate individuals to familial, communitarian, religious and authoritarian priorities.

Chapter 3

Asian Economic Governance

Synopsis: Communism is a utopia where people live together harmoniously in a natural communal state of equality, sharing and mutual support, where every individual enables everyone else to fully actualize his and her potential without private property, markets, or state governance. No mechanism however exists that assures this pipedream, so that in practice communism has come to mean whatever political authorities say it means within a loose doctrinal framework. In China, Vietnam, Laos and Cambodia, communism arguably means achieving a harmonious, prosperous, egalitarian, and socially just society through the wise administration of the communist party coordinating markets and plans. North Korea prefers criminalizing private, property, business and entrepreneurship, substituting economic command planning for markets.

Confucianism is a set of family based ethical obligations and rituals intended to eradicate individualist discord, foster harmony and promote prosperity by assigning roles, tasks and duties jointly in the emperor's (leader's), nation's and family's interest. The doctrine has been widely criticized for straitjacketing individualism and encouraging insider corruption, but familial rigidities have been greatly relaxed in Taiwan, South Korea, Singapore and Hong Kong over the last few decades.

Communalism is a collective form of governance where group welfare supersedes individual self-seeking. It can take a multiplicity of institutional forms, but always entails placing duty before self-interest, substituting group for individual preferences, and acquiescent satisficing (incomplete utility maximizing caused by the obligation to accommodate

(Continued)

(Continued)

others). Communalism and neoclassical optimizing behavior are mutually exclusive approaches to creating ideal societies.

Theravada Buddhism is a world denying religious culture that views earthly desire as the cause of human suffering, and prescribes a meditative quest for enlightenment (nirvana) as the cure. It rejects neoclassical utility (wellbeing) seeking as at best a delusion and at worst, a snare, and encourages a harmonious, spontaneous interaction with nature and community (including enlightenment seeking) as a superior mode of existence. Some material pursuits are sanctioned, but only if they accord with the dharma (spiritual law). Thailand's king promotes a "sufficiency" economy as a righteous alternative to democratic free enterprise.

Four Sovereigns

Asia has four major economic governance systems. Each is defined by its "ism", that is by a philosophical, political, or religious doctrine prescribing the proper way to govern. Communism, Confucianism and Buddhism are formal doctrines. Communalism is an informal group governance process hardwired into Japan's shame culture.

Asian Communism

Asian communism in its contemporary forms is based on the doctrines of Karl Marx, Friedrich Engels, Vladimir Lenin, and Joseph Stalin. The governance scheme was imported after the Bolshevik revolution in 1917. It formed the backbone of insurrectionary groups that seized national power in China, North Korea, Vietnam, Laos and Cambodia after World War II. The command version of Asian communism clones Joseph Stalin's model. The market communist version also has deep western antecedents, but the market building process itself has been predominantly home grown.

Communist ideology is deceptively simple. Advocates portray communism as a system of governance that enables members individually and collectively to fully actualize their human potential without physical, emotional, material or societal impediment. Beauty, intelligence, sensitivity, creativity, status, and wealth afford no advantage. Ugliness, stupidity, callousness, inertness, baseness and indigence handicap no one, and everyone harmoniously adjusts his and her behavior for the greatest mutual benefit. There is no conflict, jealously, or greed. Everyone is compassionate and equal. Life is a perpetual delight.

Communism promises salvation from every affliction. It is both a beacon to the poor, hungry and oppressed, and those who consider privilege unjust. Adherents are not chastened by the implausibility of communism's fairytale, nor Marx's failure to explain how the criminalization of private property and business in a stateless society eradicates vice. Faith is maintained merely by reiterating the mantra of an exploitation free world, and taking seemingly appropriate measures like establishing a dictatorship of the proletariat (paternalist authoritarianism) (see Chapter 1), abolishing or restricting private property and markets, imposing an egalitarian distribution of income, and repressing enemies.

This was the "beacon and sword" approach taken in the early phase of communism by Friedrich Engels, Vladimir Lenin, Joseph Stalin, Mao Tsetung, and Kim Il-sung. It features one party rule, state ownership of the means of production, central planning, and the suppression of democratic and civic opposition. During its worst Asian phase (coercive command 1950–1985), communism relied extensively on lethal forced labor.[1]

Kim Jong-un continues the tradition in contemporary North Korea,[2] but communist practice after 1985 has changed profoundly throughout the rest of Asia. Although forced labor continues, lethal repression no longer is a significant part of the Chinese, Vietnamese, Cambodian and Laotian landscapes. One party dictatorships with suppressed civil liberties remain, but political rule has been liberalized, and leasing markets were introduced. Citizens in these countries can operate for-profit private businesses, hire labor, lease residences, and accumulate personal wealth.

---

[1] see Rosefielde (2010).

[2] Amnesty International (2011), "An estimated 200,000 people are detained in the network of camps, many for 'guilt-by-association' — for being related to a detainee. The majority of prisoners, including those 'guilty-by-association', are held in 'Total Control Zones' from which they will never be released. A significant proportion of those in camps do not even know what crimes they are accused of".

As a result, individual and community conduct are closer to in some, but more distant in other respects from the precepts elaborated in Marx's and Engels's *Communist Manifesto*. The role of the state has diminished and people are encouraged to be self-sufficient. These are pluses, but private property and markets have been partly restored causing renewed labor exploitation and resurgent inegalitarianism, both negatives from a Marxist point of view. Many therefore have concluded that capitalism has displaced communism in China, Vietnam, Cambodia and Laos in everything but name.

Perhaps, however the jury is still out. As earlier, communism is not a set of contradiction free doctrines. It is a vision of the sublime, coupled with a political commitment to expediently pursue the dream, and is vulnerable to a multitude of abuses. Advocates today are right to fret that the party is too permissive from a communist standpoint, but this can be easily rectified with taxes, transfers, and an array of disciplinary measures. For this reason, it is unwise to consider communism moribund until the ruling party repudiates state freehold ownership of the means of production and the ideal of egalitarian harmony.

Confucianism

Confucianism is a body of moral philosophy and a strategy for harmonious, self-regulating societal governance devised by Kong Fuzi (Confucius) 551–479 BC, elaborated in the Analects of Confucius, and the Five Classics.[3] His aphoristic teachings begin with the premise that good laws and fear of punishment are insufficient for achieving social harmony. People should be taught the wisdom of moral conduct, and devise good laws accordingly, buttressed by ritual that inculcates a self-disciplining sense of guilt. Veneration of sage emperors, reverence for ancestors, primacy of family, respect for elders (and husbands by wives), deference to superiors, and loyalty are stressed over individual self-seeking, competitiveness, and minority empowerment. This is accomplished through the study of ancient precepts, self-evidently virtuous maxims that provide proper rules of conduct subtlety

---

[3] see Confucius (2003) and Annping (2007). Some contend that Confucianism is a religion, that is, a belief in and worship of a supernatural force such as ancestor spirits. See Hiroshi Okazaki and Richard Shek, eds., Shukyo toshite no Jukyo [Confucianism as Religion], Tokyo: Kuyuko Shoin, 2011.

tailored to suit every situation. The best government combines Weberian functional efficiency and incorruptibility,[4] with familial compassion. It is meritocratic stressing moral worthiness, rather than nepotism.

The paradigm imposes a hierarchical, sage-authoritarian social order that requires members of every station to preserve their dignity by fulfilling their duties. Confucians claim that societies of properly schooled, ritually embedded, guilt fearing worthies will assure harmonious prosperity.

This vision is akin to Marx's secular utopia. Both Confucius and communists seek sublime harmony and claim to transform consciousness, but choose different instruments. Confucius prescribes virtuous precepts, ritual and guilt avoidance; Marx the abolition of private property and personal liberation. Confucius's Shangrila is socially stratified, but otherwise just, while Marx seeks justice by eliminating class distinctions and promoting communally conditioned, individual self-actualization. Both accept the need for protecting paradise from the forces of evil. Evolutionary change is permissible within the paradigm, but fundamentals are sacrosanct.

Both also beg the question. They claim to abolish human discord without providing plausible grounds for believing that their mechanisms will compel strict adherence to assigned scripts. The institutions created are not eyewash; they are just insufficient, which means that outcomes will diverge significantly from ideals. Confucians are supposed to be forthright, sincere, honest, benevolent and compassionate, but too often are devious, deceitful, corrupt, and malevolent. They are supposed to honor the "silver rule", a variant on the Christian "golden rule": "never impose on others what you would not choose for yourself" (Analects XV, 24), however, many do not.

Confucian systems are invariably stratified, but this is not enough to make the powerful beneficent. The paradigm is compatible with markets; nonetheless, transactions are seldom comprehensively competitive. Status based networks subordinate laissez faire competition to privilege-granting and

---

[4]see Weber (1947). Confucianism is governed by three principles: Li (ritual), yi (righteousness) and ren (appropriate relationships). There are five relationship: 1) Father to Son (Kindness in the father, and filial piety in the son), 2) Elder Brother to Younger Brother (gentility in the elder brother, and humility in the younger), 3) Husband to Wife (The husband should be benevolent, and the wife should listen), 4) Elder to Junior (There should be consideration among the elders and deference among the juniors), 5) Ruler to Subject (There should be benevolence among the rulers and loyalty among the subjects). Confucianism has two distinct aspects, one institutional tied to bloodlines, the other informal and adaptive.

privilege-seeking. Confucians rhetorically embrace general prosperity creating change, but usually resist any threat to their privileges. They also encourage meritocratic advancement; however, mobility threatens the social order.

Therefore, after all is said and done, Confucian systems tend to be static, promoting law and order, family, loyalty, deference, and harmony that primarily benefits those with high status. China's poor economic performance 1500–1950 *vis-à-vis* the European Union illustrated in Fig. 4.1 underscore the paralytic potential.

Confucianism, however, has adapted during the last two and a half millennia and may already have discovered a formula for sustainable superior economic performance judged by Taiwan's, Singapore's, Hong Kong's and South Korea's economic successes in the past few decades.

The evolution of Confucian doctrine illustrates its adaptivity. During the Song dynasty, Zhu Xi (1130–1200) blended Buddhist speculation about the soul, and Taoist cosmology with Mencius's (372–289 BCE) Confucianism to create Neo-Confucianism. Later, in the 20th century Xiong Shili (1885–1968) initiated the New-Confucian movement melding Confucianism with western concepts like rationalism and humanism, paving the way for practices compatible with American free enterprise and European social democracy. However, for the moment, despite many shared beliefs, Confucianism remains chary of democracy, civic empowerment, unfettered individualistic competition, and welfare state.

Finally, it should be noted that Confucianism thrives today on the mainland and in overseas Chinese and Korean communities even when families lack any awareness of Confucius or his writings. Confucian precepts have been assimilated into Chinese and Korean families and their extended kinship networks and treated as the only right way to behave and govern. The amnesia changes little. What is important for systems theory is that family and kinship guided by moral rules of conduct similar to those formulated by Confucius take precedence over autonomous individualism in determining the supply of public and private goods.

Communalism

The term communalism applies to cultures and culturally guided economic systems where group (community) preferences powerfully influence, or determine individual choice. This seemingly innocuous substitution of social for individual preferences violates individualist utilitarian axioms and degrades Paretian economic efficiency. In the western scheme, individuals are motivated by a desire to improve themselves, not to accede to the wishes of the group, or to work altruistically for the benefit of others, even though altruism is permissible. In the neoclassical model individuals are autonomous, and act without external guidance unless persons judge that the counsel of others is best for them. Group action is different, particularly in Japan's shame culture because members are conditioned to abandon their own preferences in deference to team consensus. Individuals in Japan reflexively defer to family, team, group, organization, community and national desires, sacrificing the opportunity to follow their own stars when their dreams conflict with communal consensus.

The utilitarian losses entailed by erstwhile autonomous individuals vary with circumstances. Individual utility seeking is seldom wholly independent. Many private desires must be negotiated and reconciled directly with other transactors and derivatively through democratic processes. Insofar as group consensus building serves as a surrogate for this accommodation, communalist and individualist economic systems may approximate one another. This is particularly true during times of crisis when everyone pulls together, but less so when the need for accommodation is slight. Communalists defer to the group, while individualists typically march to their own drummer.

This affects the scope of utility searching. Individuals survey their options before determining whether accommodation is in their best interest. Communalists, operate the other way round. They accommodate before completing their individual utility searches, arbitrarily foreclosing many potentially lucrative opportunities. The greater the divergence between the competitive and communal models, the larger the utility loss incurred by would be autonomous individuals.

Buddhism

Buddhism alone among the three core Asian indigenous cultures is a religion (Confucianism does not have gods and divinities).[5] The historical

---

[5] The classification of Confucianism as a philosophy is contestable. Some claim that Confucians believe in divine spirits.

Buddha like Jesus is both human and divine. Virtuous social behavior is determined by his teaching which emphasizes the futility of mundane existence and the merit of spiritual accomplishments. Communism and communalism by contrast are secular.

Buddhists appreciate harmony and prosperity like other Asians, but these goals are subsidiary. Believers' raison d'etre is either the attainment of nirvana (enlightened extinguishment of the self, and merger with the universal spirit), or heavenly salvation (Amida Buddhism), depending on sectarian affiliation. Enlightenment and nirvana are emphasized by Theravada Buddhism. It requires adepts to pierce the veil of worldly desire, shunning materialism and false spiritual pursuits. They seek minimal material sustenance to support their spiritual search, and are tolerant of those who desire creature comforts, but oppose Confucius's and Marx's visions as false utopias. From the Theravada Buddhist perspective the pursuit of secular Shangrilas is an illusion that not only causes grief (dystopia), but obstructs *satori* (enlightenment).

Tibetan Mahayana Buddhists hold similar views, however, other sects like Amida Buddhism (Nichiren, Jodo shu) assert that people can be guaranteed rebirth merely by declaring their faith ten times (Nam-myoho-renge-kyo/namu amida butsu), enabling them to focus on earthly pursuits until the last moment. They are encouraged to discover their Buddha nature throughout their lives, but this does not require asceticism (Chan, Zen), or preoccupation with mystical enlightenment (Shingon). Adherents of Soka Gakkai (also derived from Nichiren Amida Buddhism) go even further, claiming that the morally principled pursuit of affluence is part of Buddha's scheme.

Buddhism's influence on economic culture therefore is a matter of doctrine. The more world-denying the outlook, the smaller the space allotted to material activities and wealth building. Indochinese Theravada Buddhism is comparatively world-denying, while Buddhists elsewhere are more engaged in mundane pursuits.

The combination of an Indochinese world-denying culture and predominant Theravada Buddhist population creates favorable conditions for assessing the faith's influence on economic relations and performance. As in other societies, many Buddhist compartmentalize their lives. They profit maximize in business, and utility maximize in consumption during work and shopping hours, reserving some of their leisure for spiritual endeavors. However, an unusually large segment of Theravada Buddhists withdraw from the workplace, entering monasteries and begging, while labor intensity elsewhere is visibly lax. The rhythm of Indochinese existence is half speed, and although people prefer to be rich than poor, most content themselves with little. Indeed, Thailand's king officially promotes a "sufficiency" economy where people are encouraged to live modestly in harmony with nature, rather than emulate western acquisitiveness.

Review

*There are three indigenous Asian cultural doctrines: Confucianism, Japanese communalism, and Buddhism.

*Communism is a western import.

*Taoism (Shinto) and other forms of animism are also widespread, but their impact on contemporary economic life is minor.

*The four primary cultures restrict individual utility seeking through ritual, reason, guilt, shame, and fear.

*The idea of communism of all types (from Aristophanes to Marx) is a utopian vision of the sublime that stresses harmony and social justice.

*Communists cannot achieve all their goals because they are mutually contradictory.

*There are many communisms, each shaped by how leaders prioritize different communist goals.

*Two important communist variants are command economy and market communism.

*Command communism historically has been susceptible to terror methods, but need not be.

*Terror free command communism in China, Vietnam, Laos and Cambodia proved to be underproductive.

*Market communism has generated better material results, but despite Hu Jintao's vision of the harmonious society, is conspicuously unjust.

*To date, there are no democratic, civic empowering communist states.

*Confucianism is a moral philosophy designed to foster a harmoniously imperial, self-regulating social order.

*Confucians believe that people will only obey imperial writ, if they are morally indoctrinated to automatically do what sage emperors desire.

*Confucius's moral order is hierarchical.

*It has lofty intentions, but is easily co-opted to primarily benefit authorities.

*It is intrinsically anti-democratic and socially rigid, but the doctrine is being modified to accommodate western humanistic aspirations.

*Confucian systems tend to be static, promoting law and order, family, loyalty, deference, and a harmony that primarily benefits those with high status.

*Confucianism, in its Neo-Confucian and New Confucian guises has been gradually adapting to spiritual and western cultural challenges.

*Buddhism alone among the four core Asian cultures is a religion.

*There are many varieties of Buddhism, some compatible with material self-seeking (Soka Gakkai).

*Southeast Asian Buddhism however is world denying. It teaches that material desires are illusory, and that people's primary concern should be spiritual enlightenment, and ultimately the attainment of nirvana.

*Compared with Japan, the tigers, and China; Theravada Buddhists work at half-speed.

*Communalism places the group above individual self-interest.

*Communalism powerfully affects Japanese and Thai economic behavior.

*It substitutes collective for individual utility seeking.

*Group members are shamed into suppressing their own desires for goals established through communal consensus building.

*Communal societies do not search utility possiblities as thoroughly as western individualistically organized economies do.

*Communal economies promote acquiescent satisficing (incomplete utility maximizing caused by the obligation to accommodate others).

*Communal economies can perform exceptionally in times of collective danger, but sometimes lose their bearings when the best path forward is murky.

Questions

1. Individuals can and do negotiate "rules" as well the terms of economic transactions. Why might it make sense for communities (communism, Confucianism, Buddhism and communalism) to set rules, rather than allow "anarchy" (unconditional negotiation) do this for them?

2. What are the necessary and sufficient conditions for communists to simultaneously achieve prosperity, an egalitarian distribution of income and wealth, mutual support, the fulfillment of their human potential, and harmony? Are their inherent conflicts between prosperity and egalitarianism? Are there inherent contradictions between individual fulfillment and mutual support? For example, should contemporary women sacrifice their careers to assure their husbands comfort?

3. Suppose some communards desire private property? Should their freedom be repressed by the majority? Is repression the flipside of communism?

4. Why are so many people attracted to pipedreams like communist harmony when casual observation shows the persistence of sin and human discord?

5. Is one party democracy an oxymoron?

6. Is utopianism the enemy of personal freedom and civil liberty?

7. In what sense is market communism a second best from a communist viewpoint?

8. If communist utopianism is infeasible, requiring the abandonment of this or that principle, how shall we distinguish genuine from facsimile communism?

9. Can one persuasively argue that communism is what communist parties do? Explain.

10. Is communism an evolutionary phenomenon, or is it path dependent toward some dominant form?

11. What is the difference between a moral philopsophy and a religion?

12. How have some scholars tried to make Confucianism a religion?

13. Morality for Confucianism is doing the right thing (obeying the emperor's implicit and explicit will) to achieve the supreme good (sage emperor's view of right goals and conduct). Some scholars argue that Confucius was trying to influence imperial preferences, others that he was training people to be compliant imperial servants. What do you think was his true motivation? Does your father always know best? Should you obey him anyway?

14. People have been arguing about "true" morality from time immemorial without reaching a consensus. What does this imply about the merit and limitations of the Confucian approach to state governance and social harmony?

15. How are Confucianism and Marxist utopianism alike?

16. Is it fair to say that Confucianism espouses individual and familial self-discipline as the moral foundation of utopia, where as Marx believes that property-less societies will be harmonious no matter how individuals seek to actualize their full human potential (harmonism)? Is Confucius a tough love disciplinarian, and Marx, a let-it-all-hang-out libertarian romantic? Explain.

17. Is Confucian discipline more likely to promote or impede creativity and technological progress? Explain.

18. Why is Confucianism chary of democracy and civic empowerment?

19. Theravada Buddhism gives priority to the spirit, Enlightenment and nirvana. Does this leave any room for economics?

20. Can Theravada Buddhists enjoy higher wellbeing than westerners, even though they have lower per capita incomes? If the answer is yes, then which system is better? If the answer is Theravada Buddhist, does it follow that economic wellbeing and therefore economics is over-rated?

21. Is the importance that Theravada Buddhists place on spiritual matters analogous to western anti-materialist attitudes?
22. Is communalism merely about people living in communities, or does it have deep implications for individual choice making? Explain.
23. What are the benefits of collective decision making?
24. What are the costs of collective decision making?
25. Does communal decision making curtail societal desire for western style democracy and civil liberties? If so, what are the risks and rewards of each approach?
26. Can Asia become America if it preserves its diverse cultures?

Chapter 4

Asian Economic Performance 1500–2010

Synopsis: Living standards in Asia and west were broadly similar a millennium ago, and remained that way for 500 years before Asia swooned into a protracted decline. Asian per capita GDP fell relative to the EU benchmark for nearly 400 years, before Japan began closing the gap in the late 19th century. Taiwan and South Korea followed suit after being annexed to Japan, and then continued their advance independently after the Second World War. China, Vietnam, Laos and Cambodia joined the bandwagon in the eighties after shifting from command to market communism. Thailand also has progressed, but North Korea and perhaps Myanmar continue to languish. Once upon a time, Asia's ascent seemed unstoppable. Many confidently predicted that Japan and the tigers would overtake the west and just keep going. Similar claims are now being made for China and Vietnam, but should not be taken seriously until the sources of their purported institutional superiority are convincingly elaborated. Asian economic systems have virtues, but their cultures constrain competitive utility seeking, judged from the neoclassical perspective, rendering them underproductive and inefficient. Although this clouds Asia's prospects, it does not mean that Asian systems will underperform because the west violates its own efficiency principles, and Asians may legitimately prefer their own values.

Nobel Prize winner Gunnar Myrdal argued as late as 1968 that Asia not only was economically backward, but might remain permanently so unless it discovered an effective resource mobilization strategy.[1] It might seem to follow that Asian underdevelopment was endemic. Unless Asia westernized in a liberal or Marxist fashion, it always would be impoverished.

Myrdal's concern was widely shared, but misleading in two senses. Asia's economic performance was not always laggard, and modernization was not tantamount to complete westernization. Asian economic growth paced the global mean for the first 1,500 years of the Common Era, and although the east fell behind during the ensuing centuries, Japan began successfully modernizing almost immediately after being opened by Admiral Perry in 1853. Many Asian latecomers have followed suit, without abandoning their culture governed economic systems. They are modernizing without westernizing.

The historical record is clear on the growth issue. The data demonstrate that despite diverse cultural evolutions, economic performance in Asia and the west were similar up to the European commercial revolution. Table 4.1 shows that in the first year of the Christian era, 1AD, per capita GDP in Japan and China were close to the world norm, a position they maintained for the next one and a half millennia.

After the 15th century, the situation changed dramatically. Living standards in the United Kingdom, Western Europe (including the UK), and United States steadily grew to twice the Japanese and Chinese levels, spurred by systemic change engendered by rapidly expanding exploration, international commerce, the Renaissance, Reformation and Enlightenment. This disparity widened throughout the industrial revolution from 1820–1950, when American per capita GDP exceeded China's by a factor of twenty. During the postwar years 1950–1973, Japanese living standards miraculously surged to within hailing distance of the UK, and Western Europe, but China continued languishing, despite Mao's claims of rapid advance. It was this laggard performance, together with anemic growth in Korea and Indochina 1820–1950 that prompted Myrdal's misgivings about Asian economic prospects, despite Japan's accomplishments, and the successes of niche players like Singapore, Hong Kong, and Taiwan.

---

[1] see Myrdal (1968).

Table 4.1. Per Capita GDP Growth 1–2001AD (Annual Average Compound Growth Rates).

	1–1000	1000–1500	1500–1820	1820–1870	1870–1913	1913–1950	1950–1973	1973–2001
United Kingdom			0.8	2.05	1.9	1.19	2.93	2.08
Western Europe (including UK)		0.22	0.41	1.75	2.13	1.16	4.65	2.08
Former USSR	0.06		0.47	1.61	2.4	2.15	4.84	−0.42
United States			0.86	4.2	3.94	2.84	3.93	2.94
Japan	0.1	0.18	0.31	0.41	2.44	2.21	9.29	2.71
China	0	0.17	0.41	−0.37	0.56	−0.02	5.02	6.72
World	0.01	0.15	0.32	0.93	2.11	1.82	4.9	3.05

Source: Maddison (2003).
Note: Western Europe includes: Austria, Belgium, Denmark, Finland, France, Switzerland, Germany, Italy, Netherlands, Norway, Sweden and the United Kingdom.

Table 4.2.   Population Growth 1–2001AD.

	1–1000	1000–1500	1500–1820	1820–1870	1870–1913	1913–1950	1950–1973	1973–2001
United Kingdom			0.27	1.26	1.01	0.93	2.42	1.86
12 Country Average			0.14	1.04	1.33	0.84	3.92	1.8
Former USSR	0	0.04	0.1	0.63	1.06	1.76	3.35	–0.96
United States			0.36	1.34	1.82	1.61	2.45	1.86
Japan	0.01	0.03	0.09	0.19	1.48	0.88	8.06	2.14
China	0	0.06	0	–0.25	0.1	–0.62	2.86	1.4
World	0	0.05	0.05	0.54	1.3	0.88	2.92	1.41

Source: Maddison (2003).

China should have done better. It was inventive and commercially vibrant at home and abroad.[2] It had ample opportunities to receive western technology through the silk route, and sea trade with India and the Middle East. It was dynastically stable, a great regional power, and had undergone its own maritime revolution in 1433, yet these advantages did not suffice. Nor can blame be laid at Malthus's door. Table 4.2 reveals that the British and EU populations grew more rapidly than the Chinese until 1950. Similar arguments hold for Korea and Southeast Asia. Were these national cultures fatally flawed despite their peoples' innate talents?

Perhaps, but the flaws were subsequently remedied as systems were reformed or replaced with superior alternatives. Although, communist national income statistics are suspect, there seems little reason to doubt that China made progress under Mao Tsetung 1950–1976, and that the entire Asian communist bloc (China, Vietnam, Cambodia, and Laos), with the exception of North Korea accelerated its advance after 1985, when these nations began embracing the market reforms that define their contemporary systems. The Stalinist command models providing the foundation for Chinese and Vietnamese growth before 1985 enabled them to temporarily overcome their lethargy, albeit at immense human cost,[3] and eventually transition to a more powerful system. Cambodia and Laos were latecomers to communism. North Korea is an unreformed Stalinist command system that performed well enough 1950–1991, and then collapsed after the Soviet Union disappeared echoing the post-communist former Soviet Republics 1991–2000. It has been depressed for more than two lost decades.

The performance of non-communist Asia during the postwar era has been more diverse, especially after 1985. The nationalist systems (South Korea, Taiwan, Hong Kong, Singapore), often called the tigers did well converging toward the global high frontier, but more recently are exhibiting signs of fatigue. Theravada Buddhist Thailand, with its constitutional monarchy

---

[2] China is famous for four major innovations: (1) papermaking: Cai Lun (AD 50–121); (2) printing: woodblock (circa 650) movable type: Shen Kuo (1031–1095) bookbinding: Song dynasty; (3) gunpowder: Five Dynasties and Ten Kingdoms period (907–960); (4) magnetic compass: Han Dynasty (circa first century AD). These contributions are only the tip of the iceberg.

[3] Rosefielde (2010).

Table 4.3. Communist Per Capita GDP Growth 1985–2001.

	1985–1990	1990–1995	1995–2001
China	4.1	7.4	5.1
Vietnam	2.2	6.2	4.8
Cambodia	−2.0	1.8	2.4
Laos	0.2	3.0	1.8
North Korea	0.0	−11.8	−4.5

Source: http://www.ggdc.net/maddison/Historical_Statistics/horizontal-file_03-2009xls. Statistics on World Population, GDP and Per Capita GDP 1–2006AD. (last update: March 2009, horizontal file; copyright Angus Maddison).

and open economy followed a similar trajectory, even though it was severely affected by the Asian financial crisis of 1997. Japanese experience also paralleled the Confucian nationalist systems, but its growth retardation was more pronounced converging toward stagnation. Like North Korea, its economic performance has been sluggish for more than two decades.

Thus, 40 years after Myrdal's alarm, it seems that his forebodings were mostly misplaced. China, Vietnam, South Korea, Taiwan, Singapore, Hong Kong, Thailand, and perhaps Laos and Cambodia have found disparate modernization paths that have allowed them to narrow the east–west living standard gap. North Korea, the lone command communist system, however continues to falter, and Japan is losing ground to the United States and Western Europe, raising the possibility that Asian catch up may never be permanently complete. Taiwan, South Korea and Singapore having reached high levels of development, likewise seem to be flirting with the Japanese disease. After the initial benefits of relative economic backwardness are exhausted, in a post-industrial epoch, perhaps other Asian nations will swoon into relative decline because their systems lack staying power. Those who believe that catch up is merely a matter of modernization, and that systems do not matter, harbor no doubts that Asia will match, or even surpass America, but careful sifting of the evidence does not support their optimism.

This is the new problematic. Contemporary Asian modernization is being driven by five distinctive paradigms: (1) communalism (Japan), (2) market communism (China, Vietnam, Laos, and Cambodia), (3) command communism (North Korea), (4) Confucian nationalism (South Korea, Hong Kong, Taiwan, Singapore), and (5) Theravada Buddhism (Thailand). All are more authoritarian than American democratic free enterprise and European social democracy, limiting individual, political and civic liberty. It seems likely that North Korean command communism is a dead-end. However, this leaves ample room for the other systems to prove their mettle, practically and judged from the standpoint of the inclusive (both public and private sectors) democratic competitive ideal. All may thrive or merely survive, but some are apt to outperform others over the next few decades, and some may even surpass a west stultified by over-regulation (Euroschlerosis).

These findings are further illuminated below. Figure 4.1 compares living standards in China with 12 West European nations 1500–2006,[4] using Western Europe as the benchmark indexed to 100. It reveals that Chinese per capita GDP was 80 percent of the EU norm a half millennium ago, gradually losing ground until 1820 when the divergence accelerated.

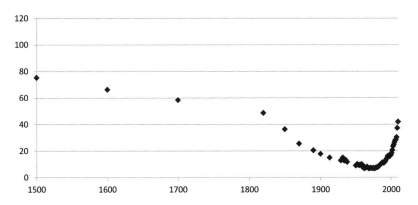

Figure 4.1. Chinese–EU Divergence and Convergence 1500–2010 Per Capita GDP (Western Europe = 100).

Source: Maddison (2003, pp. 558–563, 566). Available at http://www.ggdc.net/maddison/Historical_Statistics/horizontal-file_03-2009xls. Statistics on World Population, GDP and Per Capita GDP 1–2006AD. (last update: March 2009, horizontal file; copyright Angus Maddison). IMF GDP growth statistics 2008–2010.

---

[4] Austria, Belgium, Denmark, Finland, France, Switzerland, Germany, Italy, Netherlands, Norway, Sweden, and United Kingdom.

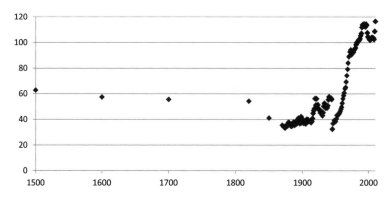

Figure 4.2. Japanese–EU Divergence and Convergence 1500–2010 Per Capita GDP (Western Europe = 100).

Source: Maddison (2003, pp. 558–563, 566). Available at http://www.ggdc.net/maddison/Historical_ Statistics/horizontal-file_03-2009xls. Statistics on World Population, GDP and Per Capita GDP 1–2006AD. (last update: March 2009, horizontal file; copyright Angus Maddison). IMF GDP growth statistics 2008–2010.

The disparity in 1950 just after Mao Tsetung seized power was more than tenfold, with China's per capita GDP just 9% of the West European level. The gap widened slightly thereafter to 7%, before a reversal started in 1977. After 477 years, China began a great ascent to 28 percent of the West European benchmark, a convergent trend that shows no sign of fading soon. Judging by the Japanese (Fig. 4.2), Taiwanese (Fig. 4.3), Singaporean (Fig. 4.4) and Hong Kong (Fig. 4.5) precedents, China could catch up completely with the Western Europe in a few decades, eliminating the east–west divide, or making allowance for the intrinsic inferiority of market communist systems, full convergence may never be achieved. Either way, however, Beijing has successfully devised modernization strategies which forestalled Myrdal's nightmare.

This inference holds even if substantial adjustments are made for the inferior quality of Chinese and Indochinese communist growth resulting from various types of forced substitution,[5] especially in the domestic

---

[5] Anti-competitive economies prevent consumers from acquiring the goods they prefer with desirable characteristics in the best assortments. This is called forced substitution, and implies that the utility consumers derive from goods produced in anti-competitive systems, and therefore their values are less than they would be if production was fully responsive to consumer demand.

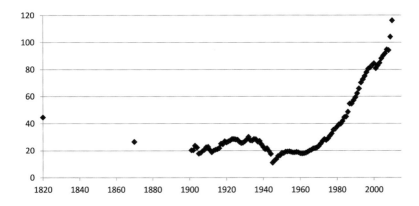

Figure 4.3. Taiwanese–EU Divergence and Convergence 1820–2010 Per Capita GDP (Western Europe = 100).

Source: Maddison (2003, pp. 558–563, 566). Available at http://www.ggdc.net/maddison/Historical_Statistics/horizontal-file_03-2009xls. Statistics on World Population, GDP and Per Capita GDP 1–2006AD. (last update: March 2009, horizontal file; copyright Angus Maddison). IMF GDP growth statistics 2008–2010.

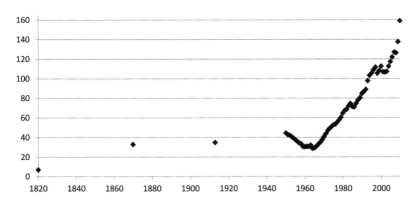

Figure 4.4. Singaporean–EU Divergence and Convergence 1820–2010 Per Capita GDP (Western Europe = 100).

Source: Maddison (2003, pp. 558–563, 566). Available at http://www.ggdc.net/maddison/Historical_Statistics/horizontal-file_03-2009xls. Statistics on World Population, GDP and Per Capita GDP 1–2006AD. (last update: March 2009, horizontal file; copyright Angus Maddison). IMF GDP growth statistics 2008–2010.

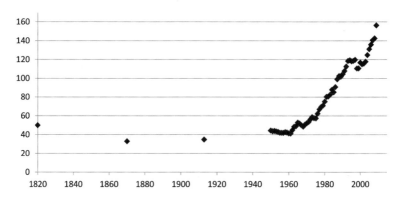

Figure 4.5.   Hong Kong–EU Divergence and Convergence 1820–2010 Per Capita GDP (Western Europe = 100).

Source: Maddison (2003, pp. 558–563, 566). Available at http://www.ggdc.net/maddison/Historical_ Statistics/horizontal-file_03-2009xls. Statistics on World Population, GDP and Per Capita GDP 1–2006AD. (last update: March 2009, horizontal file; copyright Angus Maddison). IMF GDP growth statistics 2008–2010.

market. Likewise, using the United States instead of Western Europe as benchmark merely alters the scale, not Asia–west living standard trends. America's per capita GDP was 39.6% higher than the Western Europe's in 2001. The comparative sizes of China and other Asian economies using the American benchmark therefore are correspondingly lower, but the reality of catch-up remains intact.

It should also be noted that Asian workdays during the catch up years were longer than the European, and the gap widened throughout. If Fig. 4.1 were computed on a per man-hour, instead of per capita GDP basis, the speed of Chinese and other Asian catch up would be diminished.

The systemic dimension of catch up, and perhaps fall back has two aspects: modernization and sustainability. Technology transfer provides a golden opportunity for less developed nations to increase productivity by adopting advanced technologies, skipping intermediate stages, and econo-mizing research and development costs. Any nation can modernize in this sense without making significant concessions to western individualism, but this does not mean that inferior systems will fully realize potential benefits. Moreover, even if it appears that Asian systems have boundless horizons during the early catch up phase, diminishing returns, fatigue and social adaptation seem to slow, or even reverse their progress. The

Japanese case is instructive. Although, Figure 4.2 documents its early vitality, this was partly accomplished by overwork and social arousal. There were more Japanese employed in the workforce, laboring longer hours more diligently than their West European counterparts throughout the 20th century, but recently the Japanese are reconsidering whether the material gain is worth the sacrifice in life quality. As social mobilization wanes, the demerits of its communalist system are becoming visible.

Taiwan was incorporated into Japan as a result of the First Sino–Japanese war 1894–1895, and swiftly industrialized on the Japanese model until August 15, 1945 when Hirohito surrendered to the United States. This background may partly explain the parallel postwar catch up patterns of the two nations, although the success also is a testament to positive aspects of Taiwan's Confucian nationalist system. Like Japan, Taiwan's catch up may be flagging (Fig. 4.3), particularly relative to the United States, and it will be interesting to learn whether its system, Singapore's (Fig. 4.4), and Hong Kong's (Fig. 4.5) have strong legs.

Thailand forms the middle ground. It has the same comparative size today *vis-à-vis* Western Europe that it had in 1820, after touching bottom in 1950. Its catch up has been steady, but less vigorous than the Confucian nationalist tigers. This reflects world-denying aspects of Theravada Buddhist culture that make Thai society less productively aroused, but perhaps the slow and steady approach will prove superior in the long run (Fig. 4.6).

Vietnam's postwar history like Cambodia and Laos was dominated by Mao's China, anti-colonial wars of liberation, and conflict with the United States. The damage is vividly captured in Fig. 4.7, which shows the nation's relative per capita GDP diminishing compared with Western Europe for 170 years. The switch from command to market communism has allowed it together with Laos (Fig. 4.8) and Cambodia (Fig. 4.9) to recovery some lost ground, but living standards remain less than half what they were relative to the EU in 1820. Chinese progress under Mao, offers hope for further market communist gains.

Korea provides double insight into the Asian drama. Although, it has a shared Confucian and Buddhist tradition with China, and was annexed by Japan in 1910, its people are ethnically distinct and homogeneous. Reflecting this blend of cultural influences, Korea's comparative living standard fell steadily after 1820 from 40 to 20, but recovered part of that lost ground

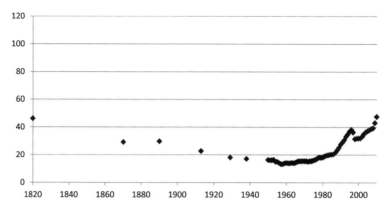

Figure 4.6. Thai–EU Divergence and Convergence 1820–2010 Per Capita GDP (Western Europe = 100).

Source: Maddison (2003, pp. 558–563, 566). Available at http://www.ggdc.net/maddison/Historical_ Statistics/horizontal-file_03-2009xls. Statistics on World Population, GDP and Per Capita GDP 1–2006AD. (last update: March 2009, horizontal file; copyright Angus Maddison). IMF GDP growth statistics 2008–2010.

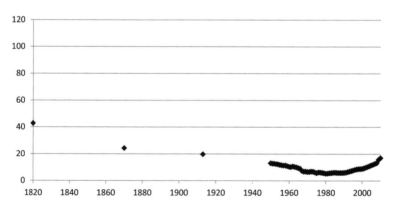

Figure 4.7. Vietnam–EU Divergence and Convergence 1820–2010 Per Capita GDP (Western Europe = 100).

Source: Maddison (2003, pp. 558–563, 566). Available at http://www.ggdc.net/maddison/Historical_ Statistics/horizontal-file_03-2009xls. Statistics on World Population, GDP and Per Capita GDP 1–2006AD. (last update: March 2009, horizontal file; copyright Angus Maddison). IMF GDP growth statistics 2008–2010.

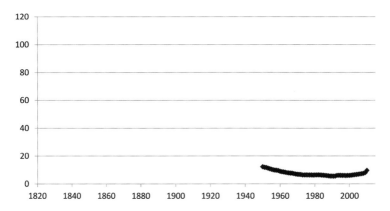

Figure 4.8. Laotian–EU Divergence and Convergence 1820–2010 Per Capita GDP (Western Europe = 100).

Source: Maddison (2003, pp. 558–563, 566). Available at http://www.ggdc.net/maddison/Historical_ Statistics/horizontal-file_03-2009xls. Statistics on World Population, GDP and Per Capita GDP 1–2006AD. (last update: March 2009, horizontal file; copyright Angus Maddison). IMF GDP growth statistics 2008–2010.

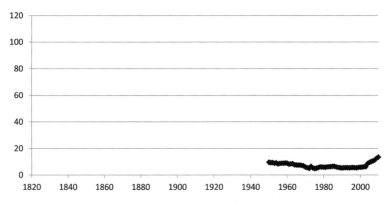

Figure 4.9. Cambodian–EU Divergence and Convergence 1820–2010 Per Capita GDP (Western Europe = 100).

Source: Maddison (2003, pp. 558–563, 566). Available at http://www.ggdc.net/maddison/Historical_ Statistics/horizontal-file_03-2009xls. Statistics on World Population, GDP and Per Capita GDP 1–2006AD. (last update: March 2009, horizontal file; copyright Angus Maddison). IMF GDP growth statistics 2008–2010.

under the Japanese yoke, only to lose the gain again toward the end of World War II when its relative backwardness was on a par with Thailand's. This was the platform from which postwar Korea would try anew to overtake the west. However, the vagaries of the Cold War divided the nation into an industrialized communist north, and agrarian Confucian nationalist south in 1947, providing an opportunity not only to test Myrdal's hypothesis, but to evaluate the comparative merit of Stalinist command communism, and Confucian managed markets under American tutelage. The results displayed in Fig. 4.10 are startling. North Korea treaded water for a quarter century *vis-à-vis* Western Europe, and then tumbled into the abyss. Its per capita income today is the lowest in the region, and its fall the deepest from the 1820 benchmark. South Korea performance was just the reverse. After a rocky start in the early 1960s, its trajectory skyrocketed, attributable in significant part to economic liberalization. Seoul recovered the 1820 parity by 1990, and is on a fast track to overtake Western Europe in the next few years, if the depression of 2008–2010 does not radically alter past trends.

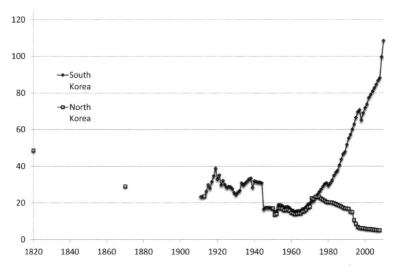

Figure 4.10.   North and South Korean Divergence and Convergence 1820–2010 Per Capita GDP (Western Europe = 100).

Source: Maddison (2003, pp. 558–563, 566). Available at http://www.ggdc.net/maddison/Historical_ Statistics/horizontal-file_03-2009xls. Statistics on World Population, GDP and Per Capita GDP 1–2006AD. (last update: March 2009, horizontal file; copyright Angus Maddison). IMF GDP growth statistics 2008–2010.

Diversity, not homogeneity or convergence is the defining characteristic of Asia's economy. A hundred flowers are blooming, under varied conditions, giving the region a broad luster it lacked 40 years ago. However, we now know that some once promising experiments did not last. Command communism failed despite high expectations in many quarters, and the full story of Asian economic systems is only beginning to unfold.

PART III

CORE ASIAN SYSTEMS

COMMUNISM

Chapter 5

North Korea

Systems Profile: North Korea

Type: Communist

Subtype: Command (Stalinist model)

Economic Sovereign: The Communist Party (Korean Workers' Party) leader's preferences control the characteristics of the system and its outcomes.

Ultimate Authority: Communist Party, not the rule of law (constitution).

Economy: (a) Formal: State ownership, central planning, directive hierarchy

(b) Informal: Bonus, forced labor, and satisficing

Government: Dictatorship

Civil Liberties: Repressed

Modernization: Low

Evolution: Little meaningful change in more than sixty years

Population (July 2012: CIA): 24.6 million

Living Standard (2011 USD, PPP: CIA): $1,800; global rank: 193

Development (EU Norm): Severely underdeveloped, falling back.

Communist Command Economy

North Korea has been dominated by Joseph Stalin's concept of communism since the country's inception in 1947.[1] The model, called command economy is best classified under the heading of an ideologically sovereign system (see Chapter 1). This means that cultural forces (in the form of Stalinist ideology) determine supply and demand rather than the autonomous preferences of individual consumers as required in the neoclassical paradigm (the democratic competitive standard). Command economy is inclusive in the sense that state governance of public services and production in what normally would be the private sector in the west are both determined by communist principles (see Chapter 3). The state which was authoritarian in Korea's pre-20th century imperial tradition remains so under North Korea's communist dictatorship, without the moral restraints formerly exerted by Confucianism (See Chapter 3). The model is a modern variant of Qin Shi Huang's tyrannical "Legalism".[2]

---

[1] Joseph Stalin, leader of the Soviet Union (1928–1953) hand-picked Kim Il-sung, a captain in the Soviet Army 1940–1945, to head the People's Provisional Committee. He made Kim Prime Minister of the Democratic People's Republic of Korea (DPRK) in 1948, after the South formally declared itself the Republic of South Korea (ROK). North Korea from its inception was a one party state that criminalized private property, business and entrepreneurship, collectivized agriculture, and pressed industrialization. It was heavily armed by the Soviet Union and exhorted by Stalin to support a war of national liberation against South Korea and American imperialism. Kim Jong-un still employs the same belligerent rhetoric.

[2] Although North Korea's communism's origins are western Marxist, despotism and command have long been elements of Asia's imperial legacy at least as far back as 221 BC when Qin Shi Huang founded China. Qin was the clan name of the royal house of the State of Qin. Shi is first. Huang refers to Three August Ones who ruled at the dawn of Chinese history, and Di is the legendary Five Di (Sovereigns) who ruled immediately after the Three Huang. After his death in 210 BC the Qin Empire collapsed, but was reconstituted under the Han first emperor in 202 BC. For clarity he is best and most simply called Qin Shi Huang (First Emperor of Qin). His personal name was Ying Zheng, King of the Chinese State of Qin 247–221 BC. Qin Shi Huang was an aspiring totalitarian, acting in accordance with the legalist principles of his Prime Minister Li Si. Although he was neither omniscient nor omnipotent, he sought insofar as humanly possible with the technologies of the day to nano-direct his subjects' lives in this world, and the next. He commanded his ministers and their staffs to execute his political, economic and civic instructions and draconian laws. Under this scheme there was no scope for independent authority above his own (although there was wiggle room created by the ambiguities and the restricted scope of the laws) including anything that might be construed as common law, and Confucian precepts (Confucianism was banned), an attitude that may well have extended to the gods. Legalism was one of four

It was pioneered by Joseph Stalin in 1929,[3] and employed by Mao Tsetung and Ho Chi Minh in China, Vietnam, Laos and Cambodia before 1950–1976. Command economy is a top-down governance scheme where the communist party leader, serving as custodian of the nationalized means of production, assumes responsibility for replacing private owner-ship and markets with a visible hand guided by central planning.[4] The unstated premise is that North Korea's Kim Jong-un and his technocrats can (1) survey the universe of all products consumers might desire, (2) compute opportunity costs, (3) ascertain the real time preferences of every North Korean, and (4) simulate the negotiations of all transactors free of capitalist distortions, allowing leaders to determine the optimal allocation of capital and labor, the best volume and assortment of goods and services, and the appropriate distribution of supplies to all users.

---

main philosophical schools during the Spring and Autumn Period (722–481 BC), and the period of the Warring States (450–221BC). The others were Confucianism, Taoism and Mohism (concept of universal love, egalitarianism, frugality, just law). One of its principal practitioners was Li Si, Prime Minister of the Kingdom, and the Empire of Qin (246–208 BC). He professed the virtues of an authoritarian system that make it possible to rule by edict (law). According to Han Fei (280–233 BC) its core teachings are Shi (position of power), shu (techniques) and fa (laws). The law code must be clearly written, public, predictable and uniformly enforced, serving as a general substitute for specific executive orders. With regard to technique, rulers should be unfathomable to minimize the risk of factional usurpation. And power requires charisma, the creation of an aura of innate authority. Qin Shi Huang outlawed Confucianism, buried many scholars alive, banned and burned books other than official decrees. The Di in his title referred to the Supreme God in Heaven, creator of the world, implying a claim to divinity. Qin Shi Huang was obsessed with immortality. Late in his life, he sought the fabled elixir of life, visiting Zhifu Island several times, and sent Xu Fu with ships carrying hundreds of young men and women in search of Mount Penglai, where the Eight Immortals lived. Legend claims that they settled in one of the Japanese islands. He died while touring Eastern China on September 10, 210 BC at the palace in Shaqiu prefecture after swallowing mercury pills devised by alchemists to make him immortal.

[3]Stalin's model has the planning features elaborated in this chapter, but was also supple-ment with lethal forced and punitive disciplinary measures that are omitted in the text to simplify the narrative. For a complete description of these coercive methods, see Rosefielde (2010). Lethal forced labor and other punitive disciplinary measure continue to be employed in Kim Jong-un's North Korea. See http://countrystudies/us.north-korea/24htm

[4]see Hare (2007), Haggard and Noland (2007), Haggard and Noland (2007), Byung-Yeon *et al.* (2007), Nanto and Chanlett-Avery (2007).

The claim is not only that the party can theoretically fulfill this mission, but that it does an excellent job in practice, despite opposition from counter-revolutionary elements.

The term command stresses the top-down aspect of North Korea's economic governance mechanism. The command principle is not absolute. Some room is provided for managerial and worker initiative guided by rules, regulations, incentives and penalties, but these actions require approval at appropriate levels in a chain of command, and can be reversed by superior authorities.

The command principle is intended to give the communist party complete control over employment, factor allocation, production and distribution. However, this is only a prerequisite for sound communist economy. The directives issued by authorities throughout the command chain also must be competent, and in the best case, optimal. North Korea's "Great Leader" Kim Il-sung and his successors Kim Jong-il and Kim Jong-un contend that planning fulfills this function at two distinct levels of the control hierarchy. Central planners gather data, process them and compute aggregate composite good production estimates as guidance for communist party leaders, and control figures for ministers supervising enterprise activity. Enterprise managers simultaneously prepare operational microplans based on past achieved levels, bonus incentives and political guidance from ministerial supervisors, who ultimately are responsible for reconciling microplans with centrally planned control figures. The result is sets of legally binding microplan directives compiled by ministerial departments into an operational enterprise work plan that forms the basis for assessing achievement in an adaptive environment subject to exogenous shocks.

These enterprise work plans have proven to be effective in a primitive sense. They have allowed North Korea to produce a wide array of goods and services and fully employ its population. But, is command planning of this sort in principle really likely to provide a level of wellbeing, fulfillment and contentment that equals or surpasses competitive markets as communists contend? The answer is easily discerned by investigating the mechanics of command communism in greater detail with the aid of an organization chart outlining the structure of Soviet-type top-down command economies (Fig. 5.1).[5] Kim Jong-un (Kim Il-sung's illegitimate

---

[5] see Rosefielde (2007).

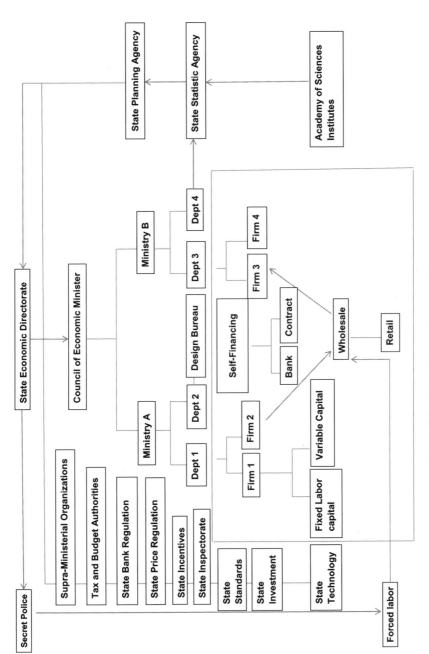

Figure 5.1. North Korean Command Communism.

grandson) is the system's "strategic" brain at the Fig. 5.1's apex. He sets the economy's goals, studies the State Planning Agency draft plan, mandates revisions, and after many revisions approves the State Planning Agency's final variant, but does not involve himself with microeconomic particulars.

The approved plan contains production targets for a small number of composite goods (textiles, autos, machines, etc). Kim forwards these control figures to the Council of Economic Ministers, which assigns oversight responsibility to appropriate ministries. Each ministry then instructs its subdepartments to disaggregate the composites into individual products based on microplans formulated in a negotiated process with enterprises under their jurisdiction. The result is sets of operational enterprise microplans covering technical, production, and financial assignments that are legally binding on enterprise managers (called "red directors"), or viewed from a different angle, de facto contracts enforceable by courts, administrators, the secret police and other communist party officials.

The process is mostly administrative, as distinct from incentive driven allocative, productive, and distributive choice making. Ministries and their departments do not compute optimal enterprise microplans, or make choices based on bonus incentives. Only red directors are materially incentivized to compute rational choice based preliminary production plans, and adjust them operationally during the plan period. Actual results never correspond with approved enterprise microplans because intermediate input supplies are not micro coordinated throughout the system, and ministerial supervisors have the power to override approved plans for the benefit of priority clients like the military, secret police and high party officials.

Directing communist enterprises is simpler than managing firms in competitive market economies. Red directors do not have to negotiate wages and sales prices, market their output or invest to maximize long run profits. They only have to supplement inputs under-allocated by the state material technical supply system using informal means; acquire labor, and maximize output in physical (tons) or value (profits) terms, subject to soft assortment and budgetary constraints.[6] North Korean enterprises are

---

[6]see Rosefielde and Pfouts (1988, pp. 1285–1299).

supposed to operate on strict principles of economic cost accounting and to be self-financing, but these obligations can be massaged.

Red directors are technically required to fulfill microplans under the penalty of law, even though planners know that strict compliance might be suboptimal. Managers might choose to fastidiously fulfill plans, when they could do better, and achieve superior results by bending input and assortment constraints. The supreme leader addresses these concerns by authorizing managerial bonuses for overfulfilling output plans in physical (tons), or value (profit) terms, and by winking at product assortment violations whenever this is expedient. The more enterprises produce, the more red directors earn. This bolsters effort, including labor discipline, but often has negative consequences. For example, enterprises dependent on secure intermediate input supplies frequently are forced to underfulfill their plans because component makers find it more lucrative to produce other goods, even though this violates microplan directives. Inter-enterprise contracting and micro-material balancing by the state wholesale network mitigate, but do not eradicate the problem.

These static efficiency problems are compounded by other systemic defects. Kim Jong-un relies on state laboratories, design bureaus and newly dedicated state enterprises to develop science and technology, create new goods including better investment durables. The relationships between scientists, engineers, designers, and their clients are mostly arms length. Established enterprises are modernized as ministers, and design bureaus see fit; not on red director, and ultimately consumer assessments of desirability. This might have some benefit, if scientists, engineers and designers clearly understand Kim's priorities, but they do not. They press their own scientific agendas, and are paid bonuses in accordance with the volume of designs completed, rather than effectiveness. Enormous resources are poured into science, technological development and new investment to increase productivity and spur economic growth, with lackluster results. Better outcomes can be achieved, if red directors are permitted to act as entrepreneurs, but North Korea's rulers consider this heresy because it raises the possibility of managerial empire building.

For similar reasons, red directors are prohibited from negotiating prices with other producers and consumers. All prices, including wages in the command system are set by the State Price Bureau on the basis of embodied labor content, as Marxist theory requires. This prevents red directors from exploiting workers and consumers for their personal gain, but it also means that prices cannot inform policymakers about competitive values. In accordance with the principle of enterprise self-financing, red directors minimize input cost to maximize bonuses, but the saving is nominal because wages are not proportional to marginal physical productivities. Likewise, under some circumstances, red directors may maximize revenue instead of the physical volume of output, but Marxist prices are not correlated with utilities, making it impossible to assess benefits, if any.

Other institutions displayed in Fig. 5.1 further constrain red director discretion. North Korean enterprise managers have little if any access to cash. Sales receipts and payments for non-labor inputs are carried out in the State Bank on a clearinghouse basis. This prevents embezzlement, but also hamstrings managerial initiative. Similarly, red directors cannot modify product specifications. The characteristics of all products are fixed by design bureaus together with the State Bureau of Standards. Red directors are barred from adulterating, but also improving them on their own volition.

Red directors are straitjacketed in these ways to prevent planning violations, rule infringement, proletarian exploitation, and the misappropriation of state assets, while incentivizing overfull production and employment. The state agrees to purchase everything red directors produce, and rewards them for overproducing. As a consequence, Kim's command economy is in a state of perpetual excess demand disequilibrium where microeconomic inefficiencies are partially offset by overwork.

The balance of countervailing forces cannot be reliably gauged because the waters are muddied further by cabals of various types that spontaneously arise to blind rulers, and enrich well placed insiders. The generic term for these rent-seeking mutual support networks is *family circle*. Administrators, red directors, and friends in high places have a common interest in diverting state assets, resources and products to private use. They conceal their tracks with elaborate accounting scams, and often pad results to obtain unearned bonuses, and in the case of administrators, undeserved advancement. Plans are fulfilled and overfulfilled on paper, but not in reality. When plan underfulfillment cannot be hidden, shortfalls are usually understated, because there is no transparency.

North Korea's rulers secretly condone some aspects of insider enrichment, but exaggerated claims of plan fulfillment are another matter. Red directors often collude with administrators and price setters to falsely claim that goods have been improved. This is called spurious innovation. The standard joke that satires this sort of behavior asks: *What is the difference between three and four star cognac?* The punch line is *the number of stars on the label.* The cognac is the same, but not the reported value-added. The fraud might seem trivial, but it is hardly innocuous. It not only allows managers to invisibly raise prices by pretending that higher prices are justified by improved quality (hidden inflation), and thereby acquire unmerited bonuses, it creates an illusion of material progress. North Korean GDP 1948–1990 seemed to be making miraculous strides (Fig. 4.10), but much of the advance was smoke and mirrors attributable to spurious innovation (hidden inflation), and other subterfuges.[7]

The system fortified with stern disciplinary methods and lethal forced labor, works.[8] Schools are constructed, curricula set by the Ministry of Education and medical services provided according to Ministry of Health protocols. Factories are built and products manufactured consistently with ministerial mission and department tasking. Engineering suffices for all these purposes, without competitive economic fine-tuning. However, this is not good enough from Kim Jong-un's standpoint.[9] He knows that the volumes, mixes, characteristics and distribution of goods and services can be better; that some insiders improperly enrich themselves; that disgruntled consumers may withhold their labor effort, and that their grievances could lead to a palace *coup d'état.*

North Korea's command system in a nutshell, as Kim Jong-un surely understands, is inefficient, subject to moral hazard, entropy, political intrigue and cannot be reformed enough to justify Marxist claims that command communism provides citizens with greater wellbeing, fulfillment and contentment than the private property based market regime that Kim Il-sung suppressed. Despite ceaseless Marxist assurances to the contrary,

---

[7] Aganbegyan (1989).
[8] Rosefielde (2010).
[9] Hobbes (1651).

close mechanical and theoretical scrutiny reveals that command systems cannot effectively (1) survey the universe of all products consumers might desire, (2) compute opportunity costs, (3) ascertain the real time preferences of every North Korean, and (4) simulate the negotiations of all transactors free of capitalist distortions. Consequently, command systems cannot determine the optimal allocation of capital and labor, the best volume and assortment of goods and services, and the appropriate distribution of supplies to all users, nor can command communism approximate these outcomes in anything thing other than the crudest fashion. It is impossible for North Korean command planning to be as productive as a democratic competitive market economy.[10] Command planning is inherently inefficient throughout, condemning communists to low levels of material wellbeing.[11] Nonetheless, Kim Jong-il did try to reform and improve the core system.

Reform

The collapse of the USSR, Pyongyang's main economic partner provided the main impetus for Kim Jong-il's reform effort. During the early 1990s, he made improvements in the production of agriculture and consumer goods. They were his top priorities, together with electricity, coal, metal and railway transportation.[12] Modernization was emphasized, and experiments conducted with 1950s style Liberman enterprise incentive liberalization granting red directors enhanced discretionary powers (reform command planning model).[13] The authority of red directors was expanded further by permitting them to buy and sell investment goods at market prices, and engage directly in foreign trade, crossing the threshold from pure command to a mixed command-market regime.

These and other tepid steps, including the introduction of farmers' markets (partly reversed in October 2005) had no visibly positive effect. The extension of farmers' markets to general markets for petty commerce

---

[10]This type of proof is widely used in economics. It has the form called an impossibility theorem. See Arrow (1950, pp. 328–346; Arrow (1951) and Rosefielde (2012).

[11]Living Standard (2009 USD, PPP: CIA): $1,800; global rank: 188 *CIA World Factbook: North Korea*.

[12]see Tselichtchev and Debroux (2009, p. 287).

[13]Liberman (1971).

was another plus, but also failed to invigorate aggregate economic growth because the state retains full ownership rights and control over the economy's commanding heights. North Korea may one day come to closely resemble Chinese and Indochinese market communism, however, there is no evidence that this will occur anytime soon.[14]

In the interim, Kim Jong-un may revert to Khrushchev's strategy of incremental reform command planning within the one-party state command framework. He may engage in what Gertrude Schroeder has called the "treadmill of administrative and economic reform".[15] Planning can be decentralized, recentralized and segmented. Weberian principles which substitute neutral, rule abiding administration for tradition and "charismatic" practices can be adopted on the supposition that command communism's success hinges on getting bureaucratic organization right.[16] Similarly, the leadership can explore enhanced industrial management techniques, derived from 19th Talyorism,[17] improved with new operations research principles, and it can continue applying the latest advances in computer based programming to central economic planning. However,

---

[14]Pyongyang closed North Korea's largest wholesale market on June 2009, redenominated its currency (won) on December 2009, and banned possession of foreign currencies on January 1, 2010. These retrenchment measures have been attributed to Kim Jong-un. They are ostensibly aimed at curbing inflation, private trade in proscribed manufactures, and confiscating *unearned* wealth, but also suggest the possibility of suppressing all vestiges of market communism except agrarian peasant production incentives. North Korea executed Pak Nam-ki, a 77 year-old planning and finance chief blamed for dragging the country into chaos by sabotaging a monetary reform in mid March 2010. Pak had been purged in January and was executed for "deliberately ruining the national economy" as a "son of a big landowner" (see Jae-Ku, 2010; Lee, 2009; Eberstadt, 2009). Astonishingly little hard data are available on the DPRK, a problem compounded by *strategic deception* designed to mislead potential adversaries about its strengths, vulnerabilities, intentions, and strategies (see Scalapino and Lee, 1972; San Oh and Hassig, 2000; Lee, 2001; Haggard and Noland, 2007; Lankov, 2007; Chol-Hwan and Rigoulot, 2001; Downs, 1999).

[15]see Schroeder (1979, pp. 312–340).

[16]Weberian Administration is a concept of rational public administration based on incorruptible performance of clearly defined administrative procedures devised by Max Weber in *Economy and Society*, 1922.

[17]Scientific enterprise efficiency management techniques devised by the American Fredrick Winslow Taylor in the 1880s, adopted and promoted by Lenin.

Soviet experience demonstrated that the more sophisticated command planning became, the more economic growth decelerated because the costs of refinements turned out to exceed benefits. North Korea might do better, but it should be remembered that impediments to computopia are probably insurmountable.[18] Even with foreseeable advances in artificial intelligence, efficiently simulating competitive markets seems hopeless out of reach.

This impossibility refutes the Marxist claim that communist civilization will provide superior material wellbeing, but does not dispose of the further issue of fulfillment and discontent. Do the command model and the North Korean communist experience provide any compelling reason for believing that criminalizing private property, private enterprise and entrepreneurship foster social harmony and provide people with higher levels of contentment than democratic free enterprise (Chapter 1, "Democratic Competitive Ideal")?

The answer is no. North Korea is a straitjacket society where personal freedoms of all kinds are prohibited or restricted including rights of residence, educational access, job choice, travel, property ownership, business, entrepreneurship, personal expression, religion, civic participation, and political opposition. Where Marx and Engels promised unbounded personal freedom, North Koreans mostly are compelled to obey. They are repressed and oppressed including being dragooned into forced labor, with no silver lining,[19] suggesting that if Kim Jong-un believes that command economy is best for him,[20] he will have to continue ruling with an iron fist.

Review

*Kim Il-sung, his son Kim Jong-il and his illegitimate grandson Kim Jong-un have sought to maximize their utility by making North Korea an impregnable, heavy industrialized, military power.

---

[18] An ideal planned economy achieved through perfect computation. The term was coined by Egon Neuberger.

[19] Amnesty International (2011).

[20] Kim Jong-Il's and Kim Jong-un's quest to make North Korea a nuclear power probably is the external aspect of this need for an iron fist.

*North Korea from its inception in 1948 was a Stalin-type communist command economy that criminalized private property, business and entrepreneurship, collectivized agriculture, pressed industrialization and employed lethal forced labor and punitive disciplinary measures.

*North and South Korea signed an armistice agreement July 17, 1953, but a peace treaty officially terminating the Korean War has yet to be concluded.

*North Korea, China and Russia are east Asia's only nuclear powers (excluding America).

*North Korea alone among Asia's communist states still proscribes private markets and entrepreneurship in everything except small scale production and petty commerce.

*Although, North Korean rulers describe their system as utopian, it is dystopic.

*According to Pierre Rigoulot, North Korea has unjustly executed 100,000 people, and forced penal servitude has claimed another 1.5 million lives.

*Command systems directors try to prepare optimal instructions by gathering expertise, information and preparing comprehensive central plans.

*They seek to engineer investment, production and social relations, but the task is beyond human capacity.

*This forces systems directors to use planning as a device for formulating soft directives (instructions) that serve as guidelines for ministers, enterprise managers, party, secret police and military production supervisors.

*The foundation stone of the North Korean economy is the criminalization of private property, business and entrepreneurship, which ipso facto outlaws markets and private activity.

*The state as sole owner of the means of production, establishes central planning as a party management mechanism for choosing production strategies, coordinating intersectoral, and interenterprise activities, issuing soft directives, and overseeing distribution to final users.

*Central planning is an administrative, not an executive operation.

*Managers, party, secret police and military supervisors are primarily responsible for interpreting and implementing soft central planning directives.

*The decisions of these actors are guided by a variety of factors, including institutional power.

*Only red directors (factor managers) and workers are materially incentivized.

*Red director bonuses are tied to various output, cost and profit targets.

*Output prices and wage rates are set by the state.

*The state purchases everything enterprises produce.

*Red directors bear no market risk. Their task is restricted to efficient production. If consumers refuse to purchase their products, this does not affect red director bonuses.

*Red directors are supposed to be financially self-supporting, but the state usually covers their debts if they run losses.

*Material incentives encourage managers to produce at full capacity, or more, but not to satisfy the intermediate input requirements of other state enterprises, or the demand of final users (state and households).

*The system promotes full capacity utilization, full employment, and GDP growth of things that Kim, but few others desire.

*This is important because there are no automatic market mechanisms permitted to guide producers to supply things buyers desire.

*There are illegal markets called the second economy, but their scope is limited by the state's status as sole legal employer, and the imposition of the death penalty for economic crimes.

*These efficiency problems are compounded by other defects. Kim relies on state laboratories, design bureaus and modernized state enterprises to develop science and technology, create new goods including better investment durables, and manufacture them for the benefit of consumers and other firms. But the design bureaus neither know the characteristics people desire, nor are incentivized to design the right products.

*Enormous resources are poured into science and technology with lackluster results.

*Better outcomes would be possible if red directors were permitted to be entrepreneurial, but this is heresy.

*Command systems straitjacket all economic actors to prevent or deter this or that undesirable behavior, but throw the baby out with the bath water, because restrictions prevent equilibrating adjustments.

*Command economies are opaque because cabals arise to blind rulers and enrich well placed insiders. The generic term for these rent-seeking, mutual support networks is family circle.

*One intractable problem is spurious innovation (hidden inflation). Documents are faked to support claims that products have been improved, and are therefore more valuable, when nothing has changed. Prices are raised to reflect the non-existent improvement giving the illusion, but not the reality of growth.

*The system works. Schools are constructed, medical services are provided, factories are built, but it is also inefficient, subject to moral hazard, entropy, and political intrigue that has made terror seem preferable to liberalization for the Kim dynasty.

*The North Korean economy has evolved and softened, but its version of market reforms has been bland. It has emphasized modernization and 1950s style productivity incentives, with only peripheral marketization.

*Someday sci-fi central planning might become a reality, but it would be foolish to bet on computopia.

Questions

1. Is North Korea's economic structure like Stalin's Russia? Hint: heavy industrialization, over-sized military, dysfunctional agriculture, etc.

2. What is North Korea's rationale for criminalizing private property, business and entrepreneurship?
3. How does central planning work in practice?
4. How are red directors incentivized?
5. Do red directors have the power to negotiate prices and wages?
6. Do red directors bear market risk? If consumers refuse to buy their products, does this affect their behavior (bonuses)?
7. Can red directors perpetually run financial deficits? If yes, does this matter, given the fact that the state sets prices and wages? Explain.
8. Red directors enjoy infinitely elastic demand for their products by the procurement agency. How does this effect plant capacity utilization?
9. If red directors receive additional capital, or better equipment would they have an incentive to produce at less than full capacity? How does this effect GDP growth possibilities?
10. Kim prioritizes full capacity utilization, full employment, and GDP growth. Does he do this at the expense of purchaser satisfaction? Explain.
11. Is there a legal market mechanism that enables Kim to better satisfy consumer demand?
12. Is there an informal market (second economy) that does this? If so, how effective do you think it could be, given the fact that the state is the sole legal employer, and that unauthorized diversion of state assets is subject to the death penalty?
13. Is the development of new products and technologies governed by purchaser's preferences and competitive opportunity costs? Explain.
14. Has North Korean civilian science and technology programs been commercially successful? Hint: Consider the GDP growth record.
15. What motivates North Korean leaders to repress competitive private demand? Does North Korea's aggregate economic performance prove that the Kims have been wise from the standpoint of consumer welfare?
16. What are "family circles" and why do their actions fog assessments of North Korean economic performance? Discuss spurious innovation and hidden inflation.
17. Despite all these deficiencies the North Korean system works. It produces basic goods and services, and provides full (overfull)

employment (including forced labor), and wage and price stability in all state activities. Given the global economic crisis 2008–2010, do you think that the costs of command outweigh its benefits compared with the western alternative? Defend your viewpoint.

18. Command economy advocates sometimes claim that the state as sole educator, employer, engineer, investor, financier, producer, and distributor can plan and provide for the nations wellbeing better than the market alternative. Can the state really ascertain purchasers' demands (including product characteristics), and organize production and distribution better than dispersed, competitive, perpetually negotiated market transactions? Can the state easily ascertain every individual's multiproduct demand functions with econometric methods, revising estimates every time individual tastes change? Can modern computers and computer programs acquire the real time data needed, and effectively process the information?

19. Has North Korean experiments with partial marketization matched China's?

20. Marx claimed that abolishing private property and profit seeking business activity would allow communards to live in a state of harmony that transformed work into blissful unpaid leisure. Has this happened in North Korea?

21. Reading the tea leaves, where do you think the North Korean economic system is heading? Explain.

Exercises

The North Korean command economy compels people and factors to overwork. Technologies are selected by designers without the advice of red directors, or final product purchasers. Training, and product characteristics are also fixed by bureaucrats without regard for purchasers and consumers demand. Factors are allocated on a plan priority basis. Priority goods are produced until marginal factor productivities are zero, causing severe overproduction. Consumer goods are underproduced from a technical standpoint. Consumer demand has no effect on output supply. Factor and product prices influence assortments within composite good categories (automobiles collectively constitute a composite composed of numerous models), if red directors' bonuses are determined by revenues, costs or profits. Products are maldistributed and mistransferred. All of North Korea's economic inefficiencies are caused by the criminalization of private property, business and entrepreneurship, the imposition of soft directive planning and fiat pricing, satisficing, rent-granting and communist party power. Command economies repress wages to enhance communist party control over the structure and distribution of national product. There is no rule of law.

Draw the Paretian ideal Edgeworth Bowley box (Fig. 1.1). Describe the impact of command communism on the length of the capital and labor vectors, the characteristics (for example work skills) of these factors, and the magnitudes (superscripts) of the isoquants. Where does North Korean production occur in this space relative to the Pareto equilibrium E? Hint: Remember that the Pareto and command communist isoquant scalings differ. Is there likely to be more than one wage-rental ratio at the command production point(s)? Explain. Hint: Wages and capital prices are fixed equally for all transactions, but there is wiggle room due to differentiated taxes and 'cherry picking' (privileged access to superior grades of goods within a given category, without appropriate price differentiation). Also, forced labor workers receive virtually no wages. Whose preferences determine the demand for public goods and civic activities, the party's or the people's?

Relocate the command communist production point(s) in the Pareto production space (Fig. 1.2). Remember that command communism reduces the isoquant values in Fig. 1.1. North Korean and Pareto production functions differ because command communist goods (qs) disregard consumer utility. Is the North Korean communist production point(s) (characteristics adjusted to the Paretian value norm) likely to be severely technically and economically efficient? Explain.

Draw the Paretian ideal Edgeworth Bowley product distribution box (Fig. 1.3). Will the North Korean product distribution box be the same size? Elaborate. Remembering that factors do not earn the value of their marginal products, will retail products be fairly distributed? Many consumer goods in North Korea are rationed. How does this affect the ability of individuals to improve their wellbeing? Some argue that it is fairer to ration than allow people to trade. Does this make utilitarian sense? Might it be more plausible in an economy of shortage where everyone lived on the margin of subsistence? Given the deficiencies of command communism, including state retail price fixing for non-rationed goods, will retail distribution likely be technically (as well as economically) inefficient? Explain. Are there likely to be multiple prices ruling in the command communist retail distribution space? Explain. Will some of this multiple pricing reflect the leadership's desire to reward insiders with discounted luxury goods?

Draw the consumer utility space (Fig. 1.4). Assume that one participant is a communist party official and the other a worker. Locate the realized utility point *vis-à-vis* the Pareto E. Is command communist wellbeing lower both due to its productive deficiencies and inegalitarianism? Explain. Is it possible that the wellbeing, fulfillment and contentment of North Korean insiders might surpass the Pareto ideal?

Draw the command communist Marshallian and Walrasian disequilibrium adjustment diagrams (Figs. 1.5 and 1.6), as well as the enterprise profit maximizing diagram (Fig. 1.7). Do Pareto efficient laws of supply and demand operate under market communism? If not, explain why equilibria achieved, if any, are distorted? Can a command communist red director simulate profit maximizing, if bonuses are tied to net revenue? Why is the simulation inadequate? Hint: Product and factor prices are set by the State Price Bureau at Marxist labor factor cost, not competitive equilibrium.

Is command communist wellbeing closer to the Pareto ideal than tiger Confucian markets, Japanese communalist markets, or Theravada Buddhist markets? Where would you rank command wellbeing, and why? Does lethal forced labor affect North Korean wellbeing? Elaborate.

Chapter 6

Market Communism: China and Southeast Asia

Systems Profile: China, Vietnam, Laos, and Cambodia

Type: Communist

Subtype: Market communist (Post-Mao model)

Economic Sovereign: The Communist Party leaders' preferences control the characteristics of the system and its outcomes.

Ultimate Authority: Communist Party, not the rule of law (constitution).

Economy: (a) Formal: State ownership, indicative central planning/ management, soft directive hierarchy, state leasing based private business, flexible exchange rate and limited price fixing. **(b) Informal:** Priority, bonus and satisficing in state owned enterprises (SOEs). The system is anti-competitive within the state sector, between the state and leasehold private sector, including foreign investors.

Government: Dictatorship

Civil Liberties: Repressed

Modernization: Uneven, but becoming institutionally sophisticated.

Evolution: Coercive command (1950–1980); reformist command planning mixed with incipient marketization (1980–1992); modernizing, open market communism (1992-present).

(*Continued*)

(*Continued*)

Population (July 2012; CIA):

China: 1.34 billion
Vietnam: 91.5 million
Laos: 6.6 million
Cambodia: 15.0 million

Living Standard (2011 USD, PPP; source, CIA):

China: $8,400; global rank: 119
Vietnam: $3,300; global rank: 167
Laos: $2,700, global rank: 175
Cambodia: $2,300; global rank: 185

Development (EU Norm): low, but rapidly catching up

Contemporary China, Vietnam, Laos and Cambodia are market communist regimes, operating in accordance with principles espoused by Deng Xiaoping and his successors. They are ideologically sovereign system (see Chapter 1). This means that communist ideology and culture determine supply and demand more than the autonomous preferences of individual consumers as required in the neoclassical paradigm (the democratic market competitive standard). The model is "inclusive" in the sense that state governance of public services and private "leasehold" production in the private "leasehold" sector are both congruent with Deng's communist principles (see Chapter 3). The state which was authoritarian in China's and Southeast Asia's pre-20th century imperial traditions remains so under China's, Vietnam's and Laos's one-party dictatorships (and to a lesser degree in Cambodia), without the moral palliatives formerly provided by Confucianism and Buddhism (see Chapters 7 and 9). The model is a "velvet" version of Qin Shi Huang's tyrannical "Legalism".[1] These characteristics distinguish Asia's communist markets from their regional and international rivals.

The market communist model is intrinsically anti-competitive and repressive. It prevents individuals from fully maximizing their utility in

---

[1] see Chapter 5, footnote 1.

work, investment (including education), job choice, production and consumption. It hinders Asian market communists from creating an affluent and diverse society where people strive to maximize their individual potentials supported by inviolable minority rights, including private property protections. Advocates of market communist economy claim that there is no need for "freehold property" (unrestricted private ownership, use, sale and bequest) and democratic protections because the communist party manages the system, guaranteeing that the people will receive everything needed for a prosperous and harmonious existence, but these promises have never been fulfilled. China and Vietnam have been growing rapidly and recovering lost ground *vis-à-vis* the west for more than two decades, however, they also have become extremely inegalitarian and disharmonious. Laos and Cambodia remain among the world's poorest nations, and may soon abandon market communism for a Theravada Buddhist system like Thailand's.

Chinese and Southeast Asian Command Communism 1950–1978

Contemporary communism in China and Southeast Asia has evolved dramatically since Mao Tsetung defeated Chiang Kaishek's nationalist Chinese government in the Fall 1949, two years after Kim Il-sung established Asia's second communist state.[2] In the beginning Mao, Kim and Ho Chi Minh (Vietnam) adopted Joseph Stalin's coercive command communist model which used lethal forced labor and other punitive methods to rouse productive effort in homeland defense against "capitalist encirclement" and in the service of rapid industrialization.[3] They criminalized private property, business and entrepreneurship, and imposed central planning. Mao, Ho, and later Pol Pot (Cambodia) modified the core model by exhorting economic mobilization from below, primarily in agriculture (communal agro-industrial complexes). More than 40 million people died prematurely during the Chinese Great Leap Forward (1956–1961), the Chinese Cultural Revolution (1969–1973), and Cambodia's dystopic killing fields (1975–1979).[4]

---

[2] The Mongolian People's Republic (outer Mongolia) was created in 1924 under the USSR's tutelage.

[3] see Rosefielde (2010, Chapter 10).

[4] *Ibid.*

These catastrophes finally prompted Asian communist leaders to disown coercive command planning (without acknowledgement, contrition or apology) in favor of reformist command planning between 1975 and 1980.[5] The main characteristics of the model were central planning, incentives and rudimentary computer based systems management.[6]

Deng Xiaoping sympathized with these technocratic and administrative reforms, but Chinese pragmatism ("seeking truth through facts", and "crossing the river by feeling the stones") induced him to push further, permitting some private productive activity to accelerate modernization, even though Marxist doctrine implied that workers and peasants might be exploited. Deng's "Bukharinite" approach led him to gradually adopt market elements from China's informal economy into the formal sphere ("socialism with Chinese characteristics"),[7] well before Mikhail Gorbachev dabbled with perestroika ("radical market reform") in 1987.[8] Deng could have widened the scope of centralized micro control as the Soviets had done before him, but chose instead to let the process evolve. Successful initiatives, often eclectically undertaken by local officials without central sanction, were soon legitimatized as standard practice, and then broadly applied throughout the country, becoming part of the formally approved market assisted, command planning scheme.

Market Communism: First Phase 1978–1989

This evolution often called Gaige Kaifang ("reforms and openness"), lasted more than a decade from the defeat of the Gang of Four (Jiang Qing, Mao's last wife; Wang Hongwen, Zhang Chunqiao, Yao Wenyuan) October 6, 1976 by Hua Guofeng, Wang Dongxing, Wu De, and Chen

---

[5] Nikita Khrushchev introduced the reformist command planning model in the USSR after 1953.

[6] see Rosefielde (2007).

[7] see Erlich (1960) and Rosefielde (2007). Nikolai Bukharin was a famous Soviet Politburo member in the mid twenties who advocated a balanced, market communist development strategy. Stalin defeated him in the political struggles, and imposed terror-command.

[8] see Shirk (1993). Large state enterprises, unable to produce various intermediate inputs, had long informally negotiated subcontracts with small state suppliers outside the purview of central planners.

Xilian) until shortly after the Tiananmen Square massacre, June 5, 1989. The idea at its core was the gradual reversal of the three ideological pillars of command economy: criminalization of private property, criminalization of private business, and criminalization of entrepreneurship. This was Marxist heresy and had to be undertaken gingerly.

The process entailed granting citizens the right to lease property from the state on a fixed term basis (as distinct from freehold proprietorship), the right to engage in for-profit business, and the right to pioneer new businesses, either privately or as state enterprise managers. Also, it necessitated granting peasants and businesses (private and state) the right to negotiate prices and wages (which required the abolition of state price-fixing and wage-fixing), providing them with access to credit, and substituting state regulation for most forms of economic control (directives, requirements and mandates). All these actions were steps toward competitive free enterprise, not free enterprise itself, because the Communist Party (CPC) fully intended to assume the role of master puppeteer, retaining its monopoly of state power (authoritarianism), restrictions on civil liberties, the criminalization of freehold property, control of the economy's "commanding heights" (banking, financial holding companies, defense, foreign trade), insider state contracting, and energetic market regulation. The Communist Party's strategy was to harness people's productive energies, including foreign investors and permit increased consumer choice, while preserving its ultimate economic sovereignty by deftly using the regulatory instruments at its disposal to pull the people's (marionettes') strings. The Communist Party's concept of power remained top-down (self-appointed authorities who control and regulate consumers), in stark contrast to democratic free enterprise which is bottom-up (consumers control private sector suppliers and elected government agents).

The years immediately after Mao Tsetung's death (1976) until the start of Gaige Kaifang were not particularly auspicious. It seemed initially that Hua's new post-coup d'etat regime would be conservative (reformist command planning), but Deng Xiaoping (whose power base was inside the communist party, rather than a state figurehead) succeeded in reversing the tide around 1978, by pressing the theme of four modernizations (agriculture, industry, science and technology, and the military), without taking a stand on the relative importance of plans and markets. He praised the "household-responsibility system" (allowing peasant family households to operate their plots relatively independently of team and communal influences) which made it possible for them to prosper by increasing productivity and selling above quota output in collective farm markets and household (cottage) industries in 1980. The principle soon thereafter was applied nationwide, even though the practice had been considered counterrevolutionary when collective farmers in Xiaogang and Fengyang informally experimented with the technique in 1978. The scheme, partly motivated by a desire to eradicate Maoist supporters through de-communalization and liberalization,[9] was not unprecedented. The Soviets permitted collective farm markets in the late twenties, and small cottage industrial undertakings with five or fewer workers always were legal, but Deng's agricultural and industrial variants were more extensive. Sometimes they merely involved incentives without markets, other times and more ambitiously incentives were combined with negotiated transactions.[10]

The household-responsibility system was quickly coupled with the "town village enterprise" (TVE) movement, an effort to transform the

---

[9] Communes were large state owned and operated farms constructed from smaller collectives, introduced by Mao Tsetung in 1958. They were locally governed, industrial and agricultural entities. Household farms and private plots were abolished, and labor assignments were carried out by production teams, production brigades and set by commune directors. After the disastrous Great Leap Forward, communes were reorganized. Their size was reduced, some autonomy was granted to local production teams, private plots reinstated, and wages differentiated in accordance with work's perceived importance. The Cultural Revolution restored central regimentation, with responsibility concentrated in the production brigades and the commune, under the direction of the Communist Party, and sometimes the military. From 1976–1979 communal autonomy was reinstated, followed by Deng's reforms which permitted households to sell some of their private plot crop in the marketplace for profit, at the same time communes themselves began being dismantled into smaller units (Shram, 1969).

[10] Pragmatism is a philosophy that claims that ideas and ideologies that do not generate practical results should be rejected, even if they are logically consistent. Conversely, concepts that yield practical results should be accepted, even if they are incomplete. The attitude is the obverse of utopianism. The concept was formally developed in the 19th century by Charles Sanders Peirce, and popularized later by William James and John Dewey. It was influential in Chinese pedagogical circles, despite its *bourgeois* pedigree.

separate profit seeking activities of individual households into a coordinated agro-industrial communal business. This hybrid institution further shifted communal management rights from superior administrators to production brigades, and households, overseen by local officials. TVE member households did not own land and capital in perpetuity (freehold property), nonetheless they had informal leasing rights to operate assets and sell produce for a long enough period to make simulating freehold profit-seeking reasonable. TVE were flexible, and enjoyed considerable discretion in choosing and implementing agro-industrial activities. The idea of integrating agriculture and industry (mostly handicrafts and light manufacturing) within an unitary institutional framework hearkened back to 1959 during the Great Leap Forward, when peasants were compelled to produce backyard steel, but Deng's version was more elastic allowing locally controlled TVEs to prosper through multiple channels. The TVE workforce quadrupled from 28 million to 135 million 1978–1993, and contributed significantly to aggregate Chinese economic growth.[11] As time passed many TVEs began operating de facto as private enterprises, despite their cooperative form,[12] and prospered in part due to the absence of freehold property owning competitors,[13] and newly decentralized state finance.[14] These halcyon days lasted until the mid-eighties when communes and collectives were broken up or abandoned and their land divided among individual households in parcels as small as a fifth of an acre. A half acre per person was the typical allotment. Although, peasants only acquired long term, renewable leasing rights, as distinct from freehold ownership, individual households strenuously contested TVEs for market share, weakening the position of TVEs in the countryside. Today, China's 700 million farmers are considered semi-independent, even though they still raise crops on government land, and sell to state-owned grain companies, because they enjoy considerable operational freedom.

Deng's command modernization initiatives were not confined to domestic production. During Mao's rule, China had repaid all its debts to

---

[11] see Naughton (2007).

[12] Wong (1988).

[13] see Kung and Lin (2007).

[14] see Oi (1992).

the Soviet Union in 1965, and banned direct foreign investment, including joint ventures between foreign companies and Chinese state enterprises. This changed with the establishment of Special Economic Zones (SEZ), the first in Shenzhen in 1980 and then in Zhuhai, Xiamen and Shantou (the "coastal strategy"), complemented by extending material incentive reforms to large scale industry, emulating Taiwanese and South Korean models. By 1989 nearly 22,000 joint ventures had been launched in the SEZs (952 with American firms like Chrysler and Coca-Cola). The bulk of the initial direct foreign investment came from overseas Chinese. SEZs developed slowly at first, but succeeded spectacularly in the nineties.

Gaige Kaifang indisputably enhanced physical productivity and real income. However, the gains were limited by forced substitution. Prices circa 1979 were fixed by the state, not competitive markets, preventing buyers from being consumer sovereign. The people could choose, but the assortments selected were determined by state set terms of trade, rather than competitive utility maximization (prices were not proportional to marginal utilities). Consumers as a consequence were compelled to purchase things they would have refused if prices had been competitively fixed. Policymakers recognized the problem in the early eighties, responding at first by setting multiple prices for the same goods in order to promote this or that objective, and then later allowed industrial enterprise managers to participate in price setting,[15] with an eye toward expanding sales and bonuses. Only a small share of industrial product prices were market determined in early 1986, but this changed rapidly so that most industrial prices were affected by the forces of supply and demand by the early 1990s. In the same spirit, import tariffs were cut in half starting a gradual process of import barrier reduction, and most other aspects of administrative regulation like tax and subsidy policy were rationalized.

Many observers based on these advances assert that China became a workably competitive capitalist market economic system (sovereignty of the capitalist class) before the Tiananmen Square massacre, but this claim is misguided. It conflates partial deregulation and Leninist New Economic Policy (NEP) style state market management with consumer sovereign

---

[15] see Fureng (1986, pp. 291–300).

competitive profit and utility seeking (See Chapter 1).[16] The Communist Party pulling billions of marionette strings remained fully in economic command. The Party, not consumers was sovereign.

Communism often employed material incentives to motivate production in ways consistent with planners' choice. Soviet workers during the thirties received progressive piece work bonuses tied to the fulfillment and over-fulfillment of production quotas. Consumer goods were rationed as rewards to the privileged on a priority basis. Some products were subsidized, and prices were freely negotiated in collective farm markets. All these expedients facilitated state goals from the command perspective, and were not construed as capitalist concessions because communist party power was preserved. Stalin's, Khrushchev's, Brezhnev's, Mao's and Deng's preferences, not those of consumers and other final purchasers determined ownership and usufruct rights, aggregate economic structure, investment, supply characteristics, assortments, distribution and finance. Any economic system can employ material incentives, and permit negotiated transactions, but only those that allow consumers' demand to govern supply are authentic neoclassical market regimes. Otherwise, they are command, controlled, administrated, managed and/or regulated economic systems.[17]

Deng Xiaoping's regime before the nineties was a communist command planning economy, administered, managed and partly regulated with material incentives, and a patchwork of local markets lacking secure business and entrepreneurial rights. The regime was authoritarian, employed forced penal labor (*laogai, laojiao*), maintained the world's largest standing army, and suppressed civil society. People had only limited rights to travel outside their locales, rationing persisted, and families

---

[16] Vladimir Lenin experimented with leasing based socialist markets from 1921–1929 in the Soviet Union. Managers were granted considerable discretion, but the state tried to guide and direct their behavior with micro-incentives and directive controls. The paradigm was called the New Economic Policy (NEP) (see Rosefielde, 2007).

[17] The term *market communism* for most Marxists is an oxymoron. Markets from their perspective are transactionary mechanisms used by capitalists to pursue private gain at the community's (workers') expense, whereas it is claimed, communism liberates the masses from market subjugation, inequality and injustice. Communism fosters the actualization of human potential through reciprocally empowering communal support. Markets and communism from the purist viewpoint are mutually exclusive.

were prohibited from having more than one child (1979 to the present). Deng Xiaoping's slogan "To get rich is glorious" may have reverberated with Confucian notions of prosperity, but communist Chinese reality was epitomized by Dickenseque command exploitation in what passed for a worker and peasant paradise. Economic liberalization was beneficial, but Chinese communism remained light years away from the true democratic free enterprise ideal.

Market Communist: Second Phase 1992-Present

The second phase of Deng Xiaoping's march to partially consumer sovereign markets (as distinct from market assisted command) can be conveniently dated at 1992, when he undertook his famous "Southern Tour" to Shenzhen. During the trip, Deng characterized China's emerging productive order as a "socialist market economy",[18] and asserted that "If China does not practice socialism, does not carry on with 'reform and opening' and economic development, does not improve the people's standard of living, then no matter what direction we go, it will be a dead end". This clarion call to reinvigorate the marketization process in the aftermath of the Communist Party's post-Tiananmen Square retrenchment was successful. Deng sidelined central planners like Chen Yun, and installed Zhu Rongji to oversee the next, more consumer empowering wave of economic liberalization, pressing forward with opening the economy, mass urbanization and development.

Deng's team promptly transformed red directors into managers of market competitive state owned enterprises (SOEs), and then ultimately into managers of private companies by expanding and codifying their powers in "The Regulations on Transforming the Management Mechanism of State-Owned Industrial Enterprises", issued in July 1992. The document

---

[18] The possibility of *market socialism* was debated in the 19th century, but rejected by most communists in 1929 when Stalin forcibly collectivized the Soviet Union. The idea was resurrected in the west by Oscar Lange in 1936–1937, and has been influential ever after (see Lange and Taylor, 1938). Stalin was impressed by Lange's theory. He summoned him to Moscow for consultations and Lange lobbied Franklin Roosevelt on Stalin's behalf regarding the government of postwar Poland. From 1961–1965 Lange served as one of four acting Chairmen of the Polish State Council (Head of State).

granted managers 14 control rights over: (1) production, (2) pricing, (3) sales, (4) procurement, (5) foreign trade, (6) investment, (7) use of retained funds, (8) disposal of assets, (9) merger and acquisitions, (10) labor, (11) personnel management, (12) wages, (13) bonuses, and (14) internal organization, and refusal to pay unauthorized charges by the government.

These rules mimicked the rights of western firms, but had less force because managers were not protected by the rule of law (independent judiciary). The communist party at its discretion could violate its own administrative decrees. Still, the new rules meant that under favorable circumstances state owned enterprises could more efficiently supply other government entities and private consumers.

The potential gains were obvious, but so too were the limitations. The command principle might still supersede the market. Managers might prefer to remain inert accepting subsidies instead of competitively profit seeking, and Deng's reforms might be distorted by moral hazard. Instead of acting scrupulously on the state's behalf, managers might employ all means fair and foul to privatize usufruct and assets to themselves. This is called adverse selection. Agents, who are supposed to serve the state, serve themselves instead at the people's expense.

Deng's Communist Party successors, Zhu Rongji, Jiang Zemin and Hu Jintao however were not daunted on this account.[19] They solved the moral hazard problem by capitulating to it, allowing managers and others including the *taizidang* (sons and daughters of high party officials often derogatorily called *princelings*) to lease state assets, close unsuccessful state enterprises, merge and acquire leased companies, enter into foreign joint ventures at home and abroad, and become billionaires,[20] while

---

[19] Hu's designated successor is Xi Jinping, the current Vice Chairman of the Communist Party.

[20] see http://princeling.askdefine.com. China had 80 billionaires in 2009, a quarter of whom derived their wealth from real estate (see http://www.forbes.com/2009/11/05/china-new-billionaire.html). Forsythe (2012), "The richest 70 members of China's legislature added more to their wealth last year than the combined net worth of all 535 members of the U.S. Congress, the president and his Cabinet, and the nine Supreme Court justices. The net worth of the 70 richest delegates in China's National People's Congress, which opens its annual session on March 5, rose to 565.8 billion yuan ($89.8 billion) in 2011, a gain of $11.5 billion from 2010, according to figures from the Hurun Report, which tracks the country's wealthy. That compares to the $7.5 billion net worth of all 660 top officials in

upholding Marxist communist principles by retaining the criminalization of freehold property.

Zhu's, Jiang's and Hu's decision to construct an asymmetric opportunity model that provided *la dolce vita* for privileged insiders, while simultaneously granting everyone else some freedom to prosper has been partly concealed behind a smoke screen of ambiguous corporate property rights. Chinese companies are classified into two broad categories: private firms and state owned enterprises (SOE). The distinction is subtle. "Privately owned" firms are leaseholds with majority private proprietorship. The state which is the sole freehold owner of all Chinese productive assets can be and simultaneously often is a minority stake leaseholder in "privately owned companies. "No Chinese private leasehold possesses freehold property rights, and in this sense China's means of production remain entirely state (people) owned. There is no freehold capitalism.

SOEs like private majority owned leasehold firms are freehold state property, but private leaseholders in these companies are minority owners. The state here variously retains sole control or leases its freehold properties on a fixed tenure basis to CEOs or groups of minority leasehold owners who operate them for-profit.[21] CEOs at their discretion are permitted

---

the three branches of the U.S. government. The income gain by NPC members reflects the imbalances in economic growth in China, where per capita annual income in 2010 was $2,425, less than in Belarus and a fraction of the $37,527 in the U.S. The disparity points to the challenges that China's new generation of leaders, to be named this year, faces in countering a rise in social unrest fueled by illegal land grabs and corruption. The National People's Congress, whose annual meeting will run for a week and a half, is legally the highest governmental body in China. While the legislature, with about 3,000 members, is often derided as a rubberstamp parliament, its members are some of China's most powerful politicians and executives, wielding power in their home provinces and weighing in on proposals such as whether to impose a nationwide property tax. Hurun, a Shanghai-based publisher of magazines targeted at the Chinese luxury consumer, uses publicly available information such as corporate filings to compile its annual list of the richest people in China. Hurun crosschecked the data with the government's list of NPC members. Zong Qinghou, chairman of beverage-maker Hangzhou Wahaha Group and China's second-richest person, with a family fortune of 68 billion yuan, is a member. So is Wu Yajun, chairwoman of Beijing-based Longfor Properties Co. She has family wealth of 42 billion yuan, according to the Hurun Report. China's top political leaders, including President Hu Jintao and Wen, do not disclose their personal finances or those of their families."

[21] The leaseholds are implicit because the CEOs are not required to pay fixed rents. Instead they must pay the freehold owner (Communist Party) whatever is demanded.

to sell their company's leasehold to insiders (including themselves) and others, domestically and on foreign stock exchanges (often described as "listed companies"). Many speak loosely of this ownership and leasehold management scheme as capitalist because of its for-profit leasing aspect, but it is thoroughly communist, including the sale of dividend streams to private portfolio investors.

The state protects its freehold interest by retaining 51% of enterprise shares, and can hire and fire CEOs and other managerial personnel at its discretion. Shareholders consequently do not have derivative freehold property rights, and merely own entitlements to revenues generated during the life of the lease. The terms of these implicit leases are fixed by the shifting power of Communist Party insiders who effectively grant custodial rights to themselves, families and friends. Thus, while SOE's are formerly state freehold property, they have become leasehold vehicles for enriching privileged members of the Communist Party, subject to regulatory supervision by the State-owned Assets Supervision and Administration Commission (SASAC).

Matters are further obfuscated by the imprecise use of the term state. Many assume that state refers to the central government in Beijing, but depending on context it also may apply to provincially and municipally owned enterprises.

There are more than 150,000 SOEs today controlled by the central, provincial and municipal governments,[22] some operating in protected (closed) sectors including defense, but the numbers are shrinking gradually due to mergers and acquisitions. The trend holds for all categories of SOEs including Red Chips (CITC, COSCO, China Resources, Beijing Enterprise, etc.) traded abroad on the Hong Kong stock exchange, which can be considered China's "commanding heights".[23] There were 159 active mega-conglomerate SOEs of this type at the end of 2006, slated to decline to 80–100 by 2010.

This consolidation, together with the disappearance of Mao era heavily industrial "dinosaurs" has led some to suppose that SOEs are vanishing, but the inference is misleading because merged SOEs are thriving.

---

[22] see Xu (2011). There were 154,000 STOs in 2008.
[23] see Tselichtchev and Debroux (2009).

SOEs control at least 40% of non-agriculture economic activity. They are profitable, vibrant and growing thanks to hidden subsidies, but remain inefficient because they are obligated to satisfy the government's political objectives.[24] Also, it is important to remember that private firms are majority private share leaseholds. They too are state owned firms, but just of another type.

Foreign joint ventures including Alcatel, Motorola, and Volkswagen are subject to similar leasing restrictions, even though they act as freehold corporations outside of China. The SASAC has substantial influence over their operations. Its sway however is less for small state and collective entities controlled by local governments, and private groups in the competitive sectors, increasingly acting like conglomerates, and small private and family collective commercial firms in the urban and rural service sectors.[25]

These developments have been accompanied by parallel stock market and banking reforms, allowing SOEs to increase equity (shares) sales to outsiders, and banks to tighten credit discipline over profligate SOEs. They also have facilitated market-driven reshuffles of corporate structure through mergers and acquisitions (M&A), neither initiated nor tightly controlled by the SASAC.

The greater good in this permissive communist variant no longer depends on protecting the people's assets from private arrogation, preventing the diversion of government usufruct, and insider rent-granting.[26] The Communist Party through the SASAC and other instruments is focused on enriching privileged SOE insiders, their families and friends

---

[24] "Of Emperors and Kings: China's State-Owned Enterprises are on the March", *The Economist*, 11 November 2011. "…, in sectors ranging from telecommunications to textiles, the government has quietly obstructed market forces. It steers cheap credit to local champions. It enforces rules selectively, to keep private-sector rivals in their place. State firms such as China Telecom can dominate local markets without running afoul of antitrust authorities; but when foreigners such as Coca-Cola try to acquire local firms, they can be blocked…" Also, see Hsueh (2011).

[25] Collective firms, discussed in the literature on "hybrid" property rights, usually have considerable autonomy. Huchet and Richet see most of these firms (TVEs) transitioning to wholly private enterprises (Huchet and Richet, 2001).

[26] The term rent-seeking means that privileged individuals try to acquire non-competitive state contracts which provide them with unearned income. Rent-granting is the granting of these non-competitive state contracts, with some kind of payoff to the grantor.

with contracts, incentives, regulations, credit access, mandates, subsidies, quotas and tariffs. This for many communists is considered a betrayal of the Marxist cause, and was Stalin's explicit justification for abolishing NEP. Deng may have agreed with Stalin through the 1980s when echoing Soviet Politburo member Nikolai Bukharin he exhorted Communists to enrich themselves in return for adding value,[27] intending to keep a lid on income inequality, but his Communist Party successors in the new millennium apparently decided otherwise.[28]

This asymmetric opportunity model providing *la dolce vita* for privileged insiders, and crumbs for the people is the distinctive feature of the second phase of China's market communism. The Party does not strive to immiserize the people, only to appropriate most of gains from market communism to itself by awarding insiders with privileged use of leased state assets, actively supporting favored SOEs with lucrative contracts, subsidies, etc., and pulling a billion marionette strings to assure their enrichment. Some call this market capitalism, but it is vintage post-Tiananmen massacre market communism.

Sources of Success

The performance of China's market communist system during the second phase was excellent judged from the standpoint of modernization, growth and development, despite the regime's anti-competitive inequities. Official statistics as is widely understood significantly exaggerate accomplishments, nonetheless, evidence from a multitude of sources confirms that China has made substantial progress building a modern infrastructure, and an export oriented industrial sector which has made it

---

[27] Bukharin (1926).

[28] see Buckley (2012). Gu Kailai, wife of Bo Xilai, one time Politburo aspirant and CPC Chongqing Committee Secretary was arrested and charged with killing British businessman Neil Heywood because he refused to move a large sum of money abroad, and threatened to expose her. This story may have come to light because the Politburo is currently engaged in a campaign to discredit the Bo's efforts to revive Maoism (Red Culture Movement) in Chongqing. Bo's reforms are sometimes labeled the "Chongqing model". Gu Kailai was subsequently convicted of murder. Bo Xilai was expelled from the party in September 2012, clearing the way for Xi Jimping to become communist party chairman.

the "workshop of the world". A quarter century ago, Beijing was congested with bicycles; today automobiles clog the roads bumper to bumper, and the same scene is repeated even in large provincial cities like Chengdu.

How can this have been accomplished in a privilege granting, anticompetitive authoritarian market communist system? In pondering the matter, it is worth recalling that the Soviet Union and Maoist China both claimed similar successes under command communism. Anticompetitiveness and privilege granting do not preclude rapid economic growth in some epochs. Stalin's and Mao's centrally planned regimes both invested heavily, provided citizens with solid technical educations, stimulated effort with material incentives, and acquired technology from abroad. Neither produced goods that consumers wanted, but this never was reflected in the official data. In an "economy of shortage" consumers bought whatever they could find.

Deng Xiaoping's reforms improved matters by making supply more responsive to demand. The growth officially claimed accordingly became more substantive than the phantom accomplishments of Mao's Great Leap Forward. Marketization moreover created the foundation for authentic economic catch up. Its contribution to China's economic growth had many aspects, but the most decisive was attracting more than a trillion dollars of foreign direct investment (FDI) to China's shores.

This inflow of foreign technology, knowhow and marketing skills worked miracles, and cost the Communist Party nothing. Foreign outsourcers drawn by the lure of cheap resources and a disciplined work force, built turnkey facilities designed to their international specifications, transferred technologies and manufactured branded products that enabled China to rapidly climb the value added ladder producing inexpensively at home and selling favorably abroad. Resources used to produce goods with Chinese characteristics in the domestic market fetched little, but the same resources redeployed to foreign outsourcers were immensely profitable. These gains were multiplied by technological diffusion. Foreign technologies were copied and soon adopted by local entrepreneurs across the economy increasing market communism's growth momentum.[29]

---

[29] see Rosefielde (2007, pp. 495–513).

Deng's gambit worked. China succeeded in modernizing far faster than it could have, if the party had chosen to rely on domestic innovation as the Maoist experience amply confirms. This does not detract from China's advance, but it does affect the assessment of market communism's prospects because potential returns to technology transfer are rapidly depleting. China's growth is decelerating, and soon will be bounded by the sustainable rate international technology progress. This means that even if Chinese market communism in the future is not hobbled by anti-competitive privilege granting, it will be unable to grow faster than a few percent per annum sometime in the near future.[30] Xi Jinping may prefer China's market communism as it is currently configured, but reality is likely to compel him to consider further radical reforms and even post-communist transition.

Market Communist: Third Phase?

What will he do?

The answer depends on which kind of puppeteer markets Communist Party insiders conclude offers them the most gratifying outcome: the "masters first, people second" model, or a more egalitarian power sharing paradigm. The first alternative which prioritizes increasingly rapacious privilege-granting over competition is apt to be destabilizing. Privilege-granting Chinese markets cannot be Pareto efficient, and growth will decelerate as the advantages of backwardness wane, intensifying social discontent. These defects may be temporarily alleviated, if privilege-seekers are permitted to acquire freehold property, but the stimulus will not be enough to offset the inherent deficiencies of the "masters first, people second" system.

The egalitarian power sharing alternative requires paring privilege-granting to the bone consonant with the rhetoric of the harmonious society. If selected, it will improve national welfare and align the system more closely with Confucian Taiwan, especially if Beijing legalizes freehold property. Should this come to pass, Chinese market communism should endure and may even prosper in the long run. Its living standard could approach Taiwan's.[31] China in this scenario will resemble an EU welfare

---

[30] This deduction might have to be revised if China unexpectedly develops a miraculously potent domestic R&D mechanism.

[31] For a more thorough description of pure neoclassical transfer model (see Meade, 1978).

state with Weberian governance,[32] some freehold property, and equal opportunity leasing overseen by communist sages protecting citizens from themselves. Individuals might be permitted to participate in state governance, enjoy limited civil rights, and the rule of law, as long as these privileges do not jeopardize party authority. It will not be utopia, but might suffice.[33]

Southeast Asian Market Communism

Contemporary Southeast Asian market communism is privilege-granting like its northern mentor, but the historical and institutional particulars differ. Although, Vietnam, Cambodia and Laos followed the dominant 20th century communist sequence passing through coercive command and reformist command planning phases before embracing market communism, their communist parties did not consolidate power within present boundaries until the Vietnamese War ended with the Fall of Saigon on April 30, 1975.

Southeast Asian communism of all varieties is younger than China's, and in the Laotian and Cambodian cases shallower. Vietnam's Marxist–Leninist Communist Party (CPV) did not exert territorial authority until 1955, while Laos's People's Revolutionary Party (LPRP) (Pathet Lao) only came into power in 1975. The Kampuchean Communist Party (CPK) formed by the Khmer Rouge seized control at the same time, and ruled during Pol Pot's reign of terror, 1975–1979, but was succeeded in a convoluted process over the years by the Cambodian People's Party (CPP). The CPP is a post-Marxist–Leninist socialist party formed from the Cambodian People's Revolution Party (KPRP) under Hun Sen, who was installed as Deputy Prime Minister by the Vietnamese when they occupied the country May 1975–December 1989. He heads a democratic coalition government with the royalist FUNCINPEC party that retains a socialist–communist orientation. Hun Sen himself is widely considered a corrupt socialist dictator.

---

[32] Weberian governance is a political and professional administrative regime devoid of Communist Party privilege granting. See Weber (2009).

[33] No theorist has yet contrived a viable institutional scheme for realizing the communist ideals elaborated by Karl Marx and Friedrich Engels in *The Communist Manifesto*. This is because eliminating private property is not enough to create a harmonious, exploitation free society that fully actualizes human potentials.

Vietnam

Vietnam's version of market communism is called Doi Moi (renewal). It began at the Sixth Communist Party Congress in 1986, superseding the Bao Cap subsidy system (1975–1986), which was gradually terminated by reducing food subsidies, and introducing cash salaries indexed to the cost of living.

Doi Moi started with the introduction of agricultural contracting in peasant cooperatives, and the privatization of some commerce, although the material incentives and the family responsibility system had been tried briefly during the period 1960–1962.[34]

Soon thereafter foreign investment, including joint ventures and outsourcing, was encouraged by the Foreign Direct Investment Law, December 9, 1987; inefficient agrarian cooperatives began being abolished by the Land Law of 1993, and farmers were given title to their plots, together with tilling rights. A Civil Code was established to define and protect these and other private property rights. Results were slight at first because the west boycotted Vietnam as long as its troops occupied Cambodia, but after 1989 the economy made notable headway.

The official objective of these reforms, replicating Deng Xiaoping's pragmatic experiment eight years earlier,[35] was the creation of a socialist oriented market economy, with a strong state industrial presence, including banking, and aspects of foreign trade (exports constituted 68% of GDP in 2007),[36] combined with agrarian cooperatives and private enterprise in the light manufacturing and service sectors.

The market dimension of Vietnam's Doi Moi socialism includes various material incentive schemes, the decriminalization of some negotiated transactions, the reduction of state price and wage fixing (regulation), and with it a lessened role for state-owned enterprises and central planning. The planning process has been decentralized with a concomitant increase in provincial and local economic power. The state owns all the non-tillable land, including resources, with private business being conducted mostly

---

[34] *Ibid.*, p. 287. By 1983 private traders controlled more than 50% of the market in foodstuffs, agricultural products, fish, and forestry products (Quinn-Judge, 2006, pp. 284–289).

[35] Vu (2009, pp. 186–226).

[36] CIA, *World Factbook*, Vietnam, 2009.

on a leasing basis. A stock exchange was established in July 2000 to expedite the partial privatization of SOEs, but foreigners are precluded from owning more than 49% of any enterprise, and cannot purchase freehold land, including residential and commercial real estate. In 2005, banks were added to the list of equitizable SOEs (majority state owned firms with minority private equity stakes).

Vietnam joined the WTO in 2007, triggering an effort to protect intellectual property rights, but the initiative has been ineffectual. Overall, Vietnam has prospered by marketizing, liberalizing, globalizing (including the receipt of billions of dollars, transferred by post-Vietnam War refugees who settled in the west), and is viewed by many as being on a Chinese-style high road to workably competitive free enterprise.

However, this characterization is misleading to the extent that it assumes communism no longer matters, or that the Communist Party of Vietnam's (CPV) power will quickly evaporate.[37] The Soviet Union's demise lends some credence to such conjectures, but not enough to carry the day. Vietnam's Doi Moi strategy has been a pragmatic exercise in devising a better mouse-trap; not a ploy for gradually relinquishing communist rule, or wholly abandoning its revolutionary agenda. The leadership from the outset has sought to kill several birds with one stone, including the retention of CPV power, the enhancement of Vietnam's wealth and influence, insider enrichment, modernization, development, and improved living standards, with foreknowledge that these benefits could not be secured without ideological concessions. It understood, and agreed to accept the fact that material incentives, partial privatization, leasing and the decriminalization of private business and entrepreneurship would dilute some insider rents, diminish communist legitimacy, reduce the CPV's span of control, increase pressure for civic empowerment and democracy, and raise the specter of extreme inegalitarianism and social strife, placing CPV sovereignty at risk.

Central Committee members could not ascertain beforehand whether rewards would exceed risks, but opted to learn by doing. Their objective was not inclusive democratic competitive free enterprise with civic

---

[37] see Chatterjee and Nankervis (2007), Chien and Truong (2005, pp. 26–47) and Collins (2009).

empowerment. They sought, and are still seeking to discover an optimal mix that preserves CPV power, and the leadership's private ambitions, while securing as many communist ideological goals as possible. Egalitarianism, individual liberty, and human fulfillment are not high priorities, but the CPV does not spurn general prosperity, and social harmony. Their policies like Hu Jintao's thus have boiled down to a strategy of masters first, people second, with rising incomes and a social safety net. They have created a one sided social contract that allows ordinary citizens to reap some of the fruits of their labor, sugar coated with revolutionary nostalgia, at the expense of egalitarianism, wellbeing, fulfillment, contentment, social justice, humanitarianism, civil liberties, and political rights. For those who assign great weight to official GDP growth statistics, and domestic winners these "birth pangs" seem a fair bargain, and no doubt will be broadly judged so by history, if blemishes fade with further communist development.

Vietnamese welfare will improve substantially if the country extends liberalization, unshackles agriculture, legalizes more aspects of private activity, reforms SOEs, embraces globalization (promoting FDI and exports) and restructures the financial sector. Corruption may subside and rent recipients become more socially conscious. However, communist moral hazard and privilege-granting could also endure, ensuring inequality (Gini coefficient estimates rose from 0.35 in 1990 to 0.43 in 2006),[38] unemployment, hardship, social injustice, authoritarianism and civic repression. Vietnamese average living standards are likely to improve for decades, given the country's relative economic backwardness and wage repression; nonetheless, both material and societal progress will be impeded if party privilege granting is not constrained. Not only will Vietnam's Gini coefficient remain stubbornly high judged from the global norm, but the inequality will be largely attributable to insider power, rather than to competitively justified differences in marginal value-added.

This behavior replicates contemporary China's in all essentials. Market communist regimes, it seems, are fundamentally alike. However,

---

[38] http://www.euromonitor.com/vietnams_income_distribution C.f. Abrami, R, E Malesky and Y Zheng, "Accountability and inequality in single party regimes: A Comparative Analysis of Vietnam and China", unpublished pdf, 5/16/08. China's Gini coefficient was 0.47 in 2004 (see World Bank, 2007).

there are some significant differences. Both GDP and inequality have grown more slowly in Vietnam than in China (if one believes the statistics), and the CPV has permitted a freer flow of imports. This has led some to claim that governing coalitions are more diverse in Vietnam, that they constrain authoritarianism, are intrinsically more competitive, and therefore superior to Beijing's brand of market communism.[39] Others stress the weakening legitimacy of the current regime, contending that the CPV is effectively dead as a source of ideals or morality, prodding the Vietnamese to rediscover their Buddhist heritage.[40] On the first view, Vietnam's brand of privilege granting market communism has a better chance than China's of surviving, while on the second, this may not be good enough to prevent Vietnam's economic system from morphing in new cultural directions.

Laos and Cambodia

Market-oriented reform started in Laos and Cambodia at the same time that Doi Moi was officially promulgated in Hanoi, but with less substance. Laos's experience with command communism was brief (the Pathet Lao came to power under Vietnamese tutelage in the mid-seventies), and the Vietnamese-occupied Khmer Rouge ravaged Cambodia for 15 years. Both criminalized private property, business and entrepreneurship, created state-owned enterprises, and central planning before 1986. Then, under their versions of Doi Moi, called the New Economic Mechanism (in Laos), gradually introduced material incentives and rudimentary markets in agriculture and commerce, followed by the legalization of some forms of private property (including direct foreign investment, outsourcing and joint ventures), and institutions to enforce property rights. Managerial and financial autonomy were encouraged in SOEs, and prices liberalized.

It is claimed that this liberalization spurred rapid growth and development, but the results are invisible to the naked eye. Neither Laos nor Cambodia displays entrepreneurial vitality (Phnom Penh was still a virtual

---

[39] *Ibid.* C.f. Gainsborough (2007 Quinn-Judge (2006, p. 289), Gandhi and Przeworski (2006, pp. 1–26), Gustafsson *et al.* (2008), Kelley (2006).
[40] Quinn-Judge (2006, p. 289).

tourist ghost town in 2009), and direct foreign investment is limited because Laos is landlocked, and Cambodia's ports are in disrepair. In principle, Cambodia's electoral democracy should have some discernible effect on the performance of its privilege granting market communist–socialist system, and Laos eventually may display some novel aspects, but for the present all that can prudently be inferred is that the privilege granting could be milder and more haphazard in Cambodia and Laos than in Vietnam and China, and that each Asian market communist system may evolve separately in its own special way.

Review

*Stalin patronized and mentored Mao Tsetung, Ho Chi Minh, and Kim Il sung. All three adopted his coercive command model in the late forties and early fifties.

*Mao, Ho and Pol Pot however soon modified Stalin's command paradigm. They exhorted economic mobilization from below, primarily in agriculture (communal agro–industrial complexes) instead of driving the peasantry off the land into urban industry. More than 40 million people were killed during the Chinese Great Leap Forward, the Chinese Cultural Revolution, and Cambodia's killing fields.

*This debacle finally induced China and Indochina to change course, first toward Khrushchev style reformist command planning during the late seventies and early eighties; and later toward market communism from the mid eighties to the present.

*Reformist command planning emphasized carrots over sticks, and strove to increase productivity with improved planning (techniques and administration), and scientific and technological progress.

*Deng Xiaoping sympathized with technocratic and administrative reform, but above all else he was a pragmatist.

*He permitted some farmers, on an experimental basis, to increase their incomes by managing their plots. This incentivized their effort, as the Soviets had always done, without free input and output markets.

*Then he enhanced the power of material incentives by allowing farmers and others to create and compete in some types of markets.

*The "Bukharinite" approach made informal aspects of Mao's system formal, creating socialism with Chinese characteristics well before Mikhail Gorbachev dabbled with perestroika in 1987.

*This evolution often called Gaige Kaifeng (reforms and openness) lasted more than a decade.

*The policy included the *four modernizations* stressing agricultural, industrial, scientific and military productivity development.

*The "household-responsibility system" provided a conceptual justification for permitting farmers a degree of independent control over production and sale.

*The household-responsibility systems was paired with the town village enterprise (TVE) movement, expanding the scope of market oriented production from individual plots to communities.

*Participants had leasing rights, not freehold ownership. Arrangements were elastic.

*The TVE workforce quadrupled from 28 million to 135 million 1978–1993.

*After agrarian communes were broken up in the mid-eighties, small independent farms (still leased) emerged that competed effectively with TVEs.

*Today, China's 700 million farmers are semi-independent.

*China was autarkic between 1966–1980 (negligible foreign trade and investment).

*Special Economic Zones (SEZ) opened enclaves like Shenzhen, Zhuhai, Xiamen and Shantou to the global economy in the early 1980s.

*Large scale industrial enterprise adopted Taiwanese and South Korean style incentives during the eighties.

*In the early stages of Gaige Kaifeng wages and prices were fixed by the state, limiting the benefits of purchase and sale operations.

*People had consumer choice; not sovereignty. They could buy and sell what was available, but not negotiate to maximum advantage.

*Price controls and regulations were relaxed in the early 1990s.

*Import tariff barriers were reduced, and subsidies rationalized.

*Although consumer influence increased, most incentives and markets were managed for the state's primary benefit.

*Any economic system can employ material incentives, and permit negotiated transactions, but only those that allow purchasers demand to dominate supply are authentic market regimes.

*Deng Xiaoping's China before 1990 was a mixed reformist command planning and rudimentary leasehold market economy.

*Laogai and laojiao forced penal labor was widespread, the military played a large economic role, and civil society and democracy was repressed.

*Despite Deng Xiaoping's slogan "To get rich is glorious" China looked like a Soviet slumscape.

*The environment brightened gradually after 1992, when Deng began emphasizing Chinese consumerism (as distinct from socialist humanism), which he called the "socialist market economy".

*This marked the start of a transition to market competitive state owned enterprises (SOEs), and then onward to leasing privatization.

*The state is the ultimate freehold owner of China's means of production.

*The state leases its freehold properties for fixed terms.

*The state owns leasehold shares. This entitles it to a share of leasehold income.

*Companies are called state owned enterprises when the state owns more than 50% of the leasehold. The state appoints its directors.

*SOEs are permitted to sell shares in the leasehold to leasehold directors, outsiders and foreigners. This is often done on stock exchanges.

*Companies are misleadingly called private when the state owns a minority stake in leasehold companies, even though the state retains ultimate freehold rights.

*SOE and private leaseholds (majority non-state lease ownership) are operated on a for profit commercial basis.

*SOEs are supervised by the State-owned Assets Supervision and Administration Commission (SASAC).

*There are more than 150,000 SOEs.

*The number of SOEs has been declining due to mergers and acquisitions.

*Foreign joint ventures operate under the same rules.

*Beijing has substantial control over foreign joint ventures with major western companies like Motorola.

*Banks recently have been encouraged to allocate credit more stringently to all companies.

*China's major financial holding companies in the public sector are state owned/controlled, with substantial minority equity stakes held abroad and traded on the Hong Kong Stock Exchange.

*These institutional reforms mimicked the rights of western firms, but still were not buttressed by the rule of law (independent judiciary), so that communist party power remained an ever present aspect of the production and distribution mechanism.

*Also, SOE directors were able to game the environment to their advantage, sometimes acting competitively, but also seeking government subsidies and the easy life.

*The new arrangements are vulnerable to moral hazard, whereby agents who were supposed to serve the state, serve themselves at the people's expense.

*Deng's successors, Zhu Rongji, Jiang Zemin and Hu Jintao solved the moral hazard problem by capitulating to it, allowing red directors and others including *taizidang* (princelings) to lease state assets, close unsuccessful state enterprises and become billionaires.

*SOEs are increasingly influenced by market forces, indicated by the evolution of their corporate structures.

*Most of these developments are driven by the priority of insider enrichment rather than social welfare.

*The balance of Communist Party priorities from Deng to Hu has gradually shifted from great power enhancement to insider personal enrichment.

*Insiders also can divert funds to themselves through taxes and transfers.

*Control of privilege-seeking tends to be lax and inefficient.

*Hu has made China's work adequately despite these perils through a mixture of material incentives, market competition and bureaucratic discipline.

*The modern communist dream is Hu Jintao's harmonious society, but this is mostly window dressing.

*Unlike the EU which prioritizes social justice over growth, China's sacrifices equality for development.

*Hu Jintao's promise is that this will eventually change with communist China achieving higher social welfare than social democratic Europe.

*China seems to have devised a Communist Party managed, self-regulating, normal, market regime. However, this is deceptive because Hu's markets are rent-granting, rent-seeking and rent-controlling mechanisms serving privileged insiders and the communist party, rather than competitively maximizing consumer utility.

*All behavioral and institutional forms have become permissible, except freehold property, if they empower the Communist Party, the state and the privileged.

*China welcomes direct foreign investment and has begun aggressively purchasing minerals and companies abroad with an eye toward capturing overseas rents.

*Subsidies to state enterprises have been reduced, and many SOEs have been forcibly merged or disbanded.

*Tariffs and quota have been reduced.

*The bureaucracy has been enlisted to promote constructive activities and eschew bribes.

*The RMB exchange rate has been kept below equilibrium to foster exports and hot house national economic development.

*China has many potential futures, all of which depend on how its privilege-granting evolves, or whether it transitions to western workable market competition.

*Southeast Asian communism is younger than China's, and in the Laotian and Cambodian cases shallower.

*Vietnam's version of market communism began in 1979 with the introduction of agricultural contracting in peasant cooperatives and the privatization of some commerce.

*Marketization proceeded in fits and starts until 1986 when it was formalized with the slogan Doi Moi (renewal).

*The goal was the creation of a socialist oriented market economy with a strong state industrial presence including banking, and aspects of foreign trade, combined with agrarian cooperatives and private enterprise in the light manufacturing and service sectors.

*Laotian and Cambodian economic evolution parallels Vietnam's after 1975. Vietnam occupied Cambodia until the mid nineties.

*Like Vietnam, it is claimed that their versions of Doi Moi were successful, but the gains are invisible to the naked eye.

*Cambodia is a communist–socialist system with multiparty elections, and Laos's rent-controlling seems comparatively mild.

*Both seem to be evolving in their own special ways.

Questions

1. How did Mao, Ho and Pol Pot modify Stalin's coercive command model?
2. Did Deng Xiaoping set out to create market communism, or did he stumble into it? Explain.
3. What were the main elements of Gaige Kaifeng?
4. What was the economic logic behind the household responsibility system and the Town Village Enterprise phenomenon? Did these initiatives require markets? Explain.
5. How did TVEs differ from private freehold business in the west? Explain.
6. Most Chinese farms today are semi-independent. In what sense are they dependent on the government, village and communist party?
7. What is the difference between consumer choice and consumer sovereignty?
8. Why are negotiated prices superior to state fixed prices and wages? Explain.
9. Do fixed prices tend to cause forced substitution? Explain.
10. Why did Mao impose fixed prices and wages? What were the costs and benefits as he perceived them?
11. In what sense are tariffs and subsidies devices for achieving forced substitution?
12. What are the traditional arguments supporting tariffs and subsidies? Were these arguments validated by Chinese economic performance 1990–2012? Explain.
13. Why are Chinese style state managed markets inferior from the purchaser's perspective?
14. Why is it misleading to infer that Chinese market economy makes China a normal society? Discuss one party "democracy", civil liberties, the role of the secret police, forced labor, the military and great power ambitions.
15. China's markets had little visible impact on the quality of life until Deng Xiaoping embraced consumerism. Why do you suppose that this was the case?

16. China has transformed its SOEs by making their survival depend on market profitability. The government has pressed state enterprises to sell equity shares to the public. This makes it seem as if SOEs are just like non-state leasehold firms. Why might this be misleading? Hint: Ponder their monopoly power.

17. Chinese SOEs are not freehold companies, and are not disciplined by the rule of law (in the western sense where contract disputes are judged by an independent judiciary). Why does freehold property matter, and why might SOEs be above the rule of law? Explain.

18. Is the state the ultimate freehold owner of China's means of production? Explain.

19. What is the structure of Chinese leaseholdership?

20. What benefit does the state receive from its lease-granting?

21. What are the key characteristics of SOEs.

22. Are SOEs permitted to sell shares in the leasehold to leasehold directors, outsiders and foreigners? Where are these sales made?

23. Are private leaseholds wholly privately owned?

24. Are SOE and private leaseholds operated on a for-profit commercial basis?

25. What is the State-owned Assets Supervision and Administration Commission (SASAC), and what is its function?

26. Are the number of SOEs declining? Is this due to the waning role of SOEs in the economy, or mergers and acquisitions?

27. Do foreign joint ventures operate under the same rules as SOEs.

28. Are banks being assigned a regulatory role over leaseholds. If so, what is the role?

29. Are the new arrangements vulnerable to moral hazard, whereby agents who were supposed to serve the state, serve themselves at the people's expense.

30. Can the Communist Party divert funds to insiders through taxes and transfers? Explain.

31. Do Chinese SOEs always have the possibility of seeking government assistance if managers prefer the easy life? Explain.

32. What are the *taizidang*? Would Marx be aghast to learn that party officials are able to use their offices to become billionaires?

33. Are foreign joint ventures extraordinarily vulnerable to communist party pressures? How might this affect the moral hazard problem?
34. One way to interpret changes in Chinese corporate structure is to view them as institutional modernization rather than a fundamental revision of the privilege-granting paradigm? Why might this insight be useful? Elaborate.
35. Are small private firms, especially those that have become conglomerates subject to many of the problems impairing the efficiency of SOEs? Explain.
36. What is Hu Jintao's concept of the harmonious society? Does the concept imply that the current regime is socially ideal?
37. What changes would be required in methods and goals to achieve a harmonious society consistent with traditional communist principles?
38. Is market communism competitively viable in the long run? Explain.
39. How might communist ideology have contributed to limiting the destructive force of privilege-granting?
40. What is Doi Moi? Elaborate.
41. How does Southeast Asian market communism differ from the Chinese paradigm?
42. China seems to have outperformed its Southeast Asian market communist clones. What factors appear to explain the divergence?
43. Based on the evidence introduced in the text, is Asian market communism more likely to evolve along a common path, or diverge? Explain.

Exercises

Market communist economies are only partly responsive to consumer demand. Goods and factors have dispreferred characteristics, are produced with the wrong technologies using inferior factor supplies. Factors do not earn the value of their generally competitive marginal products, and products are maldistributed, and mistransferred. These inefficiencies have many causes including prohibitions on freehold property, the absence of the rule of law, satisficing, privilege-granting and communist party power. Market communist countries repress wages to facilitate exports to the west.

Draw the Paretian ideal Edgeworth Bowley box (Fig. 1.1). Describe the impact of market communism on the length of the capital and labor vectors, the characteristics (for example work skills) of these factors, and the magnitudes (superscripts) of the isoquants. Where does market communist production occur in this space relative to the Pareto equilibrium E? Hint: Remember that the Pareto and market communist isoquant scalings differ. Is there likely to be more than one wage-rental ratio at the market communist production point(s)? Explain. Hint: Privileged firms have monopsony power (facilitated by worker and consumer satsificing). Whose preferences determine the demand for public goods and civic activities: the party or the people?

Relocate the market communist production point(s) in the Pareto production space (Fig. 1.2). Remember that market communism reduces the isoquant values in Fig. 1.1 (Market communist and Pareto production functions differ because market communist goods(qs) do not fully optimize consumer utility). Is the market communist production point(s) (characteristics adjusted to Pareto standard equivalent worth) likely to be severely technically and economically efficient? Explain.

Draw the Paretian ideal Edgeworth Bowley product distribution box (Fig. 1.3). Will the market communist product distribution box be the same size? Elaborate. Will retail products be fairly distributed, remembering that factors do not earn the value of their marginal products? Also given the deficiencies of market communism, will retail distribution likely be technically (as well as economically) inefficient? Explain. Are there likely to be multiple prices ruling in the market communist retail distribution space? Explain.

Draw the consumer utility space (Fig. 1.4). Assume that one participant is a communist party official and the other a worker. Locate the realized utility point *vis-à-vis* the Pareto E. Is communist market wellbeing lower both due to its productive deficiencies and inegalitarianism? Explain. Is it possible that the wellbeing of market communist insiders might surpass the Pareto ideal? Recall that China's and Vietnam's Gini coefficients are among the world's highest.

Draw the market communist Marshallian and Walrasian disequilibrium adjustment diagrams (Figs. 1.5 and 1.6), as well as the enterprise profit maximizing diagram (Fig. 1.7). Do Pareto efficient laws of supply and demand operate under market communism? If not, explain why equilibria achieved, if any, are distorted?

Is market communist wellbeing closer to the Pareto ideal than tiger Confucian markets, Japanese communalist markets, Theravada Buddhist markets, or North Korean command planning? Where would you rank market communist markets, and why?

CONFUCIANISM

Chapter 7

Taiwan, Singapore, Hong Kong and South Korea

Systems Profile: Taiwan, South Korea, Singapore, Hong Kong

Type: Confucian

Subtype: Liberal authoritarian/liberal democratic

Economic Sovereign: Confucian culture and networks control the characteristics of the system and its outcomes.

Ultimate Authority: Confucian cultural attitudes; not the rule of law (constitution).

Economy: (a) Formal: Freehold ownership, private business, rule of law, state management through indicative planning, contracting, financing, subsidization, flexible exchange rates, negotiated pricing and macroeconomic regulation. **(b) Informal:** Confucian family based networking, privilege-granting and privilege-seeking between the state and private sector.

Government: Emergent democracy with authoritarian residue

Civil Liberties: Mildly repressive

Modernization: Advanced

Evolution: Confucian authoritarianism (1950–1985); democratizing, liberalizing Confucianism (1985-present)

(Continued)

Population (July 2012; CIA):

Taiwan: 23.1 million
South Korea: 48.9 million
Singapore: 5.4 million
Hong Kong: 7.2 million

Living Standard (2012 USD, PPP; source, CIA):

Taiwan: $37,900; global rank: 28
South Korea: $21,700; global rank: 40
Singapore: $59,900, global rank: 9
Hong Kong: $49,300; global rank: 10

Development (EU Norm): Advanced, converged to or above EU level.

Contemporary Confucian Economic Systems

The economies of contemporary Taiwan, Singapore, Hong Kong and South Korea are strongly influenced by classical Confucianism and its evolution in the modern period after 1950. They are best classified under the heading of culturally sovereign systems (see Chapter 1). This means that cultural forces determine supply and demand more than the autonomous preferences of individual consumers as required in the neoclassical paradigm (the democratic competitive standard). The model is "inclusive" in the sense that state governance and the private sector are both compatible with Confucian principles. The state in Taiwan's, Singapore's, Hong Kong's and South Korea's imperial traditions is inclined toward authoritarianism, although this is waning, and the private sector is "paternalistic" as befits family-centric societies. These characteristics are fundamental because they undermine the autonomous, individualistic premises of democratic free enterprise. The Confucian model is intrinsically anti-competitive and socially conservative. It prevents individuals from fully maximizing their utility in work, investment (including education), job choice, production and consumption, and it deters governments from vigorously promoting the wide range of social programs that are the core of what western countries describe as the welfare state. Other things equal, it might be supposed that culturally sovereign Confucian systems might be severely underproductive, but the paradigm can be very competitive from a familial, rather than individualist perspective. Likewise, while Confucian systems resist the west's governmental approach to individual protection, they compensate with extended family based forms of security and mutual aid. Confucians recognize that the rigidities of their system impose costs, but feel that the trade-off enhances their community's wellbeing.

Confucianism

Confucianism is a utopian prescription for constructing ideal imperial states with harmonious societies, founded on virtuous patriarchal households. The philosophy has profoundly influenced East Asia for two and a half millennia.[1] It began as an assemblage of precepts propounded by the Chinese philosopher Kong Fuzi (Confucius) [551–479 BC, Zhou dynasty] in his analects before China became a unified state in 221BC under the reign of Qin Shi Huang, and has continuously evolved with the region's political vicissitudes (see Chapter 3). Despite periodic ups and downs, aspects of Confucianism today are easily observed in Taiwan, Singapore, Hong Kong, Macao, South Korea, communist China and Vietnam, Thailand, and Japan. They are most conspicuous in Taiwan, where the contemporary variant is partly traceable to Chiang Kaishek's (and his wife Soong Mayling's) New Life Movement (1934), which blended Confucianism, nationalism and authoritarianism in a doctrine that rejected western individualism and capitalist values.[2] Singaporean

---

[1] Edith Terry contends that Confucius was primarily interested in devising norms for effective imperial governance, and sees the idealized patriarchal family as a metaphor. In the analects of Mencius the text solely consists of advice to kings. The patriarchal family however regardless of Confucius's intent plays a strong role in Chinese culture. Even though, Confucian communities in the 20th century rejected imperial rule, they retained the patriarchal family as an inspirational ideal for education, entrepreneurship, loyalty, trust, prosperity and beneficence. Email December 8, 2009.

[2] The program was a reformulation of Sun Yatsen's "Three Principles of the People", nationalism, democracy, and government guided economic welfare (see Chiang Kai-shek (1934). Essentials of the new life movement. Speech). Many overseas Chinese consider the New Life Movement shallow agitational rhetoric.

Confucianism, concentrated in the Chinese community has a late Ching dynasty flavor, while South Koreans often claim that their neo-Confucianism is the most pristine version of the master's teachings. All three societies are influenced by other traditions including Taoism, Buddhism, Christianity, and western social philosophies from Enlightenment libertarianism to Marxist socialism. Thirty five years of Japanese occupation (1910–1945) also has left a residue on South Korea's shame culture and communalism.

Confucianism thus cannot explain every aspect of the Taiwanese, Singaporean, Hong Kong and South Korean governance systems, but its impacts on individual psychology, values (including personal integrity, ancestral duties, liberty and self-fulfillment), communal norms, networking, hierarchy, minority empowerment, social stability and political control are profound. It accepts the legitimacy of personal utility seeking, however, only with stringent cultural constraints that compel most people to satisfice (including character formation) rather than utility maximize, subject to their status, position, role, and trans-generational duties.

The cornerstone of the ideal social order for Confucians of every persuasion is a set of moral precepts inculcated from birth intended to promote personal, communal, societal and national harmony autonomously, without higher legal, imperial, transcendental, or divine guidance. The approach is the antithesis of Qin Shi Huang's top-down governance,[3] predicated on blind obedience to imperial edicts and administrative laws ("legalism").[4] The legalist tradition still holds sway in Beijing and Hanoi, in sharp contrast to the Confucianism of Taiwan, Singapore, Hong Kong and South Korea, creating a real life contest between these two ancient sinic cultural rivals.

Confucianism teaches that every individual's supreme moral obligation is familial (dynastic) wellbeing; not God, country, administrative law, or Kantian categorical imperatives. It is duty to family understood as an hereditary unit deferentially orchestrated according to Confucian rules that is the summum bonum,[5] rather than personal appraisals of precepts' merit, or specific outcomes. This makes Confucius an institutionalist. Wellbeing in his governance scheme is intrinsic to the orderly performance of the

---

[3] see Chapter 5, footnote 1.
[4] see Chapter 5, footnote 1.
[5] The emperor's extended family in this scheme is the nation.

familial ballet, and does not depend on individuals realizing their potentials. Confucians, of course, claim that faithful performance of choreographed familial duty is a prerequisite for individual psychological wellbeing, reflected in self-perceptions of wellbeing, fulfillment and contentment.

Confucius's ethics, as distinct for Confucian praxis are broadly sensible. Men and women are exhorted to avoid treating others badly to discourage them from being hurt in return (the "silver rule").[6] This is supposed to make it self-evident that people should never harm other people by being hurtful, discourteous, imperious, dishonest, deceptive, false, envious, rancorous, manipulative, seductive, obscene, bawdy, treacherous, impious, unjust, or malicious. They should not conspire, inveigle, traduce, slander, demean, debase, degrade, embarrass, humiliate, steal, burgle, defile, profane, injure, pillage, kidnap, molest, rape, torture, or murder. Instead, they should be enlightened (educated), refined, cultured, discrete, polite, thoughtful, fair, benevolent, considerate, compassionate, generous, philanthropic, chaste, loyal, trustworthy, prudent, hardworking, frugal, farsighted, provident and wise. These behaviors which are echoed by the Protestant ethic, advance familial wellbeing by avoiding conflicts and vendettas; promoting prosperity, respect, friendship, love, peace, tranquility, harmony, serenity, prosperity and happiness.

Confucian virtue is its own reward, and a benefice to society, just as it was for Plato. There cannot be wellbeing without moral integrity. Those who do good deeds are enriched by their benevolence, and serve further as paragons for those who cannot find their bearings. They enable the less worthy, and lost souls to quickly perceive the folly of their transgressions, and save themselves.

Confucian societies build on these ethical pillars by instilling senses of guilt for wrongdoing, and shame for disgraceful conduct that transform ethical precepts into a self-regulating familial and communitarian order. Plato's Republic mimics Kong Fuzi's moral logic, but relies on the righteous behavior of autonomous individuals clustered in three estates: philosopher kings (wisdom), warriors (courage), and commoners (temperance).

---

[6] "Do not to do unto others as they would have others not do unto them". This is a negative formulation of the Christian golden rule: Do unto others as you would have others do unto you).

Their collective action, instead of Confucian families and communities, jointly insure prosperity, security, national welfare, and justice.

Confucius also invokes the notion of sage emperor (philosopher king), responsible for guiding his flock, but argues explicitly that familial and communitarian rectitude is a precondition for effective, virtuous state governance. Emperors in his universe, as heads of the national family, need only promulgate their benevolent programs, and inform their subjects, who will loyally and harmoniously comply.

There is no place in the orthodox Confucian paradigm, or even Hsiung Shih-li's (1887–1968) neo-idealist Confucianism which blends Confucian ritual with Buddhist ethics for individualist self-discovery fulfillment, and minority empowerment.[7] Fung Yu-lan's neo-rationalist (Kant) Confucianism combining Cheng-Chu's Song dynasty teachings with neo-realist philosophy incorporates some westernizing values, but his Confucian outlook remains staunchly conservative, despite concessions to social mobility, and socialism.[8]

Confucian households are hierarchical. Everyone has a fixed role. Fathers rule and are guardians of family welfare. Women bear children and perform sundry chores. Children obey their parents, and care for them in their dotage. Everyone respects ancestors, is filially pious, loyal and self-sacrificing for the greater family good. The hierarchy defines status. Husbands as wise lords and protectors are the most revered. Wives follow behind a distant second, appreciated by their husbands and esteemed by their children; an arrangement reminiscent of Thomas More's Utopia.[9]

No one voluntarily lives for himself or herself, or seeks personal fulfillment at the family's and nation's expense. Selfish behavior for Confucians, commonplace in the west and increasingly observable in overseas Chinese communities is immoral. It creates disharmonies that poison human relations, debase familial wellbeing, generate adversarial productive regimes, and impair productivity; spawning inequalities, strife and injustice. Just as in Plato's and More's universes, there exists one and

---

[7] see Chan (1986).
[8] see Fung (1952–1953), Rozman (1991), and Wright (1961).
[9] see More (2002). The original text was published in 1516.

only one ideal moral socio-economic system requiring everyone to know his or her place, and faithfully fulfills assigned roles.

Some may agree, but many Asians do not see things this way. They challenge the idea that indoctrination, discipline, subordination, self-abnegation, self-sacrifice and loyalty really are individually and socially best because reliance on precepts implies that people do not think things through for themselves; they simply obey. Obedience is virtuous in some contexts, but not necessarily in others. Contemporary women and children may find Confucian obligations stifling, even though men might yearn for paradise lost. Female, male and juvenile misfits could adjust their attitudes under duress, acquiescing to necessity, but in doing so they would be compelled to satisfice in numerous senses that preclude maximizing their wellbeing. Thus, even if people were morally compliant in Confucius's system, they might be profoundly unfulfilled and discontent.

These shortcomings apply with still greater force in the imperfect world mortals inhabit where people may espouse Confucian virtue, but play by very different rules. Husbands may be despots, wives conniving, and children vicious. Family units may advance themselves by preying on other families, and disregard their communitarian obligations. Nepotism and corruption may be endemic. Communities may be rigidly divided into respected estates [Shi (scholars), Nong (peasants), Gong (craftsmen) and Shang (commerce)] and outcasts (soldiers, entertainers, prostitutes, etc.) under the supervision of emperors and nobles. The educated, especially those serving the imperial bureaucracy may be privileged at the expense of productive businessmen, workers and peasants. Individual fortunes may be determined by birth, gender and ethnicity rather than ability because mobility across occupations and within families and communities is blocked. Greed and power may take precedence over harmony and justice.

Under such degenerate circumstances, Confucianism is turned upside down. Having started as a strategy for creating a virtuous, prosperous and harmonious society founded on ethically guided familial institutions, Kong Fuzi's teachings may end up as a rationale for corruption, privilege and subjugation. Instead of promoting material progress and national wellbeing, Confucianism may impair both in favor of entrenching the prevailing order. China's inferior economic performance 1500–1950 displayed in Fig. 4.1, including Chiang Kaishek's nationalist Confucian interlude 1934–1950 exemplifies the danger, while Taiwan's, Singapore's, Hong Kong's and South Korea's experiences during 1950–2012 highlight the benefits of Confucian rejuvenation.

Confucian Rejuvenation

Asia's premier contemporary Confucian societies are Taiwan, Singapore, Hong Kong, and South Korea. Their superlative economic performance during the past half century prompted some to dub them Asian Tigers or Four Little Dragons.[10] Many factors explain their successes. Among them, and perhaps most importantly has been Confucianism's surprising adaptivity. Asia's tigers learned by doing how to relax familial restrictions, increasing member's degrees of freedom, and fostering a surge in productivity without paying too great a price in foregone familial protection and mutual aid.

The new found adaptivity may have been forced upon some by necessity. Mao Tsetung's conquest of mainland China and the cold war provided a powerful motive for adjusting to new realities.

This new priority drew women out of the household into the labor force and substantially increased their status within the nuclear family. In the process, attitudes toward optimal family size have shifted from large to small units, often with only a single child, and increasingly toward families with no children at all. Two breadwinners tend to equalize the status of husbands and wives, diminish the importance of ancestors, alter dynastic expectations, and augment the power of increasingly entitled children. Extended families and fictitious kinship partly mitigate the obsolescence of the Confucian family archetype, but individuals rather than groups nonetheless are becoming the epicenter of a new Confucian morality as family units are reduced to heterosexual pairings, and same sex partnerships.

---

[10] Taiwan, Singapore, Hong Kong and South Korea are frequently described as Asian tigers, or little dragons to stress their economic vibrance (1960–1990), and the emergence of a second cluster of successful Asian economies following Japan's earlier example. Their accomplishments are sometimes attributed to "Asian values", particularly education attainment and harmonious labor-management relations (see Kinzley, 1991).

The rigidities of Confucian social structures and rituals also have been weakened. Industrialization and the burgeoning service sector have increased social mobility, raising the importance of value-adding accomplishment at the expense of hereditary stature.[11] Attitudes toward entrepreneurship and profit seeking have been modified, and the state is displacing communities as the primary guarantor of local wellbeing. Nonetheless, traditional values continue to coexist with modern lifestyles, constraining the scope of utility searching, supporting anticompetitive networking, nepotism and the corruption underlying the Confucian moral facade. Economic performance in Taiwan, Singapore, Hong Kong, and South Korea have been very good, reflecting the benefits of resource mobilization, modernization and partial westernization, but they could reach a ceiling if Confucian rigidities reemerge or residual restrictions are not softened.

Entrepreneurship and socialism are especially important in both these regards. Confucianism, unlike Theravada Buddhism has always promised prosperity and social welfare. It commended education, hard work, self-reliance and technological progress insofar as they strengthened family and community, but frowned on any behavior that made personal self-seeking, or state welfare dependency highest goods. Families and communities of families, first and foremost were morally self-regulating, guided by sage and compassionate emperors.

These are the notions that Chiang Kaishek appealed to when he condemned capitalism and socialism alike in his "New Life Program". But the genie could not be put back in the bottle. The collapse of the Ching dynasty in 1911, liberationist rhetoric, entrepreneurial opportunism and

---

[11] Taiwan not only benefited from inexpensive factors of production (including labor), easy access to American and Japanese markets, and technology transfer, but the traditional Confucian reverence for education swiftly became a vehicle for steadily elevating productive skills. Foreign demand disciplined Taiwanese suppliers to produce goods with desirable characteristics. Technology transfer raised factor productivity, while authoritarianism repressed trade unions, and Confucian ethics facilitated cooperative labor-management relations and cost efficiency. Like Deng Xiaoping's subsequent market liberalization on the mainland, Chiang's authoritarian modernization program was bolstered further by the advantages of relative economic backwardness. Microeconomic inefficiencies associated with Confucian restrictions on individualism were more than offset by climbing the value-added ladder from a low to a high productivity regime.

communist promises (1925–1949) gradually altered cultural attitudes, legitimating family based and individual acquisitiveness at the community's expense on one hand, and state paternalism on the other, beyond what Confucius would have thought desirable. Entrepreneurship sparked material progress, and paternalist government provided a social safety net, but the two forces pulled Taiwan's, Singapore's, Hong Kong's and South Korea's economic systems in opposing directions; the first toward individualist free enterprise, and the second toward socialism. The tensions can be partially or fully reconciled in various ways, but each solution has distinct ramifications for the economic potential of modern Confucian economic systems. Asian tigers may westernize as globalizers predict, subordinate growth to state provided social welfare, or choose diverse middle paths, all within Confucian frameworks.

For the present, it seems that the increase in the material wellbeing of Confucian Taiwan, Singapore, South Korea and Hong Kong, illustrated for Taiwan in Fig. 4.3 has more than amply justified bending the democratic competitive standard to suit sinic cultural needs. The latent intra and inter-familial discontents in prewar Confucian Asia also appear to have been alleviated by increased mobility and gender equality,[12] without eradicating the psychological benefits of Confucian family structures.[13] Ironically, Confucian family institutions are making Taiwanese more autonomous than America's erstwhile "individualists", who have become entrepreneurially straitjacketed by and dependent on "big government". The game obviously is not over, but it can be concluded nonetheless that for the last quarter century, evolving Confucian civilization has had a greater positive effect on Asian wellbeing and contentment than most observers might dared to have hoped.

---

[12] The proportion of three or more generation households in Taiwan has declined, while single-person households have steadily increased driven in part by rising divorce rates and single-parent families. Likewise, female employment outside the household has increased substantially for both single and married women, due to enhanced educational attainment, shifting public attitudes, and reduced reliance on male bread-winning. This has sparked a host of social problems that have challenged the nation, prompting the government to respond by increasing funding for social wellbeing.

[13] These accomplishments were accompanied by a marked decline in inequality. The Gini coefficient fell from 0.56 to 0.3 between 1953 and 1980, just the reverse of communist Chinese experience under Deng Xiaoping and Hu Jintao.

Trajectory

Asia's tigers recognize that they must be continuously adaptive.[14] They cannot stop the entrepreneurial clock in deference to traditionalist sensibilities because global comparative advantages are perpetually in flux. Once upon a time, the little dragons could compete in labor intensive industries with China and Vietnam, but that is ancient history. Now they are compelled to excel in information technology, LCD, LED flat-panel TVs, biotechnology, and other high tech industries, outsourcing wherever they can including China.

Likewise, although emerging Asian tiger state welfare systems have many distinctive characteristics,[15] they are evolving in liberal directions compatible with enhanced global competitiveness. Social insurance, labor assistance, family responsibility, and supplementary private protective reforms are motivated as much by economic efficiency concerns as they are national wellbeing.

Modernization and globalization are also prodding Asia's tigers toward the inclusive democratic competitive model, that is, toward democracy, increased market competitiveness, openness, and civic empowerment, and away from traditional reliance on family discipline and social conformity. Nonetheless, democracy is still embryonic and febrile. Electoral multiparty democracy started in South Korea in 1988, followed soon thereafter in Taiwan. Hong Kong has British democratic institutions, but remains compliant to Beijing's pressure, while Singapore is still considered by most experts to be a one-party authoritarian regime. A westernizing liberal trend toward democracy and civic tolerance is taking root, but still falls far short of the ideal.

The sum and substance of these intricate matters is that Asia's tigers despite notable advances toward westernization still retain a strong residue from the imperial/20th century Confucian past. Market, political and

---

[14] see Tselichtchev and Debroux (2009). The authors stress that the tigers, and market communist nations are shifting from enterprises relying on state loans to equity capital, and adopting market oriented corporate governance.

[15] Social welfare expenditures as GDP shares in 2002 were: Japan 18.4, America 11.9, South Korea 5.5, Germany 28.4, Taiwan 4.9, France 28.6, Singapore 1.8, UK 22.4, China 0.3. (see Chan, 2008).

civic freedoms are restricted by state management, limited popular sovereignty and selective civic repression, combined with familial and communitarian satisficing. Spokesmen for the little dragons conceal these blemishes by showcasing their successes in closing the Asia-west living standards divide (see Figs. 4.3, 4.4, 4.5, and 4.10). This is accurate as far as it goes, but requires qualification. The best way to appreciate the composite properties of modern Confucian market economies is through the prism of the Pareto standard elaborated in Chapter 1, which exposes sundry deficiencies beneath the statistical gloss of rapid growth and modernization (see Exercise section, this chapter). Asia's tigers are microeconomically inefficient (partly concealed by forced substitution), inadequately representative, and civically circumscribed. These negatives are often swept under the rug, but they should not be. They degrade national wellbeing and fulfillment behind a facade of misleading macroeconomic accomplishment.

Confucians can and do object to this net assessment, asserting the superiority of their cultural values. They claim that market, governmental and civic restrictions placed on individual utility-seeking are for the greater good, and yield superior results. This position deserves a balanced hearing. Readers should ponder the intrinsic merits of Confucian ethics, discounted for ambiguities, contradictions, biases and social consequences observable in Taiwan, Singapore, Hong Kong and South Korea in reaching their own verdicts.

Let us consider this issue further by examining the particularities of the Taiwanese and South Korean economic systems.

Taiwan

Taiwan was a Japanese colony from 1895 to 1945. The Qing dynasty legally transferred the territory to Japan in the treaty of Shimonoseki. From 1945 to 1952 Taiwan belonged to Japan, but was administered by American occupation forces, delegated to the Republic of China (ROC) led by Chiang Kaishek (head of the Chinese Nationalist Party, Kuomintang). When the People's Republic of China (PRC) was founded in 1949, Chiang fled to Taiwan and unlawfully established a dictatorship 1949–1987, even though Japan initially retained ownership. Tokyo renounced its claim to Taiwan and Penghu in the San Francisco Peace Treaty 1952 ending World War II.[16] Mao's People's Republic of China was excluded and is not a signatory. This diplomatic precedent bolstered Chiang's position, but still left open the question of whether Japan had renounced its claim in favor of the ROC or PRC.

This brief historical sketch reveals that Taiwan's Confucian economic system was forged under complex conditions dominated more by political than ethical factors. Communists and PRC sympathizers were enemies and rivals for sovereignty in Taiwan and abroad, making it imperative from Chiang's perspective to adopt a social mobilization strategy that simultaneously promoted rapid modernization and dampened dissidence, just as Stalin and Mao had done before him. Chiang had not embraced economic mobilization before 1952. The construction of this authoritarian development model was easily accomplished, at least conceptually, because it only required adapting his New Life Movement initiated in 1934 to a rapid industrialization agenda.

Chiang harnessed familial aspirations for prosperity by encouraging private business, while simultaneously channeling these energies into state preferred projects through various means including banks and four year national planning. This involved public works of the sort that the Chinese have always excelled from the time of Qin Shi Huang, as well as an export driven growth strategy designed both to skirt domestic market rigidities and capture the benefits of superior western purchasing power. Simply put, goods produced for export generated higher value added than import substitutes. Occupation networks created during 1945–1952 between the Kuomintang and American businessmen facilitated this process, as did historical links with Japan, allowing Chiang to subsidize exports, while protecting import substitutes.

Neither authoritarianism, nor civic repression appears to have seriously hampered Chiang's modernization initiative. Taiwan not only benefited from inexpensive factors of production (including labor), easy access to American and Japanese markets, and technology transfer, but the

---

[16] The Soviet Union never signed the treaty and Russia is still technically in an armistice with Japan. The Sino–Japanese war was concluded separately April 28, 1952 by the Treaty of Taipei, signed by Republic of China and Japan.

traditional Confucian reverence for education swiftly became a vehicle for steadily elevating productive skills. Foreign demand disciplined Taiwanese suppliers to produce goods with desirable characteristics. Technology transfer raised factor productivity, while authoritarianism repressed trade unions, and Confucian ethics facilitated cooperative labor-management relations and cost efficiency. Like Deng Xiaoping's subsequent market liberalization on the mainland, Chiang's authoritarian modernization program was bolstered further by the advantages of relative economic backwardness. Microeconomic inefficiencies associated with Confucian restrictions on individualism were more than offset by climbing the value-added ladder from a low to a high productivity regime.[17]

Moreover, these accomplishments were accompanied by a marked decline in inequality. The Gini coefficient fell from 0.56 to 0.3 between 1953 and 1980, just the reverse of communist Chinese experience under Deng Xiaoping and Hu Jintao. Confucians take credit for this positive development, and may well deserve it. The reverse trend occurred during communist China's market liberalization surge.

---

[17] Chiang's Taiwan had various other advantages. When the Kuomintang fled China, it brought the ROC's entire stock of precious metals and foreign currency reserves with it. Refugees from the PRC were well educated, comprising much of the mainland's intellectual and business elites. The Japanese had built an excellent agricultural and industrial infrastructure, and accumulated large chemical, material and food reserves. The US government provided four billion dollars of financial aid and soft credit during the period 1945–1965. The KMT instituted land reforms and market liberalization in Taiwan that it had steadfastly resisted on the mainland. These reforms increased agrarian productivity, and provided a pool of industrial laborers released from agricultural employment. USAID assisted in the creation of a massive industrial infrastructure, communications, and developed the educational system. A 19 point program of Economic and Financial Reform was adopted in 1959, liberalizing market controls to stimulate exports and attract direct foreign investment. General Instruments pioneered outsourcing electronic assembly in Taiwan in 1964, but the nucleus of industrial production remained internal family business, financed with family savings and savings cooperatives (Hui), assisted with government subsidies and bank credit. Family business coalitioned with foreign companies, but direct foreign investment never accounted for a large share of production, except in the electronics industry. Direct foreign investment comprised only 2% of GDP in 1981, but foreign firms accounted for 25% of exports. No large multinational corporations were created as they were in Singapore, and the Taiwanese eschewed chaebols. However, some domestic family firms did become big international players.

Success however also bred social change, and systemic adaptation. Independent trade unions began to form in the 1970s. Taiwanese companies began outsourcing abroad, particularly in mainland China, and agitation for enhanced civic empowerment emerged, culminating in a movement to create a well-functioning democratic order, and a shift in government priorities from fostering production to social welfare.

During the 1990s, the government increased the size and scope of social welfare programs, allowing families to lighten their obligations to elder care, education, and unemployment assistance. It also provided coverage for those living outside familial safety nets, including disadvantaged groups, supported some feminist aspirations, and had the further effect of transferring income from the rich to the poor. The government established National Health insurance targeted at the elderly, children and disabled and handicapped in 1985–1991. It tackled unemployment insurance in 1994 and gender issues like juvenile prostitution, and sexual assault in 1995–1997, before invading the sanctity of the Confucian household with legislation on domestic violence prevention and assistance to women and households in difficulty 1998–2000. A gender equality employment law was passed in 2002 to ameliorate the Confucian preference for male workers.[18]

These changes are not impressive judged from a western benchmark, but they should not be belittled because they illustrate the kind of adaptiveness required for nations to prosper in an increasingly competitive international environment,[19] complicated by an aging population, declining fertility (Tables 7.1 and 7.2), and defamilialization.[20] The proportion of three or more generation households in Taiwan has declined, while single-person households have steadily increased driven in part by rising divorce rates and single-parent families (Tables 7.3 and 7.4). Female employment outside the household has increased substantially for both single and married women (Table 7.5), due to variously improved educational attainment, shifting public attitudes, and reduced reliance on male bread-winning. This has sparked a host of social problems that have challenged the nation, prompting the government to respond by increasing funding for social wellbeing.

---

[18] see Lan (2009).

[19] see Peng and Ito (2004, pp. 289–425).

[20] see Esping-Andersen (1999).

Table 7.1. Graying of Taiwan's Population (Population Over 65: Percent).

1980	1990	2000	2006	2007
4	6	9	10	10.2

Source: Council for Economic Planning and Development (2008). *Projections of the Population for Taiwan Area and Taiwan Statistical Data Book.*

Table 7.2. Fertility Rate in Taiwan, 1960–2003 (Percent).

1960–1965	1985–1990	1995–2000	2003	2007	2008
3.59	1.63	1.39	1.01	0.89	0.62

Source: Council for Economic Planning and Development (2008). *Projections of the Population for Taiwan Area.*

Table 7.3. Taiwanese Family Structure (Percent).

	1990	2000
Nuclear	60	55
Three generations	25	16
Single	13	21

Source: National Statistics, Directorate General of Budget, Accounting and Statistics, Executive Yuan.

Table 7.4. Divorce Rates in Taiwan (Percent).

1980	2000	2006	2007
8	24	28	26

Source: *National Statistics*, Directorate General of Budget, Accounting Statistic, Executive Yuan.

Table 7.5. Female Labor Market Participation Rates (Percent).

	1979	1980	2000	2006
All women	32	33	50	53
Married woman	29	31	35	34

Source: *National Statistics,* Directorate General of Budget, Accounting and Statistics, Executive Yuan.

This new orientation is at variance with the classical Confucian model, but perhaps not with a liberal reading of Kong Fuzi's ethics that might apply to new globalist economic, social, political and diplomatic realities. It may well contribute positively to the solution of the deeper challenge posed to Taiwan's prosperity by the depletion of the sources of its economic growth (post catch up effect),[21] and the ongoing problem of reconciling Confucian satisficing (restricted individual utility-seeking in deference to family obligations) with competition from less individually encumbered, individual utility maximizing economic systems.

South Korea

South Korea (Republic of Korea (ROC)), like Taiwan has a turbulent past and only came of age recently. The entire Korean peninsula, which had been part of the Japanese empire since 1910, was supposed to be transformed into a single independent country after Japan surrendered to the United States September 2, 1945, but the interim occupation arrangements in the Soviet controlled North, and American administered South led to the creation of two separate regimes. Kim Il-sung established a communist state in the North under Stalin's tutelage, while Syngman Rhee launched a democratic government with strong American support run in an authoritarian manner 1948–1960. Like Chiang Kaishek, Rhee was a Methodist, but South Korea's culture was a mixture of Japanese influenced communalism and indigenous neo-Confucianism.

Korean state governance before Japanese annexation followed the Chinese post-Tang dynasty Confucian imperial paradigm during the Goreyo dynasty 918–1392 and Neo-Confucianism emphasizing loyalty, filial piety, benevolence and trust during the Joseon dynasty 1392–1910. Given China's chaotic late Ching dynastic and Republican experiences, only the foolhardy would have predicted a smooth postwar transition to western democratic free enterprise with or without Soviet and American occupation. Japan had taken many important strides in this direction during the late Meiji and early Taisho periods, but succumbed to imperialist militarism. This too should have lowered expectations.

---

[21] see Krugman (1994).

Some of these misgivings were confirmed during the succeeding 40 years. Despite constitutional formalities, electoral democracy was not established in the South until 1988 when President Roh Tae-Woo replaced Chun Doo-Hwan. Lee Myung-bak's inauguration February 25, 2008 made only the second time that power was peacefully transferred from one party to political opponents. Likewise, while the South Korean variant of Confucianism enabled family businesses to flourish for several decades, the institutions of the early years may be losing their effectiveness, and civic rigidities remain a serious problem.

One way to appreciate the limitations of the South Korean Confucian economic model is through the lens of the rule of law (where individual economic and civic rights trump familial and state edicts). During the Goreyo, Joseon, and Japanese colonial periods public, private and civic participation were circumscribed and tightly regulated by state directives and Confucian precepts. The people did not craft laws consensually binding their actions, implemented and adjudicated by independent courts, but had laws imposed on them for patriarchs' and the sovereign's convenience. South Korea's Chiang Kaishek-type military dictatorships may be fading memories, but the culture of insider sovereignty perpetuated by the rule of men persists within a framework of private property, business and entrepreneurship. South Korea's civilian presidents and the conservative establishment over which they preside (including chaebols) use public money for private purposes. They rent-grant, draft preferential laws, disregard statutes with impunity, and control judicial verdicts, despite the achievement of free and fair elections, universal adult suffrage, multiparty competition, civil liberties and a free press. Freedom House lists South Korea as only one of six Asian countries that is politically free.

The problem is not unique, but in South Korea takes a distinctive Confucian form featuring symbiotic relationships between politicians, ministers and technocrats linked by clan, family and shared elite values on one hand, and chaebols (familial business conglomerates) on the other. The arrangement, which echoes autocratic relations between the landed nobility and wealthy merchants before 1910, began in 1961 shortly after General Park Chung Hee came to power with an industrializing mission diversely driven by security needs, a desire for political legitimation and a Confucian penchant for prosperity. Park, faced with a credible North Korean communist threat (like Chiang *vis-à-vis* Mao's China) sought to expedite economic development by creating a directive planning system to mobilize and channel private resources

The center piece of this planning regime was the Economic Planning Board (EPB), an organization similar to Economic Planning Agency of Japan (EPA) and Ministry of Economy, Trade and Industry (METI). The EPB acquired standard national income accounting data (not enterprise draft plans as in North Korea), assessed development prospects with sectoral production functions, and forged programs (plans) according to Park's priorities. Had the EPB done nothing more, its plans would have been indicative in line with contemporary European Union (EU) practice. However, Park made them directive by nationalizing the banking system (including merging the agricultural cooperative movement with a state Agricultural Bank), allocating credit only to private sector firms agreeing to micro implement the EPB's sectoral plans.

The tactic, anticipated by Oscar Lange and Fred Taylor in their *On the Economic Theory of Socialism* (1938) was technically sound, but its effectiveness depended on the prowess of recipient firms. Park decided to enhance this weak link by favoring friendly (often filially related) companies with state contracts and other assistance, encouraging them to become mega conglomerates spanning multiple sectors, except banking which remained a state monopoly. He also nurtured state owned enterprises, creating a system closer to North Korea's than anyone cared to acknowledge, overseen at the top by the EPB [now Ministry of Strategy and Finance (MOSF)] which commanded and indirectly financed state companies (later supplemented by Ministries, the Korean Development Institute and the Office of the President), and outsourced to chaebols. Power in this original and pristine form was concentrated in the hands of the state, but the balance subsequently shifted with the political tides. After Roh Tae Woo assumed the presidency, it became increasingly difficult to distinguish the dog (state) from the tail (chaebols). Chaebols measured in terms of revenues (2004) emerged as global giants: Samsung ($89.2 billion), Hyundai Motor company ($57.2 billion), LG ($50.4 billion), SK ($46.4 billion), Hanhwa ($4.4 billion) and Kumho Asiana ($2.8 billion) capable of doing the state's bidding, receiving subsidies, and providing reciprocal political support. However, they also developed sufficient power to impose their will on the government. The independence of chaebols was increased by access to foreign loans, and equity financing.

Judging from South Korea's rapid economic development, it can be inferred that neither the military dictator-chaebol alliance, nor its fractious democratic successor were destructive enough to significantly offset the gains from enhanced occupational mobility, urbanization, education, capital widening, American assistance, foreign outsourcing and technology transfer. But as South Korea's 1997 financial meltdown proved, clan governance bred massive corruption and wasteful subsidization.[22] The crisis prompted various efforts at reform under President Kim Dae-Jung. Chaebols have been pressured to focus on core businesses, spinning off unrelated enterprises. They were encouraged to hire professionals, instead of family managers, and various tax laws were enacted to limit private family wealth. These modifications however are subsidiary from a systems perspective. What counts is state-chaebol constrained competitiveness, which significantly circumscribes the scope of permissible individual utility seeking both in the public and private household sectors, and deters the empowerment of excluded strata.

South Korea's civic sector likewise is wanting from the Pareto benchmark. In accordance with Confucian principles, the state and society are inseparable, and therefore individual South Koreans have no independent moral basis for pressing their rights against the state-society. This encourages conformism and impedes pluralism, phenomena reinforced by the state-chaebol alliance. Western businessmen often view the state as hostile, but in South Korea the norm is collaboration. Women's roles are particularly tightly constrained, preventing them from actualizing their full human potential. According to the World Economic Forum Gender Gap Index, South Korean women find themselves near the bottom of the global hierarchy, 54th out of 65, above India and below Jordon.

As with the public and household sectors, civil society has made significant strides since electoral democracy blossomed in 1987. There were 7,600 NGOs active in the ROK as early as 1999. Specialists however, insist that South Korean civic groups lack civility (the desire

---

[22] For example, the Daewoo Group's bankruptcy left 80 billion dollars of debt to the government unpaid.

to compromise and achieve peaceful consensus), and as a corollary, undervalue pluralism (the dark side of Confucianism). They believe that Confucian South Korea will continue to differ substantially from the inclusive western democratic competitive ideal.[23] Social welfare east and west consequently cannot be the same, with appraisals of comparative merit turning on material performance, national subjective judgments, and the values of independent observers (see Chapter 1).

If one considers the west a worthy standard, South Korea probably stands second or third behind Japan in its degree of westernization. Its electoral democracy and perhaps its rudimentary rule of law seem better than Singapore's and Hong Kong's. Unlike China it accepts freehold property, its economy is comparatively open, and its civic institutions may well improve. Still details matter. Japan too appears western to novices, but experts know it is not. Culture not only caps potential changes, but also affects the social and political dynamics of transition. When critical cultural thresholds are breeched, there is always an acute risk of destabilization.

The cultural forces at play in South Korea are diverse, including Confucianism (pervasive), Christianity (26% Protestant; 6.6% Roman Catholic), Buddhism (23.2%), other/unknown (1.3%), and none (49.3%) as reported in the 1995 census. These religions (and ethical systems) rest on a guilt culture with pronounced shame cultural elements which in their entirety make Koreans simultaneously and often contradictorily autonomous (entrepreneurial) and conformist (including overworking). Until recently South Koreans worked 54 hour weeks.

South Koreans are individualistic, ethical, and self-regulating within Confucian parameters, but they are also comparatively intolerant of diversity, and bureaucratic with a proclivity toward insider corruption, capping effectiveness in the global marketplace. Many observers brush aside these blemishes arguing that hard work and the South Korean brand of neo-Confucian ethics will overcome all obstacles. Such assurances should be taken with a grain of salt because Confucian ethics are not immutable and do not guarantee economic success as Korea's pre-1960 economic performance attests. Seoul has proven that the chaebol model is effective in some epochs, however it remains at risk for many types of decay, and mostly relies on an

---

[23] see Koo (2002, pp.40–45).

inner Confucian moral light to guide it to safe harbors, instead of the robust and dense defenses of western systems predicated on the rule of law.

Singapore and Hong Kong

Taiwan, South Korea, Singapore and Hong Kong are classified as tigers or four little dragons because they shared many common characteristics during 1950–1997: Confucianism, authoritarianism, a postwar resource mobilization mentality, state led development, private property, export fueled growth, competitive open market economy, global integration, and emergent rule of law. These characteristics are still shared, but the change in Hong Kong's sovereign status from a British crown colony to a semi-autonomous administrative entity under communist Beijing's control probably justifies its reclassification. Hong Kong's performance after 1997 seems to have been shaped as much by its role as a Chinese administrative unit under Beijing's one country, two systems formula as by Confucian culture. Its status today is unique.

Hong Kong and Singapore also differ from Taiwan and South Korea in other important ways. Taiwan and South Korea spent the first half of the 20th century under Japanese control, whereas Singapore and Hong Kong were British port colonies (Singapore 1824–1940; Hong Kong 1842–1997) that ultimately benefited from a comparatively strong respect for the rule of contract law. After Japanese occupation (1941–1945), Singapore evolved into a multi-ethnic (predominantly Chinese) independent island city state on the southern tip of the Malay Peninsula in 1965 (a micro-state and the smallest country in Asia), but Hong Kong never acquired full sovereignty. It went from being a British to a Chinese possession.

The British imperial connection also was a plus in other ways. It fostered Hong Kong's and Singapore's transformation into enclaves for western multinational corporations and facilitated the influx of low cost foreign workers. These special features are reflected in Singaporean statistics by the gap between indigenous and aggregate per capita GDP. Resident workers and Singaporean owned companies contribute less per capita to GDP than foreign entities. Non-indigenous businesses generated 41.6 percent of Singapore's GDP in 2008. GDP per capita was 57,410 Singaporean dollars (SGD), but the indigenous figure was 43,107 (see Table 7.6), implying that the indigenous living standard expressed in

Table 7.6. Indigenous Singaporean Per Capita Income (Yearbook of Statistics Singapore, 2012).

	Indigenous Gross National Income (At Current Market Prices)						
	2001	2006	2007	2008	2009	2010	2011
Million Dollars							
Total Gross Domestic Product	157,136.1	231,580.6	267,630.4	268,772.4	270,012.7	310,036.8	326,832.4
Share of Resident Foreigners & Resident Foreign Companies in GDP	61,542.6	101,458.8	115,999.6	111,746.0	115,863.1	132,207.4	144,228.2
Indigenous GDP	95,593.5	130,121.8	151,630.8	157,026.4	154,149.6	177,829.4	182,604.2
Net Factor Receipts of Singaporeans from Rest of the World	15,064.5	38,126.9	53,163.8	30,671.0	41,504.9	48,264.1	48,987.8
Indigenous GNI	110,658.0	168,248.7	204,794.6	187,697.4	195,654.5	226,093.5	231,592.0
Per Capita Indigenous GNI ($)	33,272	47,718	57,156	51,527	52,400	59,945	61,117
Per Capita Indigenous GDP ($)	28,742	36,905	42,318	43,107	41,284	47,148	48,189
Percentage Change Over Previous Year							
Total Gross Domestic Product	−3.4	10.9	15.6	0.4	0.5	14.8	5.4
Share of Resident Foreigners & Resident Foreign Companies in GDP	3.2	18.9	14.3	−3.7	3.7	14.1	9.1
Indigenous GDP	−7.1	5.4	16.5	3.6	−1.8	15.4	2.7
Net Factor Receipts of Singaporeans from Rest of the World	−30.6	41.3	39.4	−42.3	35.3	16.3	1.5
Indigenous GNI	−11.2	11.8	21.7	−8.3	4.2	15.6	2.4
Per Capita Indigenous GNI ($)	−12.6	10.0	19.8	−9.8	1.7	14.4	2.0
Per Capita Indigenous GDP ($)	−8.6	3.7	14.7	1.9	−4.2	14.2	2.2

Sources: Singstat http:www.singstat.gov.sg/stats/themes/economy/natac.html. National Income and Balance of Payment listing.

constant 1990 USD (Maddison, 2003) was 20,188 [0.75 × 26,886]. This figure is lower than Taiwan's (20,858), and South Korea's (19,608) computed consistently in Maddison's constant dollars. Hong Kong's indigenous income is very close to Singapore's. It was 49.9% of GDP in 2008. The data needed to compute the full income of indigenous Hong Kong citizens including earnings from abroad (GNP basis) are not published, but the adjusted figure is probably similar. [24]

The combination of foreign multinational activities in finance, services, manufactures and high tech export industries together with relatively low labor costs (kept under control by the fresh inflow of migrants) has enabled these alpha cities to attain living standards using the GDP benchmark near or at the American level,[25] which however is misleading judged from the indigenous income benchmark.

Both cities are considered the most business friendly in the world, and have reaped the benefits. The Heritage Foundation's and *Wall Street Journal*'s economic freedom index ranks Hong Kong number 1, and Singapore number 2, ahead of the United States which holds the fifth spot. Nonetheless, the disparity between their achievements before and after account is taken of earnings received by foreign nationals and multinational corporations, suggests that the benefits of Confucian pragmatism are partly offset by other cultural rigidities.

Future Shock

Taiwan and South Korea today are no longer the authoritarian mobilization systems they once were. Their survival does not depend on rapid development. Their private sectors are fully modernized (within cultural limits). Men and women have increased educational and vocational opportunities, labor is more mobile, and managerial practices are state of the arts. Democracy and civic empowerment are burgeoning, and social

---

[24] Hong Kong does not report "indigenous" income *per se*, but provides the data essential to calculate it. These data are "External Factor Income Flows". The outflows as in Singapore are to resident foreigners and resident foreign companies. They are included in GDP. See 2009, Gross Domestic Product, Census and Statistics Department Hong Kong Special Administrative Region, February 2010, Table A, p. 153.

[25] "Alpha" cities are considered key global economic nodes.

safety nets are widening. There is still some room for catching up to, and perhaps overtaking American living standards, but not enough to significantly augment near term growth. Singapore and Hong Kong are apt to face similar changes in the not too distant future.

This puts Taiwan and South Korea at a crossroads. They must choose between liberalized Confucianism with residual anti-competitive networking characteristics, or a full-fledged inclusive democratic competitive system. If they stay the course, full catch up living standards may elude them. If they switch, they must master an alien cultural technology. Both alternatives are risky because either way the tigers will have to cope with the realization that they cannot have it all (Confucian networking, free competition, true democracy and full civic empowerment). The resulting disorientation may take many forms, and could be bewildering. Japanese economic stagnation suggests one possible outcome.

These complexities should be borne in mind when contemplating the costs and benefits of Taiwanese reincorporation into China on the basis of Beijing's one country, two systems formula. China's "legalist" market communism and Taiwan's Confucian system are moving along non-convergent systemic trajectories obscured by short and intermediate term commercial possibilities. What might appear to be a comfortable fit today may turn out to be counterproductive for both parties tomorrow.

Review

*The Confucian mindset has profoundly affected Chinese societies across the globe for two and a half millennia.

*Confucian precepts are an assemblage of ancient proverbs that have evolved throughout the centuries in response to changing circumstances, designed to achieve wise, efficient, just and stable imperial rule.

*Confucian attitudes are manifest in Taiwan, Singapore, Hong Kong, Macao, South Korea, communist China and Vietnam, Thailand, and Japan.

*Confucianism, instilled into everyone including the emperor, teaches that his or her supreme moral obligation is familial wellbeing.

*All family members, headed by the emperor as the nation's father, ideally should be enlightened, discrete, polite, thoughtful, fair, benevolent, considerate, compassionate, generous, hardworking and wise.

*Prosperity, harmony, happiness, wisdom (education), and longevity are the ingredients of Confucian bliss.

*China is a guilt culture. Violating Confucian precepts is a sin, not just a shame because it is the ethical principles, not the attitudes of others that count.

*Loyal, deference and submission to authority are fundamental moral precepts.

*The rules however become fuzzy when emperors and patriarch are immoral.

*Hypocrisy is a problem. Confucians may preach righteousness, and act viciously. This leads to hypocracy; the rule of hypocrites.

*Hypocrisy is not a Confucian monopoly, but many Asians distain Confucian authority because they distrust it.

*Confucianism historically has been more concerned with preserving the established order than economic mobilization.

*The North Korean and Chinese communist threats however prodded Syngman Rhee and Chiang Kaishek to make economic mobilization Confucianism's interim highest good.

*Taiwan, South Korea, Hong Kong and Singapore are often called the four tigers, or four little dragons.

*Postwar tiger Confucianism has been tugged in two opposing directions; towards individualistic entrepreneurship, and the welfare state. Both have merits, but threaten to erode the positive prosperity enhancing influence of family solidarity.

*The tigers have become high labor cost nations that depend more and more on entrepreneurship and high technology for employment and growth.

*The growth of tiger welfare states supports the development of high tech culture, but if abused also encourages anti-entrepreneurial dependencies.

*Democracy is still in its infancy in Taiwan, South Korea and Hong Kong, and is not on the radar screen yet in Singapore.

*Democracy and civic empowerment are elements of economic wellbeing.

*Likewise the satisficing aspect Confucian family and communal behavior (restricted utility seeking in deference to family and community) prevent society from being Pareto efficient.

*Asia's tigers are microeconomically inefficient, inadequately democratically representative, and civically circumscribed.

*Confucians counter argue that the constraints placed on individual utility self-seeking are wellbeing enhancing, and better than the Pareto ideal. The counterclaims cannot be definitively adjudicated.

*Taiwan immediately after the Treaty of Taipei concluding the war with Japan in 1952, was an authoritarian mobilization economy.

*Foreign demand disciplined suppliers to produce desirable products, and Confucian ethics facilitated cooperative labor-management relations and cost efficiency.

*Microeconomic inefficiencies associated with Confucian restrictions on individualism were more than offset by climbing the value-added ladder from a low to a high productivity regime.

*These accomplishments were accompanied by a marked decline in inequality.

*Chiang Kaishek's authoritarian mobilization regime gradually became more socially benevolent. Independent trade unions began to form in the 1970s. Civic empowerment and democracy movements emerged.

*The economy began globalizing beyond the export of local manufactures, by outsourcing in mainland China.

*The welfare state gradually superseded economic mobilization as the government's primary objective.

*This reduced and altered the role of family, increased egalitarianism, provided a social safety net (including unemployment insurance), and promoted some feminist goals like protection against patriarchal abuse.

*A gender equality employment law was passed in 2002 to insure that women enjoyed equal opportunity.

*Taiwan is experiencing defamilialization, reflected by diminished family size, fewer generations cohabitating, and the steady rise in divorce and single parent households.

*Democracy only came to South Korea in 1988, and remains fragile.

*The South Korean Confucian culture of insider sovereignty persists.

*South Korean civilian presidents use public money for private purposes, rent-granting, draft preferential laws, disregard statutes, and control judicial verdicts.

*These violations of democratic competitive principles emphasize symbiotic relationships between politicians, ministers and technocrats linked by clan, family and shared Confucian values.

*The heart of the South Korean Confucian development model is the Economic Planning Board (EPB) which mobilizes and channels private resources in accordance with the president's priorities.

*This indicative planning was transformed into a directive system by nationalizing banks (including merging the agricultural cooperative movement with a state Agricultural Bank), allocating credit only to private sector firms agreeing to micro implement the EPB's sectoral planning.

*Directive planning was further enhanced by favoring friendly companies with state contracts and encouraging them to become mega conglomerates called chaebols.

*State owned companies also were fostered, creating an industrial planning structure closer to North Korea's than people wished to acknowledge.

*However, as chaebols flourished they gradually became less state dependent, both pursuing ventures without government blessing, and influencing the EPB [Contemporary Ministry of Strategy and Finance (MOSF)] priorities.

*The financial crisis of 1997 exposed the fragility of many chaebols, prompting reform. Chaebols have been pressured to focus on core businesses, spinning off unrelated enterprises. They have been coaxed to hire professionals, instead of family managers, and laws enacted to limit private family wealth.

*Contemporary chaebols behave much like their market communist counterparts. The main distinction is the controlling equity stake held by the Chinese government in China's largest companies.

*Also, like China there are two kinds of for-profit economies, one state favored, the other operating under disadvantageous circumstances.

*South Korea enjoys greater civil liberties than communist China, including democratic participation, but Confucianism remains a restrictive force. The state and society are inseparable in this respect, leaving individuals in a weak moral position for pressing their rights against the state-society.

*Many women consider themselves particularly disadvantaged.

*Pluralism is inadequately prized.

*In sum, despite substantial material progress, South Korean has not transitioned to either EU social democracy, or an inclusive democratic competitive system. It relies on an inner Confucian moral light to guide it to safe harbors, instead of the robust and dense defenses of western systems predicated on the rule of law.

*Taiwan and South Korea are approaching the performance limits of their Confucian systems.

*They cannot significantly improve their relative performance within the Confucian mold.

*They must choose between Confucianism and inclusive democratic competition.

*Both paths are risky. People may respond adversely if Taiwan and South Korea stay their courses, but also could become disoriented trying to master a new culture.

*Taiwan is moving on a political and socially liberalizing course that may increasingly diverge from China's market communist trajectory.

*The prospect of amicably reuniting Taiwan and China under Beijing's one country, two systems formula is becoming increasing problematic for both parties, even though burgeoning commercial relations mask systemic difficulties.

Questions

1. What is Confucianism? Is it a religion or a blueprint for state governance founded on familial moral order? Hint: Religion requires a deity.
2. What are the principal elements of the Confucian moral code?
3. Can Confucianism be hypocritical? How might Confucian practice differ from the ideal?
4. What are the pros and cons of loyalty, trust and deference from the standpoint of individual wellbeing?
5. If Confucianism supports the imperial state, why did Qin Shi Huang despise Confucians?
6. In what ways is Confucianism compatible with modern economic growth and development?
7. In what ways is Confucianism anti-modern?
8. Could anti-modern aspects of Confucianism be a long run trammel on Confucian economic systems? Explain.
9. Confucianism is adopting modern western values. Could the results be dysfunctional? Explain. Hint: Discuss socialist, welfare state and hyper-individualistic possibilities.
10. The tigers, like their counterparts in the west are looking toward high tech as the key to sustained rapid economic growth, now that they have become high labor cost producers. Could global competition greatly impair these expected benefits? Explain.
11. Is democracy a threat to Confucianism? Explain.
12. Is civil empowerment a threat to Confucianism? Explain.
13. Could satisficing become a greater trammel on economic growth as the advantages of economic backwardness fade?
14. Why are the tigers inefficient from a Paretian perspective?
15. What is the Confucian counter-position on this issue?
16. Describe the evolution of the Taiwanese economic system since 1950.
17. There is a possibility that Taiwan might abandon its sovereignty and merge with China under the formula "one country, two systems". Are

the evolutionary trends in Taiwan and China conducive to union? Elaborate.

18. In a unified China, with one compromise system, Taiwan might be compelled to become inegalitarian. Why is this ironic?

19. List the similarities between Taiwanese and South Korean Confucian economies.

20. Identify the differences between them. Hint: Do both economies rely on chaebols, and does this matter?

21. Which country seems the most competitive: Taiwan, South Korea or China? Elaborate.

22. Do the benefits of economic mobilization diminish as the tigers catch up with the west?

23. Other things equal, is Taiwanese or South Korean Confucian economy better positioned to cope with global devitalization?

24. It can be argued that authoritarian growth has been stronger than democratic development in Asia. Is this hypothesis valid? Assume that democracy and autocracy choose the same development strategy. What are the costs and benefits of adopting autocracy versus democracy?

25. Market communism probably offers women more economic opportunities than Confucian economies. It suppresses democracy, but might have some civic advantages. What in your opinion is the net benefit of either market communism or Confucianism with regard to democracy and civil rights? Which system on balance better promotes human wellbeing?

26. Why cannot Taiwan and South Korea improve their relative performance significantly within the confines of their Confucian culture? Elaborate.

27. Why must they choose either/or, rather than mix and match? Elaborate.

28. Why are Taiwan and market communist China moving along opposing systemic trajectories? Can China retain its communist party political and civic monopolies, and still genuinely democratize and support full civic liberties? Elaborate.

29. Why do so many observers claim that Taiwan's and China's systems are converging? Are they conflating modernization with westernization? Elaborate.

Exercises

The tiger economies are competitive, subject to authoritarian public programs and satisficing. They enjoy freehold private property and greater political and civic freedom than under market communism. It can be argued that the relatively small size of the tigers' social welfare programs is attributable to the weakness of the people's electoral influence. Confucian culture encourages hard work and longer work years than the Pareto ideal. Nonetheless domestic goods and factors have dispreferred characteristics, are produced with the wrong technologies, using inferior factor supplies (judged from the Paretian benchmark). These inefficiencies have many causes including weak rule of law, privilege-granting, authoritarian power, and Confucian satisficing. Still, the greater competitiveness of tiger economies at home and abroad compared with market communism is reflected in isoquant values closer to the Pareto optimum. Confucian culture relies on networking that benefits powerful families.

Draw the Paretian ideal Edgeworth Bowley box (Fig. 1.1). Describe the impact of tiger Confucian principles on the length of the capital and labor vectors, the characteristics (for example work skills) of these factors, and the magnitudes (superscripts) of the isoquants. Where does tiger production occur in this space relative to the Pareto equilibrium E? Hint: Remember that the Pareto and tiger isoquant scalings differ (especially in the domestic sector where networking restricts competition). Is there likely to be more than one wage-rental ratio at the tiger production point(s)? Explain. Hint: Powerful Confucian firms have market power. Is the associated distortion likely to be as great as under market communism? How does Confucian satsificing effect monopsony power and gender opportunity? How does it affect public programs and civic freedom? Whose preferences determine the demand for public goods and civic activities: state insiders or the people?

Relocate the tiger production point(s) in the Pareto production space (Fig. 1.2). Remember that satisficing reduces the isoquant values in Figure 1.1. Tiger and Pareto production functions differ because tiger goods (qs) don't fully optimize consumer utility. Is the tiger production point(s) (characteristics adjusted to Pareto equivalent worth) likely to be technically and economically efficient? Explain.

Draw the Paretian ideal Edgeworth Bowley product distribution box (Fig. 1.3). Will the tiger product distribution box be the same size? Elaborate. Remembering that factors do not earn the value their generally competitive marginal products, will retail products be fairly distributed? Also given tiger market deficiencies, will retail distribution likely be technically (as well as economically) inefficient? Explain. Are there likely to be multiple prices ruling in tiger retail distribution space? Explain.

Draw the consumer utility space (Fig. 1.4). Assume that one participant is a patrician Confucian family head and the other a single household female worker (no family). Locate the realized utility point *vis-à-vis* the Pareto E. Is tiger wellbeing lower both due to its productive deficiencies and inegalitarianism? Which is greater: tiger or market communist inegalitarianism? Elucidate. Is it possible that the wellbeing of tiger insiders might surpass the Pareto ideal? Take into account the importance of family harmony and other Confucian virtues.

Draw the tiger Marshallian and Walrasian disequilibrium adjustment diagrams (Figs. 1.5 and 1.6), as well as the enterprise profit maximizing diagram (Fig. 1.7). Do Pareto efficient laws of supply and demand operate in tigerland? If not, explain why equilibria achieved, if any, are distorted?

Is tiger wellbeing closer to the Pareto ideal than the market communism, Japanese communalist markets, Theravada Buddhist markets, or North Korean command? Where would you rank the tiger Confucian system, and why?

COMMUNALISM

Chapter 8

Japan

Systems Profile: Japan.

Type: Communalist.

Subtype: Shame culture guided; liberal.

Economic Sovereign: Communalist shame culture and networks control the characteristics of the system and its outcomes.

Ultimate Authority: Emperor, communalist cultural attitudes; not the rule of law (constitution).

Economy: (a) Formal: Freehold ownership, private business, markets, rule of law, communalist networks (keiretsu, Keidanren), state management through indicative planning, contracting, financing, subsidization, flexible exchange rates, negotiated market pricing and macroeconomic regulation. **(b) Informal:** Dominance of communalist role assignment, communalist networking and consensus building. Marginalized rule of law.

Government: Communalist, emperor deferential democracy.

Civil Liberties: High, communally constrained.

Modernization: Advanced

Evolution: Bellicose, imperial communalism with limited parliamentary democracy (1930–1945); peaceful, imperially deferential, liberalizing parliamentary democratic communalism (1950-present).

Population (July 2012; CIA): 127.4

(Continued)

(Continued)

> **Living Standard (2012; USD, PPP; source, CIA):** $34,300; global rank: 37
>
> **Development (EU Norm):** Advanced, but falling back relative to EU.

Japan's Communalist Economic System

Japan's economy is strongly influenced by its 2,500 year old communalist tradition, which remains steadfastly in force today despite significant institutional reforms imposed on the nation after its defeat in the Second World War. It is best classified under the heading of culturally sovereign systems (see Chapter 1). This means that cultural forces determine supply and demand more than the autonomous preferences of individual consumers as required in the neoclassical paradigm (the democratic competitive standard). The model is "inclusive" in the sense that state governance and the private sector are both compatible with "imperial" communalist principles. The state in Japan's imperial tradition is inclined toward authoritarianism, softened by communalist consensus building across social strata, and the private sector is similarly organized as befits a nation that places as much or even greater emphasis on communitarian harmony than kinship. These characteristics are fundamental because they undermine the autonomous, individualistic premises of democratic free enterprise. The communalist model is intrinsically anti-competitive and mutually supportive. It prevents individuals from fully maximizing their utility in work, investment (including education), job choice, production and consumption, and it deters governments from vigorously promoting the wide range of social programs that are the core of what western countries describe as the welfare state. Japanese depend more on each other than the state, substituting direct communitarian assistance for government tax-transfer schemes. Other things equal, it might be supposed that culturally sovereign communalist systems might be severely underproductive, but the paradigm requires Japanese to labor unstintingly for the group, always attentive to high quality production. Likewise, while Japan's communalist system resists the west's governmental approach to individual protection, it compensates with communitarian forms of security and mutual aid. Japanese recognize that the rigidities of their system impose costs, but feel that the trade-off enhances the nation's wellbeing.

Communalism

Japanese culture, like Chinese Confucianism has never left responsibility for solving the problems of wellbeing, fulfillment and discontent to individual utility seeking. It provides citizens with ethical codes, rituals, disciplinary and adaptive mechanisms that cushion modernization, material shocks and psychological distress, relying on group norms rather than Confucian precepts. Unlike China, the community is sovereign in the land of the rising sun, not the family or universal values. Family loyalty is important, but roles differ from the Confucian paradigm, both internally and with respect to outsiders. Confucians treat nuclear and extended families, where members have well defined roles, as allies supporting and defending common interests against others. Individuals utility maximize within this framework. Japanese by contrast are conditioned to place obligations to groups above self-betterment.[1] Individuals either mostly adopt group preferences, or subordinate their desires to the community's will.

Japanese satisfice under social constraint (incompletely searching individual utility possibilities to accommodate the group), more often than they individualistically utility maximize. Communal welfare supersedes personal self-seeking. Japanese sometimes act like western *homo economicus* (utility seeking for their own benefit, paying limited attention to

---

[1]Anthropologists sometimes distinguish the self in isolation from people's social selves. Economists seldom make the distinction treating the individual as the primary unit with the capacity to include social concerns to any extent rationally deemed optimal. The economist's attitude reflects the discipline's rationalist assumption, while some anthropologists take the view that people may not have core selves. A mixed position is taken in the text above. It is assumed that Japanese are acculturated to merge their core identities with group interest without rational evaluation in some, but not all instances. Japanese satisfice whenever they refrain from rationally considering their private interests. They optimize whenever actions are fully weighed.

the preferences of others, including extended families, groups and communities), but group and community obligations are more important, profoundly altering the laws of Japanese economic motion.

The term group covers a broad range of collectives including families, workplace organizations, teams, large corporate structures, communities, and governmental institutions crowned by the Emperor. Group wellbeing in Japan is an end in itself, not just a means to individual utilitarian betterment. Doing the right thing *vis-à-vis* other members takes priority over competitive efficiency and the accumulation of wealth. Confucian and Japanese cultures both strive for harmony, but their methods differ. Confucians advocate ritualized, family based social orchestration where everyone acts in accordance with their station and duties, whereas the Japanese cultural ballet emphasizes group consensus building and adaptive social accommodation. Both approaches have pluses and minuses. Their satisficing constrains wellbeing and fulfillment, influences income disparities, ameliorates some and aggravates other types of discontent.

The Japanese paradigm is conflict averse within families and across society. It is particularly effective in dealing with distributive and interpersonal emotional aspects of wellbeing, fulfillment and discontent. Companies and communities strive to avert discord by retaining workers whose marginal value added is less than their wage, rewarding them equally, providing special assistance when required, building consensus on issues of mutual concern, treating everyone with dignity, and shunning destabilizing business practices including entrepreneurship. Satisficing attitude adjustment (avoidance of group conflict) diminishes anxieties further. Japanese culture encourages acceptance of adversity and discourages resentment. People are trained not to begrudge sacrifices for the communitarian good, and to take pride in their civility. It is shameful to be selfish, and virtuous to be communally altruistic.

These cultural mechanisms are not always effective. Chinese families and Japanese groups sometimes are antagonistic and dysfunctional. Communalism did not forestall social turmoil and imperial expansionism during the Meiji, Taisho and Showa modernization periods, even though it did mitigate the traumas. Likewise, while the model has generated a lofty, relatively egalitarian distribution of income and social contentment, real growth in the new millennium has been sluggish.[2] A decade ago, Japan was the king of Asia's economic mountain. Today, it remains affluent, but is slipping against all regional competitors, except North Korea, and needs rejuvenation. Apparently, Japanese adaptability helps individuals solve the complex choice problems posed by communitarianism, but it is not a panacea.

Shame and Guilt

The secret ingredient that makes Japanese more communally attentive and self-disciplined than most other cultures is its shame regime. Shame is revulsion felt when people violate social norms even when actions are not criminal. For example, ladies may feel ashamed if they are inappropriately dressed, even though the transgression is not sinful.

Japanese communalists are primarily governed by shame, unlike Confucians who rely predominately on universal precepts of righteous ethical behavior, guilt and ritual to regulate personal conduct. Group attitudes, approval, and fear of communal reproach determine what the Japanese consider the right and wrong way of doing things. They are taught from the cradle that they are duty bound to do the right thing, seek approval, and abhor incurring group censure. Right and wrong for Japanese is contextual. The same behavior may be appropriate in one setting, but inexcusable in another. Social status, role, location and circumstances all matter, and Japanese are coached to know precisely how to act in every conceivable circumstance. Group members are ubiquitously obliged to do their utmost for their groups' benefit, according to their station. If teams deem overwork appropriate, shame will compel members to comply even when employees have legitimate grounds for refusal. This implicit moral code is extremely complex, nuanced and demanding, but once mastered greatly shrinks the domain of rational choice making (optimizing), expands satisficing and reduces associated anxiety. Japanese do

---

[2] What would be the implication — structure reform of the past was not as bad as it's expected? Available at http://www.oecd.org/dataoecd/45/57/41527303.pdf; http://www.oecd.org/document/25/0,3343.en_2649_201185_41530009_1_1_1_1_1,00,00.html. OECD (2008).

not have to talk incessantly with others about the right things to do (outside of formal consensus building conclaves), because context and situational ethics settle matters. Cross cultural studies confirm this claim.

Japanese intellectuals fully appreciate the power of their shame based situational ethics and consider the mechanism superior to inflexible Confucian and western universal morality and guilt based discipline. They believe that their moral order is tailored better to life's complexities and provides superior communal wellbeing and emotional health, but recognize that the shame principle may be deficient for effectively engaging other cultures.

The primacy of shame is the heart of Japanese social control. Leaders do not have to convince teams that policies conform to established moral precepts (guilt culture), or are in each member's personal interest. They only have to build a consensus on tradition and duty. Once, groups inculcate an agenda, issues like labor exploitation vanish. Firms are able to mobilize teams to overwork because team members want to do it, even though members may appreciate at some level that they would be better off working less.

The shame based priority of duty over self-interest encompasses most aspects of economic activity. Japanese firms are able to muster loyalty, effort, commitment to superior quality (*ichiban* mentality) more than individualistic guilt based cultures, even though few are rewarded in accordance with the value of their marginal products. This self-sacrifice may partly be altruistic, but here too what counts is the team's attitude, not the merit of duties. If teams decided to under-work, under-exert, disregard quality, and adopt inegalitarianism, then shame would discipline members accordingly.

Shame is not a standard of virtue. It is a collective economic governance device for achieving group discipline and conformity. It is communally rational and beneficial in many ways when group attitudes are constructive and deleterious otherwise. It may surpass the guilt principle when autonomous individuals disregard their consciences, and underperform when personal utility seeking empowers everyone to fully actualize potentials in accordance with democratic competitive economic theory. The democratic free enterprise paradigm yields better results from an individualistic perspective because the shame utility search engine is not exhaustive.

The shame principle is not restricted to productive teams. It pervades all aspects of Japanese life from filial obligations to imperial deference. The structure can be visualized as a stack of nested, concentric rings tapering toward the apex, reminiscent of a Buddhist stupa (pagoda). Individuals comprise the lowest and widest ring. Shame subordinates everyone beneath the emperor to the state, communities, business institutions and family. Roles are rigid, enabling Japanese to easily ascertain their duties. Men and women have distinct functional assignments, dress and codes of etiquette. They are expected to marry and procreate. Men head households, but women control family expenditures (derived from Samurai tradition). Juniors are subordinated to elders. Productive teams have informal leaders and are subordinated to supervisory and managerial hierarchies. Inter-firm relations likewise are tightly structured. Corporations enter into cross shareholding alliances called keiretsu,[3] including main banks, and cooperate with business associations like Keidanren.[4] Communities and state governance have superior and inferior aspects too. Only the emperor is independent in his sphere of competence.

This delineation of roles is both a partial cause and consequence of shame control. Attitudes need to be expeditiously formed in communalist regimes, a process facilitated by rank recognition. Likewise, role awareness enables everyone to effectively fulfill group obligations.

Consensus Building

Japanese society is a consensus building, hierarchy of deferential relationships where group welfare supersedes individual utility-seeking. Shame-based norms of right and wrong are not dictated by authorities, although the opinion of high ranking individuals carries great weight. Instead groups assemble members for exhaustive policy discussions, guided by strict rules of politeness that continue until everyone agrees that solutions are best. Some individuals may still harbor reservations. Nonetheless, they embrace and support the group consensus with greater commitment than under the

---

[3] Japanese business affiliated group economic coordination founded on cross shareholding by related companies and their suppliers.

[4] Japanese business policy advocacy association.

principle of majority rule where losers often are disgruntled. They substitute group preferences for their own, or maintain a secret inner life.

Either way, the sphere of non-deferential individual utility-seeking is severely restricted compared with western and some Asian nations. Once Japanese decide to rationally or emotionally conform, subsequent actions are communally, not individually determined.

Shame control does not necessitate consensus building, but the Japanese have widely adopted the technique as a device for nurturing loyalty and fostering acquiescence. Indeed, Japanese communal utility searching can be aptly viewed as a perpetual consensus building and enforcement process where members of the nation communicate, reconcile and validate their missions. The system is sensitive to communal concerns throughout the shame regulated "stupa" hierarchy.

Western scholars rarely grasp the distinctions between individual and communal utility searching, leading many to conflate consensus building coordination with monopoly and other forms of collusive profit maximizing. In competitive individualistic economies people are assumed to seek the most advantageous transaction terms they can, exerting market power wherever possible at the expense of others. Self-seeking is only limited by competitive actions of third parties. In Japan no man is an island. Although, individuals realize that market power can be personally rewarding, the impulse is checked by a maze of shame cultural obligations that make fairness and mutual support more important than profit augmenting market restriction and manipulation. Communal utility search therefore is distinctive. Groups endeavor to better themselves, but prefer to satisfice in the community's interest rather than individually utility maximize.[5] Japanese are content with enough, without being acculturated to crave more as is too often the case in the west.[6]

Satisficing is intrinsic to shame cultures and is one of its most distinctive economic features, but differs from culture to culture. Japanese satisficing for example is hitched to meeting the community's material requirements, whereas, it serves a more spiritual function in Thailand.

---

[5] Conflicts between Japanese domestic corporations and communities more often than not are settled through oblique informal discussions rather than litigation as in the west.

[6] see Tawney (1920).

Satisficing also affects the quality of Japanese lives, although this is difficult to quantify.[7] People find solace in their station, roles, circumstances and Japanese are unusually discerning. They are attentive to etiquette, the needs of others and aesthetic aspects of life.[8]

---

[7] Japanese society displays all of civilization's contradictions and discontents. Powerful people often act unscrupulously in their own interest, disregarding communalist obligations. Although, corporate salaries are egalitarian by American standards, business expense accounts frequently fund lavish lifestyles. "Favors" among businesses and politicians are legendary. Nonetheless, daily life can be burdensome even for the privileged. It has the character of a Kabuki play with everyone performing his and her role. People are not what they seem. They must abide by assigned scripts, seizing private moments here and there as catch can. This choreography mitigates group and interpersonal conflict, but also creates a superficial existence that the postmodern artist Takashi Murakami stigmatizes as *superflat*, that is, a cheerfully superficial consumer culture. Masao Miyamoto looking at the kabuki way of life from a bureaucratic perspective portrays Japan as a *straitjacket society* (see Miyamoto, 1995). There always have been cracks in the facade. Elements of each successive postwar Japanese generation have rebelled, but as time passed the kabuki drama continued with new customs and makeovers that left the cultural core intact. The latest fads are young men dubbed *herbivores* or grass eating men (*soshokukei danshi*) who eschew high salary jobs and hot cars, favoring shopping and fashion to sex, (see Japan's Samurai back in vogue. *Economist*, October 29, 2009), and a trend toward one-of-a-kind luxuries, and away from brand names. The "grass eating men" phenomenon appears to have sociological traction. Half of Japanese men 20–34 are unmarried and only 20% have girlfriends, creating difficulties for young women looking to marry successful salarymen. Many seem to be sublimating by playing video games romanticizing Samurai heroes. Assessing the quality of Japanese life is complicated further by the disparity between publicly extolled virtues and culturally approved counter-values. For example, Japan's "sunshine" culture depicts women as dutiful handmaidens, submissively fulfilling their roles as daughters, mothers and grandmothers, but the "shadow" culture alternative is more complex. Although, Japanese women may seem powerless, they control household finance in the Samurai tradition, doling out small allowances to their husbands, while pampering themselves. Likewise, while men are supposed to be upright patriarchs, "adult" entertainment is ubiquitous. These and a multitude of other contradictions could be disorienting, but usually are not because shame culture tutors everyone what is and is not contextually appropriate. Finally, there is the metaphysical question of what life quality means to a population dominated by group egos, where personality is sacrificed to persona. If shame culture assigns people to be content, and the communal ego complies, can anything at all be inferred about private wellbeing behind the kabuki mask?

[8] Steven Rosefielde, *Asian Economic Culture: Visualizations of the Ideal*, available on request.

Pareto Inefficiency

Japanese shame based communalism is intrinsically anti-competitive, a defect that is apt to place it at a long run disadvantage. The communalist aversion to market incentives is pervasive. This is most easily appreciated by pondering the meaning of profit maximizing. Maximizing in western classical theory is superlative. It means that transactors exhaustively explore every legitimate opportunity for reducing competitively determined costs and increasing revenues. Passively accepting established wages, prices and technologies is not good enough. As the North Korean example shows, maximizing accounting profits computed at state set wages and prices disconnected from value-added leads to degenerate results, and the Japanese shame based obligation to fix wages and prices fairly, instead of at the competitive margin is similarly distortive.

Communalist incomplete profit seeking is satisficing, not maximizing. Neither workers nor managers completely search workplace utility and profit possibilities during perpetual consensus building sessions. Likewise, keiretsu firms and main banks do not coordinate their activities on a profit maximizing basis. Companies instead set just wages and equitably coordinate with little regard for value-added. They fix customary rather than competitive market prices and choose technologies on a similar basis. Moreover, in the Japanese version of communalism most workers enjoy jobs for life, causing sustained overfull employment. The rules for overriding Walrasian and Marshallian automatic price and quantity adjustments differ in the Japanese and North Korean systems,[9] but the resulting distortions take similar forms. People overwork, factors are misallocated from a democratic competitive perspective, and goods are produced with the wrong characteristics,[10] in the wrong assortments, at the wrong prices and are over-exported. Product characteristics, assortments and quantities are sub-optimal. Forced substitution dominates competition, impairing returns on capital and financial assets (dividends and

---

[9] There are two basic microeconomic adjustment mechanism: Marshallian and Walrasian. See Chapter 1.

[10] For example, although road worthiness rules restrict auto service life to five years, Japanese automakers design their cars to last three times as long, incurring unnecessary expense and thereby reducing profits.

interest). It might be supposed that these deficiencies could be offset by positive aspects of Japanese consensus building, but corporate bottom lines show that benefits are outweighed by the costs. Pareto competition quite simply is more productive.

Some consequences of communalism are visible to the naked eye. The Japanese work twice as many person hours annually than the Germans to obtain the same per capita income. Therefore, Japanese economic welfare (living standard) is exaggerated to the extent that leisure has positive utility. Interest rates and dividends likewise are well below international standards because the claims of outside shareholders are subordinated to insider needs.[11]

Most distortions however are invisible. Aggregate statistics tell us virtually nothing about forced substitution (communally imposed product choice). Japanese regularly over-consume and overpay for local and native products to support their communities. Team loyalty causes them to overwork, even though neither the law nor personal utility require it. The utility of labor and personal consumption thus are far lower than they appear judged from an individualistic perspective.

This anomaly is vividly exemplified by the Japanese labor market. The Japanese overwork for free. Both employers and employees feel communally obligated to work overtime without direct material compensation. Supervisors stay at their posts after the nominal workday is finished to show their dedication, and loyalty compels employees to stay on the job until the day's tasks are done. This means that everyone works more hours than they would in the individualistic competitive model, even though devotion does not directly augment income (however, the extra labor does indirectly augment remuneration by increasing the pool of distributable net revenue).

Figure 8.1 illustrates the problem. It arrays the wage rate (w) on the ordinate and person hours (l) on the abscissa. The labor demand curve in the employment space is downward sloping reflecting the diminishing marginal value of hourly labor service as the workday expands. Employers never willingly pay more than worker marginal value-added. The labor supply curve is kinked. It is upward sloping until point E, and then is horizontal along the abscissa from l_e to l_f.

---

[11] Japanese banks lend funds to locals below competitive rates.

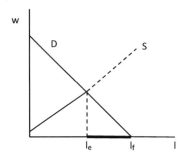

Figure 8.1.   Japanese Communalist Labor Supply.

Assume for simplicity that point E happens to be the general competitive equilibrium so that Japanese and western firms behave identically. l_e is the normal workday, and w_e, the competitive wage rate. In the west, everyone goes home at 5 pm, or receives overtime wages; usually some multiple of the base rate. In Japan, employers and employees voluntarily work overtime without compensation until point l_f where marginal value-add is precisely zero. Value-added along the demand curve from l_e to l_f is everywhere greater than the marginal cost of labor. Shareholders thus benefit from their employees' selfless dedication. Workers should bristle at these exploitative terms, but do not out of a sense of team spirit, and perhaps in part because they understand that their total remuneration would diminish if they insisted on working nine to five.

Similar disequilibrium behavior can be observed in egalitarian labor managed cooperatives.[12] The Japanese case therefore is not unique. Nonetheless Fig. 8.1 makes it clear that Japanese firms will only operate at the competitive equilibrium accidently, and normally will be in a state of acute disequilibrium invisible to those using macroeconomic efficiency criteria as their benchmark. Moreover, and equally important, communalist labor practices are impervious to the invisible hand. The willingness of Japanese employers and employees to work overtime for free disables the Walrasian wage adjustment mechanism, and disorients the Marshallian

---

[12] see Rosefielde and Pfouts (1986). Egalitarian labor managed enterprises maximize per work dividends instead of profits, which causes them to incompletely utility maximize.

quantity adjustment (profit maximizing) mechanism. Where communalism reigns; the invisible hand withers.

This means that Japanese workers and their supervisors incompletely
utility maximize (satisfice). They could enjoy more leisure without reducing their total utility, just as shareholders could enhance their wellbeing if
Japanese firms completely profit maximized. Every time communal culture
and consensus building misallocate factors, over(under) remunerate inputs,
force substitute factors and outputs, over(under) price products, ration
credit, over(under) price finance, and suboptimally diffuse technology, they
reduce utility below consumer sovereign competitive potential. The losses
are endemic to the system and indisputable from a positivist perspective.

In inclusive democratic market economies, higgling and piggling
cause transitory losses that are quickly dispelled by competition. People
try to create monopolistic advantages, or protect their privileges, but
Walrasian and Marshallian automatic price and quantity adjustment
mechanisms defeat their machinations. Japanese anticompetitive communal firewalls however are too strong. They are impervious to the invesible
hand despite the inroads of globalization. Superficially, Japan gives the
appearance of being a textbook, individual utility seeking market economy, but these appearances are deceptive because the nation rejects subordinating group welfare to individual utility and profit seeking.

The loses entailed could be compensated by Masahiko Aoki's "economies of trust" (gains from trustworthy labor-management relations),[13] but
flagging Japanese comparative international productivity indicates that
whatever communalism's normative virtues might be, it is materially
underproductive.

The Japanese would enjoy a higher material standard of living, if they
discarded communalism in favor of democratic free enterprise. Most
Japanese economists appreciate the loss incurred by maintaining the current system. Yet more than any other nation in Asia, Japan steadfastly has
clung to communalism. It has modernized, and embraced many aspects of
westernization including democracy and civic empowerment, but has kept
Adam Smith at bay. One could concoct innumerable explanations for this
tenacity; however there is a common denominator. Unlike the Confucian

---

[13] see Aoki (2001) and Lorenz (1988, pp. 194–210).

zone, Japan is primarily a shame culture, where individual conduct is regulated by group attitudes rather than universal norms of ethical behavior characteristic of guilt cultures. Group consensus trumps personal preferences, including foreign norms of right and wrong.

Social Efficiency

The Pareto inefficiency of the Japanese economy is real. Despite, Japan's well deserved reputation for high quality export products, its economic system misallocates factors, under-produces, overworks, misdistributes and mistransfers goods and services. It operates below the neoclassical production possibilities frontier, on the wrong vector. Retail distribution lies off the contract curve and aggregate utility is inferior.

More subtly, team attitudes seldom reflect a deep understanding of the local and national net benefits, and team choices dominate the social interest. This truncates the system-wide utility search producing inferior outcomes judged from the standpoint of communalist potential. On one hand, team consensus building is circumscribed by taboos, incomplete scrutiny and restricted competence. On the other, society frequently acquiesces to team judgments, foregoing independent pan-societal review. If teams and the nation were fully apprised of the opportunity costs, they could achieve better results, but the possibilities are concealed in the communal process, outside the invisible hand's sway.

These problems are handled in the inclusive democratic free enterprise model through market competition, the state's adept use of taxes, transfers, programs, mandates and regulation.[14] The Japanese by contrast prefer to settle both issues locally in teams, and throughout their communal group hierarchy, bypassing the government whenever they can because they trust each other more than state institutions.[15] They believe that

---

[14] see Bergson (1954, pp. 233–252) and Samuelson (1977, pp. 81–88).

[15] Modern economic optimization theory requires that citizens competitively negotiate all their transactions privately up to the point where elected officials have a comparative advantage serving the people with programs (including transfers), laws, mandates and regulations. This fluid boundary depends on the people's shifting preferences and its assessment of elected agents' technical competence. Officials should never be permitted to undertake tasks unless it can be rigorously demonstrated that they can do the job better than the

microeconomic efficiency losses, including incomplete intergroup welfare optimization are more than offset by the benefits of direct, hands-on communal intervention. Tax-transfer authorities from their perspective are far removed from those they claim to serve, and good results are uncertain. The Daiichi nuclear meltdown provides a clear example of government ineptitude. The Japanese therefore prefer to be safe than sorry, providing sound group protection that prevents most from falling between the cracks. They know that the inclusive democratic free enterprise solution should be better in theory, but chose instead to forego two birds in the bush for one bird in the hand.

Democracy

The western preference for transfers is rooted in the concept of "Enlightenment democracy", which places the preferences of individuals' above those of Japanese shame culture.[16] The quality and variety of democratic transfers take society's desires into account only insofar as individuals warrant. Therefore, in assessing the merit of Japan's economic system, it must be fully appreciated that shame culture is not only Pareto inefficient; it is intrinsically undemocratic despite aspects of social efficiency. The group principle dominates individualist based, one person-one vote state governance.

Epochs

The Japanese communalist model proved to be a formidable engine of economic modernization and development from the start of the Meiji era

---

people. The burden of proof should always fall on elected agents, not their sovereigns. The people here means the majority of the electorate subject to fundamental property and civil rights guarantees, not minority segments of the electorate acting on their own behalf claiming to be the conscience of society. Optimization theory further requires that agents fully inform themselves about the people's preferences when it is appropriate to act on their behalf. Government may have to act as a good parent instead of obeying its inexperienced children from time to time, but should never act cavalierly. A true democratic best is an integrated optimum where individuals privately maximize their utility and government efficiently fills in the gaps as the people's agent to further improve the national wellbeing.
[16] see Rosefielde and Mills (2013).

September 1868 until the great bubble of 1989. Many claimed that the Japanese model was miraculous, and inherently superior to its rivals.[17] Then suddenly, and without warning Japan lost its former vitality. The post bubble period is now referred to as "two lost decades", with an end to stagnation nowhere in sight. The change has been partly attributed to an aging population, "zombie banks",[18] deflation, growing Asian competition, disorienting effects of liberalization, the financial crisis of 2008, an appreciating yen, and the March 11, 2011 tsunami.

There is no reason to reject any of these factors as contributory causes, but there is another intriguing possibility. The burst bubble of 1989 may have shifted the priorities of Japan's shame based consensus from Asian economic hegemony to domestic tranquility. Although, the government has pressed liberalization as the antidote for fatigue, the Japanese seem to prefer lowering their aspirations and living in splendid isolation.[19]

This preference has merit, even though it entails abandoning the globalization bandwagon for a sufficiently affluent and harmonious way of life, in accordance with its Yamato tradition.[20] Japanese per capita income and employment are high. The yen's purchasing power abroad is favorable, income is fairly distributed and there is little social discord. The best from society's standpoint may be the enemy of the good.

Reform

This bodes badly for Japan's frequently touted western liberalization (Big Bang)[21] or other reform initiatives such as European Union style social

---

[17] see Johnson (1982) and Forsberg (2000).

[18] see Akiyoshi and Kobayashi (2008) and Krugman (1994, pp. 62–79).

[19] Young people do not want to study abroad and participate in international business. They are content to stay at home and take pleasure in what they have.

[20] The Yamato are indigenous Japanese who established a domain from Asuka to Kurume from approximately 250–710AD. The name derives from a fourth century court, and the character can be read either as capitol of the mountain people, or people of the great harmony.

[21] The Financial System Reform, "Japanese Big Bang", commenced in November 1996 under the three principles of "free, fair and global", aiming to rebuild the Japanese financial market into an international market comparable to the New York and London markets.

democracy, or entry into a supranational Asian Union.[22] It is difficult to abolish the matrix of relationships undergirding loyalty, diligence, self-sacrifice, exertion, perfectionism and mutual support.[23] Policymakers continue to advocate profit maximizing, and open economic competition widely employed in overseas subsidiaries, but there is little enthusiasm for unfettered individual utility seeking at home that infringes communal solidarity. The resistance is buttressed by the intricacies of reengineering a shame culture into one that simulates autonomous guilt principles, or substitute's guilt for shame. This is terra incognita,[24] and the problematic itself is only dimly understood. Consequently, it should be expected that while Japan will continue experimenting with liberal economic and democratic reform, improvements will be gradual.

Tokyo's malaise has five distinct components. First, weak entrepreneurship hampers growth by failing to fully capitalize on the potential benefits of technological progress at home and abroad. Second, communalism impairs microeconomic efficiency. Even though the Japanese work more man-years than their rivals, per capita GDP is well below the American norm and falling back. Third, the over-valued yen is encouraging offshore manufacturing and hollowing out the economy. Fourth, high national debt (more than 200 percent of GDP), and macroeconomic risk aversion constrain the government's ability to successfully stimulate aggregate economic activity. Finally, demography and cultural change are becoming increasingly burdensome. The population is graying, and people are gradually reducing their effort as the west's leisure ethic lessens

---

[22] see Rosefielde *et al.* (2012).

[23] The Japanese achieve these goals by conflict avoiding. This is facilitated by *tatemae*, that is, politeness intended to avoid conflict, even if it requires concealing the truth (*honne*). The Kenkyusha (New Japanese English Dictionary) defines tatemae as a principle, or rule. It is one's words, or public position, as distinct from hone (truth). There is a big gap between what people say and really think; between public declarations and private intention. Many Japanese feel that Tatemai is an admirable principle which cannot be openly rejected.

[24] Japanese learn how to behave in shame cultural fashion by participating in group activities. This is why they exhibit a strong preference for group travel. If the Japanese were to suddenly abandon their shame culture, they would not know which set of universal principles to adopt; those of the *sunshine* or *shadow* culture, and would find themselves disoriented.

the attraction of working selflessly for the common good. Compensatory factors which once masked communalism's shortcomings are now exacerbating them, making it unlikely that Japan will regain its lost Asian preeminence.

Communalism has many appealing virtues, but its rapidly mounting costs indicate that a strong case can be made for relaxing Japan's shame trammels to facilitate some forms of individual utility seeking like entrepreneurship. Unlike the west and many parts of Asia, affinity groups more than individual utility seeking dominate economic action, creating consensus that curtails competitive incentives in pursuit of team harmony. Consensus building can be seen as a surrogate for market efficiency incentives, but the accumulating evidence suggests that the approach is less effective than scholars like Aoki once hoped.[25]

The power of affinity groups is pervasive and operates in subtle ways. With respect to aggregate economic growth, on the surface deference to teams and groups seems entirely positive. Japanese scientists and engineers are inventive. Designers and marketing managers are attentive to consumer desires, and the quality of goods and services is high. Firms invest heavily in research and development. Corporate culture encourages worker dedication, exports, and adept salesmanship. Yet despite these and other formidable advantages, aggregate technological progress and diffusion have been anemic because new processes must be team friendly. If profit maximizing options entail in-house job losses, or burdensome adjustments, they will be shunned or only adopted in foreign subsidiaries. Aspiring Japanese entrepreneurs grasp the problem, and understand how it should be solved, but can do little more than tinker around the margins. Where entrepreneurs, CEOs and investors in the west would press ahead, maximizing profits within the limits of the law, and trade union counterpressure, no Japanese corporate director can be right against the team consensus. It is the duty of teams in Japan to abridge individual utility self-seeking (including shareholders), and the obligation of decision makers to place the team above their personal welfare. The team is king, not shareholders or the market.

---

[25] see Aoki (2001), Aoki *et al.* (2007), Aoki and Dore (1994). Consensus building need not be incompatible with competitive market incentives, but is so in the Japanese case.

Wellbeing, Fulfillment and Contentment

The Japanese experience sheds considerable light on why some nations might choose a culturally sovereign economic system which marginalizes true democracy over the inclusive democratic free enterprise ideal. First, and foremost Japanese communalism makes it plain that there is more to national wellbeing than Pareto efficient factor supply, production, distribution and state provided democratically sovereign public transfers. Nations may decide on ethical and humanist grounds (such egalitarianism and mutually aid) that they disprefer some or all aspects of Pareto efficient outcomes, and judge that as a practical matter culturally sovereign economic systems provide citizens with greater wellbeing, fulfillment and contentment than imperfectly competitive markets and arms-length government. Japanese communalist shame culture fosters moderation, self-improvement, egalitarianism (inheritance tax is almost confiscatory), appreciativeness, compassion, social justice, attentiveness to special member needs, and harmony to degrees unlikely to be achieved in individualistically organized societies. Institutions matter.[26] Second, it demonstrates that these benefits observable in Confucian kinship-centric regimes can be extended more broadly throughout communities and the nation.

The Japanese case accordingly merits very careful monitoring both with respect to its material and psychological aspects in an age where western government policymakers are simultaneously straitjacketing economies with excessive and often dysfunctional regulation, and are accumulating potentially catastrophic foreign debts with little regard for national wellbeing. Japanese shame cultural risk averseness in the aftermath of the bubble debacle, and its attentiveness to the socio-psychological dimension of wellbeing during its recent two lost decades, suggests that it may be better positioned to provide its people with greater wellbeing, fulfillment and contentment in the decades ahead than the America or the European Union systems, despite the ideal conceptual advantages of democratic free enterprises and social democracy.[27]

---

[26] see Landes (2000).
[27] see Rosefielde and Mills (2012).

Review

*Japanese economic men and women routinely substitute communal for their private preferences, either preferring the results of the collective mind, or subordinating their desires to group will.

*They behave like western *homo economicus* in private contexts, but otherwise violate the axioms of neoclassical utility theory, and its laws of economic motion.

*Japanese economic behavior therefore deviates fundamentally from the neoclassical norm.

*There are many styles of group behavior. Postwar Japanese communalism stresses hard work, high quality, and benefit sharing.

*It is consumer oriented, rather than abstemious or bellicose.

*Japan is relatively egalitarian and tranquil.

*Real GDP growth however has been negligible for decades, and may diminish further.

*Japan is affluent, but needs rejuvenation.

*Japan's malaise is attributable to weak entrepreneurship, communal inefficiency, an aging population and cultural change (eroding work ethic).

*These problems are not transitory and jeopardize Japan's global economic standing.

*Adaptation may provide a solution. Japan can widen the ambit of individual utility seeking at the expense of group deference.

*Team harmony and competitiveness are seldom complements, contrary to Masahiko Aoki's expectation.

*Japanese society is rationally structured and integrated, just like ideal command communism.

*However, many productive possibilities are rejected for the sake of team harmony.

*The problem can be fixed technically, but the culture ties society's hands.

*The team is king, not the market.

*As under communism, it can be argued that communal benefits outweigh anemic growth.

*Nonetheless, it is worth noting that communalist utility searches are intrinsically self-limiting and less exhaustive than the neoclassical ideal.

*Consensus building is cumbersome, acquiescent and incomplete.

*Teams and the nation are not fully apprised of opportunity costs.

*This degrades the efficiency of Walrasian and Marshallian mechanisms.

*Another way to look at Japanese communalism is to recognize that social welfare is addressed directly, rather than through transfers.

*The western strategy is to maximize the pie, and then redistribute to the needy. In Japan things work the other way round. Groups discuss member needs, and then individuals adjust their behavior for the communal good, obviating transfers. The end result is similar, but the scope of the utility search differs. The west is more thorough on the production side, Japan is better at ascertaining communal needs.

*Japanese communalism constrains profit maximizing and is intrinsically anti-competitive. Inclusive democratic competitive economies solve both problems, but are bureaucratically encumbered in providing welfare services and transfers.

*The constraints imposed on profit maximizing and competition by contemporary Japanese communalism cause people to overwork. They are misincentivized and misrewarded. Product characteristics, assortments and quantities are sub-optimal. Forced substitution dominates competition.

*Some of this distortion is reflected in the aggregate statistics. The Japanese work twice as many person-hours annually than the Germans to obtain the same per capita income.

*Communalist dividends and interest rates are below the competitive standard.

*The Japanese labor market is in double disequilibrium. People overwork, and are under-remunerated because they are required by communalist custom to provide unpaid overtime labor.

*The Japanese labor market is not self-adjusting because unpaid overtime disables the Walrasian automatic wage adjustment mechanism, and disorients the Marshallian quantity adjustment (profit maximizing) mechanism.

*Where communalism rules, the invisible hand withers.

*Japan's devotion to communalism is attributable to its shame culture, where individual conduct is regulated by group attitudes rather than universal norms of ethical behavior characteristic of guilt cultures.

*Group consensus trumps personal preferences, including external norms of right and wrong.

*Leaders do not have to convince teams that policies are in each member's personal interest, or are morally correct. They only have to build a consensus on tradition and duty.

*The shame principle is not restricted to productive teams. It pervades all aspects of Japanese life from filial obligations to imperial deference.

*Shame controlled communal hierarchy has the appearance of Confucian order, but is more malleable because it does not have a fixed ethical structure.

*However, at any given moment, roles are rigid.

*Hierarchy is essential in shame based communalism because it facilitates goal setting.

*Japanese hierarchical goal setting is unusual because it enlists consensus building in support of authority. This nurtures loyalty and satisficing.

*Japan's anti-competitiveness is not motivated by oligopolistic and monopolistic profit-seeking. Fairness and mutual support are more important than profit augmenting market restriction and manipulation.

*Japanese are content with enough, without craving more as is too often the case in the west. This is an essential aspect of Japanese satisficing.

*Japan and Thailand both have shame cultures, but their motivational content differs. Thai Buddhism preaches compassion and charity, but Japanese communalism is more effective at supporting society's material needs.

*Japanese communalism fosters national wellbeing.

*Japanese technical inefficiency is mitigated by the effectiveness of communalist sharing.

*Communal solidarity and the basic effectiveness of the Japanese system impede fundamental reform.

*No one knows how to efficiently replace shame culture based communalism with western democratic free enterprise.

Questions

1. Have you ever found it easier to follow the crowd, than to go your own way? Did you do this because you assumed the crowd might know best, or you did not want to reveal that you did not fit in?
2. Suppose that the crowd's decision had resulted from lengthy group discussion ending in a consensus where everyone agreed except you. Would this have made it more difficult for you to be a maverick?
3. Suppose that you routinely defer to group will, would you be a Paretian utility maximizer, or satisficer?
4. Are individual utility maximizers and satisficers equally thorough in searching possibilities for enhancing their wellbeing? Elaborate.
5. The Japanese are satisficers whenever they feel that they are being monitored by others including family, ancestral spirits, neighbors, communities, voluntary associations, religious organizations, labor unions, employers, employer associations (keidanren), cross shareholding entities (keiretsu), political entities, and the emperor. Communalism is used as a generic term for the phenomenon. It implies that Japanese feel closely watched. Does this mean that Japanese never individualistically utility seek? What sorts of choices might be made on a purely individualistic basis? Provide examples.
6. Japanese communalism is a matter of degree. Westerners routinely behave communally in some contexts; that is, they satisfice deferring

to group preferences. The concept of "majority rule", implies this sort of accommodation. Nonetheless, if the scope of Japanese satisficing is significantly greater than accommodative behavior in the west, could this justify the claim that Japan violates the axioms of the neo-classical paradigm? Elaborate.

7. Confucianism, Theravada Buddhism and communism have explicit credos. Virtuous systems of these types should advance their values. Is communalism similarly constrained? Compare Japanese values before and after WWII. Compare Japanese with Thai shame ideals.

8. How does Japanese communalism promote egalitarianism?

9. In what ways might Japanese communalism be responsible for its economic stagnation?

10. Why might cultural change (attitude adjustment) within the communalist paradigm be a contributing cause to Japan's economic devitalization.

11. Are Japan's economic woes likely to be self-healing?

12. What adaptive options are open to Japan, if it chooses to retain communalism?

13. Why are team harmony and competitiveness substitutes?

14. Does communalism prevent Japan from being a good engineering society?

15. Why is communalism uncomfortable with entrepreneurship and labor-saving technologies?

16. Why is the team king, rather than the market?

17. Could the deficiencies of communalist growth be counterbalanced by other benefits? Discuss the determinants of wellbeing, fulfillment and contentment.

18. Philosophical speculation aside, what is the deep utilitarian shortcoming of communalist choice making? Explain. Hint: The scope of utilitarian search.

19. Why is consensus building cumbersome, especially in a Japanese setting where conflict avoidance is obligatory?

20. Why is it difficult to appraise opportunity cost through consensus building processes?

21. Why does deficient opportunity costing impair Walrasian and Marshallian equilibrium adjustment?

22. Why are government transfers unimportant in Japan's communalist economy?

23. How do Japanese and western approaches to creating social safety nets differ?

24. What are the comparative merits of the two approaches? Which do you think is better and why?

25. How does Japanese communalism constrain profit maximizing, and why is it intrinsically anti-competitive? Explain.

26. How does the Japanese labor market differ from the Pareto ideal. Illustrate your point using Fig. 8.1. Is the behavior competitively efficient? How do Japanese rules affect factor allocation, work effort, the length of the workday, and communal welfare? Hint: How do the Japanese limit the impact of business cycles fluctuations on unemployment?

27. Which is better: Mass American involuntary unemployment during the crisis of 2008–2010 or Japanese full employment with implicit group wage reductions?

28. Japan's banks pay depositors zero interest, and then lend the funds to community members at rates below Paretian competitive equilibrium. Why is this bad? Can you find a silver lining?

29. Why is the Japanese labor market in double disequilibrium? Why does Japanese per capita income performance overstate worker welfare? How is this connected to the double disequilibrium? Explain.

30. How is Japan's shame culture related to its communalism? Would Japanese communalism be more or less effective if it were based on the guilt principle? Hint: The guilt principle fosters individualistic utility-seeking.

31. Can it be argued that the shame principle facilitated Japanese aggression before 1946? Can it be argued that the shame principle facilitated the Nanjing Massacre?

32. Can satisficing be ethically perilous?

33. How does Japanese communal behavior differ from Confucian order?

34. Why is hierarchy facilitated by communalism? Hint: Consider the advantage of authority in expediting consensus building.

35. How does consensus building nurture authoritarian loyalty? Does it strengthen Japanese respect for the emperor?

36. The Japanese widely engage in collusive corporate price-fixing. This could be a consequence of monopsony and oligopoly price exploitation. But the Japanese never restrict output to augment marginal revenue, and do not manipulate employment to minimize wage rates. Can an alternative explanation be found based on communalist principles? Elaborate.

37. The Japanese are easily contented. Is this a virtue or vice? Elaborate from the standpoint of wellbeing, fulfillment and contentment.

38. Japan's uniqueness can be highlighted by comparing it with another shame culture. Compile a list of Japanese and Thai attitudes toward work and performance. Are the differences explained by Theravada Buddhist and Japanese material precepts?

39. Why is it difficult to efficiently transition to guilt based system? Elaborate.

40. Does culture matter?

Exercises

Draw the Paretian ideal Edgeworth Bowley box (Fig. 1.1). Describe the impact of Japanese communalist principles on the length of the capital and labor vectors, the characteristics (for example work skills) of these factors, and the magnitudes (superscripts) of the isoquants. Where does commualist production occur in this space relative to the Pareto equilibrium E? Hint: Remember that the Pareto and Japanese isoquant scalings differ (especially in the domestic sector where networking restricts competition). Is there likely to be more than one wage-rental ratio at the Japanese production point(s)? Explain. Hint: Japanese consensus building is group specific, with limited wider coordination. Factors consequently are not universally allocated to best use, or in ways that competitively maximize individual worker utility. Is the associated distortion likely to be as great as under market communism? Whose preferences determine the demand for public goods and civic activities: elected officials or consensus building communal actors?

Relocate the Japanese production point(s) in the Pareto production space (Fig. 1.2). Remember that satisficing reduces the isoquant values in Fig. 1.1. (Japanese and Pareto production functions differ because Japanese goods (qs) do not fully optimize consumer utility). Is the

Japanese production point(s) (characteristics adjusted to Pareto equivalent worth) likely to be moderately technically and economically efficient? Explain. Would your evaluation be more favorable to Japan, if it is assumed that in the final analysis fully informed Japanese conclude that the wellbeing they achieve through satisficing is greater than what could be expected from adhering to the inclusive democratic, consumer sovereign, competitive paradigm?

Draw the Paretian ideal Edgeworth Bowley product distribution box (Fig. 1.3). Will the Japanese product distribution box be the same size? Elaborate. Remembering that factors do not earn the value of their competitive marginal products, will retail products be fairly distributed? Also given Japanese market deficiencies, will retail distribution likely be technically (as well as economically) inefficient? Explain. Are there likely to be multiple prices ruling in Japanese retail distribution space? Explain. Hint: Group member receive preferential treatment, but Japanese shame culture requires that all Japanese outsiders (and usually foreigners too) be treated fairly.

Draw the consumer utility space (Fig. 1.4). Assume that one participant is of high social rank and the other a commoner. Locate the realized utility point *vis-à-vis* the Pareto E. Hint: The spectrum of corporate remuneration is exceedingly narrow in Japan compared with other Asian nations and the west. Is Japanese wellbeing lower both due to its productive deficiencies and egalitarianism? Which is greater: Japanese or market communist egalitarianism? Elucidate. Is it likely that the wellbeing of high ranking Japanese will surpass the Pareto ideal as their counterparts in tigerland? Figure 1.4 can be construed to include Paretian government transfers. Could the Japanese be better off relying on communalist care than welfare state programs? Explain.

Draw the Japanese Marshallian and Walrasian disequilibrium adjustment diagrams (Figs. 1.5 and 1.6), as well as the enterprise profit maximizing diagram (Fig. 1.7). Do Pareto efficient laws of supply and demand operate in Japan? Hint: Are Japanese domestic prices and wages set competitively in consensus building firms? If not, explain why equilibria achieved, if any, are distorted?

Is Japanese wellbeing closer to the Pareto ideal than the market communism, tiger Confucian markets, Theravada Buddhist markets, or North Korean command? How would you rank the Japanese communalist system, and why?

BUDDHISM

Chapter 9

Thailand

Systems Profile: Thailand

Type: Theravada Buddhist

Subtype: Liberal constitutional monarchy, open market economy.

Economic Sovereign: Theravada Buddhist culture, king, state service elites, and various ethnic networks control the characteristics of the system and its outcomes.

Ultimate Authority: King, Theravada cultural attitudes; not rule of law (constitution).

Economy: (a) Formal: Freehold ownership, private business, markets, rule of law, open economy, state management through indicative planning, contracting, financing, subsidization, flexible exchange rates, negotiated market pricing, and macroeconomic regulation. **(b) Informal:** Dominance of royal businesses, ethnic networks, and world denying attitudes. Marginalized rule of law and acceptance of labor exploitation.

Government: Intermittent fractious democracy and military rule disciplined by royal deference.

Civil Liberties: Moderate (admixture of tolerance and repression)

Modernization: Dualistic: advanced and traditional segments.

Evolution: Theravada Buddhist monarchy before 1932 with open markets; intermittently democratizing, parliamentary Theravada constitutional monarchy with open markets, 1932-present.

(Continued)

(Continued)

Population (July 2012; CIA): 67.1 million

Living Standard (2012 USD, PPP; source, CIA): $9,700; global rank: 112.

Development (EU Norm): Moderate, gradually catching up to EU.

Thailand's Theravada Buddhist Economic System

Thailand's economy is strongly influenced by more than 1,000 years of Theravada Buddhist culture, a faith which remains vibrant today despite aspects of secular modernization. It is best classified as a theocratic subtype of a culturally sovereign system (see Chapter 1). This means that religious cultural forces determine supply and demand more than the autonomous preferences of individual consumers as usually assumed in the neoclassical paradigm (the inclusive democractic competitive standard). The model is "inclusive" in the sense that state governance and the private sector are both informed by Theravada Buddhist sensibilities. The state in Thailand's imperial tradition is occasionally inclined toward authoritarianism (periodic military control loyal to the king), softened by Buddhist tolerance and compassion, and private self-seeking is restrained by Buddhist moral and spiritual duty. These characteristics are fundamental because they make Pareto utility maximization subsidiary to the higher purpose of individual spiritual Enlightenment. Devout Thai Theravada Buddhists do not consider maximizing profits or mass consuming important. An opulent existence is considered nothing compared to the attainment of true knowledge through self-disciplined mental management and transcendence in Nirvana. The goal is to escape the "self" (soul), not to wallow in luxury. The inclusive democratic competitive paradigm from this perspective is a minor virtue, or worse, a distraction obstructing escape from mundane desire and suffering. The Theravada Buddhist model is intrinsically a-competitive. It discourages individuals from fully maximizing their potential utility in work, investment (including secular education), job choice, production and consumption, and it deters

governments from vigorously promoting the wide range of social programs that are considered indispensible in modern secular nations. Thais
depend more on their communities than the state, and are world denying.
They care little about competitive efficiency. This makes them comparatively under productive. Thailand's growth rate is subpar for a country at
its stage of development. Thais recognize that Theravada Buddhist values
restrict their material possibilities, but strongly believe that spiritual gains
vastly outweigh the affluence foregone. They embrace the King's desire
to create a "sufficiency economy" compatible with the Theravada
Buddhist concept of worthy existence. Theravada Buddhism is not the
only influence shaping Thailand's economic performance. There are other
factors including communalism, a competitive market, foreign investment, and the king. Nonetheless, Theravada Buddhism provides a window
into what Thais consider the sufficiency economy ideal.

Thai Economy

The Thai economic system is governed by four cultural forces: Theravada
Buddhism,[1] shame, imperial authority and westernization filtered through
a multi-ethnic sieve. The combination of the first two influences diminishes the role of individualism as the primary explanation of productive
behavior and tilts the economy toward communalism, and away from
Sino-Korean Confucian kinship systems. Imperial hierarchy centralizes
the system as it did throughout pre-modern Asia, and westernization
encourages competitive individual utility seeking.

---

[1]Theravada is a Pali word meaning "the Teachings of the Elders", connected with the
"Teaching of Analysis", and derives from the earliest Buddhism. It flourishes in Sri Lanka,
Cambodia, Laos, Burma and Thailand, and is practiced by minorities in Yunnan (Shan and
Tai ethnic groups), Vietnam (by the Khmer Krom), Bangladesh (by the Baruas, Chakma and
Magh), Malaysia and Indonesia, and is gaining popularity in Singapore and the west.
Adherents are estimated between 100 and 200 million. Its teachings are traced to the
Vibhajjavada and the prevalent doctrine at the time of the Third Buddhist Council around 250
BC during the reign of Emperor Asoka. The religion was adopted by the royal houses in Sri
Lanka and Southeast Asia. It arrived in Suvarnabhumi (Indochina) around 250 BC brought
by two monks Sona and Uttara. The Mon (earliest people to inhabit lower Burma) are thought
to have been Theravadin since the third century BC. The Thai adopted the Mon religion when
the Lanna Kingdom conquered Hariphunchai (modern Lamphun, near Chiangmai) in 1292.

Theravada Buddhism

Theravada Buddhism is pivotal because it sets a world denying, satisficing agenda that is opposed to the prosperity seeking cultures of China, Taiwan, South Korea and Japan. The goal of devout Thais and others in Sri Lanka and Southeast Asia is *self-less* enlightenment beyond mundane marginalist utilitarian concerns paradoxically achieved through a self-initiated search (self-motivated search to achieve selflessness), rather than secular guidance (state, group, family) or obedience to the imperial throne.[2] Thais, like Japanese can take cues from their communities, but cannot allow group expectations to deter their pursuit of enlightenment whenever goals conflict. Theravada Buddhists cannot relegate the attainment of nirvana to the attitudes of others. This makes them more autonomous than Japanese who are always conscious of group obligations, and therefore less independent.

Enlightenment is more than apperception: assimilating new information with the benefit of experience, and attaining knowledge of the inner self. It is transformative.[3] As one comes to appreciate the insubstantiality of self in a universe of perpetual change, and comprehends the unity of all transient selves, individuals achieve ever higher states of transformative consciousness until ultimately souls are freed from the cycle of reincarnation, extinguished and mystically merged into cosmic nirvana.[4] The truth (or even the precise meaning) of Theravada Buddhist metaphysics is

---

[2]The "Teaching of Analysis" stressed that insight must come from the aspirant's experience, critical investigation and reasoning facilitated by heeding the advice of the wise, instead of blind faith. Ritual also is futile.

[3]Every action has karmic results that affect the spiritual process.

[4]Buddhism has an elaborate trans-temporal eschatological cosmology linked to reincarnation. Some sources suggest that the ego of enlightened souls live eternally in heavenly realms: others stress ego extinguishment. Theravadin doctrine usually holds that the soul is separate from the body, and that enlightenment only involves the soul. The unity of body and soul, or as psychoanalysts would have it body and mind is inessential. Enlightenment and transcendence are attained through clarification of the soul, not the full actualization of body and mind, which is an unnecessary complication, and therefore a hinderance to salvation. The Theravadin position is closer to early Christianity than renaissance humanism (see Promta, 2007). Promta argues that the body should be integrated into Theravadin doctrine in a manner consistent with genetics, without departing fundamentally from the Theravadin stress on transcendent enlightenment.

unimportant from a behavioral perspective.[5] It is the concept of value-seeking that is decisive. Individuals enhance their utility through the pursuit of material consumption and some strive for high forms of personal fulfillment in the west, China, and Confucian Asia. The Japanese strive to improve group material welfare, fulfillment and contentment. Theravada Buddhists reject both approaches as delusory. They view mundane desires including a comfortable life, shallow contentment and secular fulfillment as the cause of suffering and impediments to spiritual progress. Mobilizing resources, effort and technology to achieve high living standards and rapid economic growth together with self-cultivation and daily visits to a psychiatrist may seem sensible, but are snares. They are worthwhile, but only insofar as these pursuits facilitate the quest for nirvana.

Theravada Buddhism does not require poverty. The doctrine is balanced. Thais are encouraged to engage in right occupations, design products as they should be, perform tasks competently, concentrate, utilize resources efficiently and exert themselves. They are expected to be productive and *green*. Given right technology, people should have sufficient sustenance, and something more for a satisfactory life, but given the low priority accorded to acquisitiveness they are apt to underperform Asian neighbors. Harmony and transcendence in this life and across cycles of reincarnation take precedence over riches.

This Thervadin paradigm, predicated on an ontology of ceaseless change (without Aristotle's unmoved prime mover) and an anti-Lockean epistemology of fallible perception (reality is illusory, not transparent) is codified by The Four Noble Truths, and The Eightfold Path.[6] The Four

---

[5] Metaphysics is best understood as "like" physics (following Karl Popper); that is aspects of reality that have some scientific content, but not enough to assure exact prediction, or provide tangible proof. The word is often interpreted as meaning "after" physics, hence cosmology and ontology, but the "after" refers only to texts posthumously added to Aristotle physics, not to transcendental topics. Not everything is "like" physics. Some things are "mysteries", logical and existential paradoxes that cannot be treated even loosely with scientific methods.

[6] Theravada Buddhists believe that transience is eternal; that there never was, nor will be beginnings and ends of time. Aristotle, among others in the western tradition, take the opposite stance. Their analysis begins with the "unmoved prime mover", that is, an existence before change. On western theories of perception (see Locke, 1641).

Noble Truths succinctly characterize the human predicament; the Eightfold Path provides a roadmap to salvation. Like the Christian concept that life is a vale of tears,[7] Theravadins assert that the primary noble truth is suffering (*dukkha*), arising from birth, aging, diseases, death, pain, love, and hate; as well as the impermanence of things people cherish. Suffering is partly physical, but primarily the mental and spiritual distress felt by unenlightened souls who cannot comprehend the human condition. The underlying cause of suffering (*dukkha samudaya*) is desire (both innocent and sinful) which leads to attachments and bondage including yearning for immortality. People cannot face their own mutability. Although they have no fixed, unchanging identity (*Anatta*; not self or permanent essence), like western utilitarians some Thais make the illusory self the center of their reality. Their physical form, feelings, perceptions, cognitive structures and consciousness change moment by moment, yet many people persuade themselves that their essence (soul) is eternal.

The third noble truth is the good news that salvation exists (*dukkha nirodha*), even though it is futile to pursue permanence in this life. Suffering can be conquered by accepting the immutable transcendental truth of Theravada Buddhism.[8] It cannot be effortlessly accomplished by a flash of insight (Chan and Zen Buddhism), nor through good deeds. The fourth noble truth is that freedom lies in following the Noble Eightfold Path, until the enlightened are freed from the cycle of rebirth.

The Noble Eightfold Path is the fourth Noble Truth, and is known as the Middle Way, represented by the dharma wheel. It has three divisions: wisdom, ethical conduct and concentration. Wisdom lies in acknowledging the immutable truth of Buddhism [1] holding the right view, and having the [2] right intention to act accordingly. Ethical conduct requires shunning activities incompatible with the right view, namely [3] wrong speech (lies including those people tell themselves), [4] wrong action (evil

---

[7]Vale of tears refers to the sufferings virtuous people leave behind on earth when they enter heaven. The expression derives from Salve Regina and alludes to Psalm 23. Early Christianity until the time of Constantine rejected worldly vanities, concentrating instead on the attainment of salvation and eternal life in the hereafter. The notion of a mystic union with God was also prevalent.

[8]It is not clear to the author whether physical laws like gravity or the speed of light are fixed or mutable in Theravadin doctrine. Transcendentals may be immutable.

deeds like killing, stealing, despoiling nature) and [5] wrong occupation (evil occupations like prostitution and racketeering). Enlightened beings shun harming others, are respectful of others and compassionate. Once wisdom and ethical conduct are assured, then attaining enlightenment only requires concentration: [6] right effort, [7] right mindfulness, and [8] right concentration. Adherence to the Noble Eightfold Path enlightens souls with knowledge that ultimately allows them to be extinguished and mysteriously absorbed into the eternal cosmic spirit.[9]

The protocol is more reflective and meditative than prescriptive like the Ten Commandments or Confucian codes of conduct. It has many things in common with humanist psychoanalysis (false consciousness which in Theravada Buddhism is a form of wrong speech), but even more with western religious and philosophical concerns with conscience, moral self-scrutiny, discipline and self-purification. However, while virtuous behavior is required, and universal human wellbeing and social justice desired, they are not the ultimate end (summum bonum). Even if Buddhists lived in an earthly utopia (such ideal as inclusive democratic competitive free enterprise) their quest would be incomplete until they achieved full spiritual enlightenment and nirvana, a goal necessitating both mundane and transcendental understanding.

This Buddhist truth is hidden from ordinary people among other things by sexual passion, fear of death,[10] self-deception and moral confusions. These desires, fears, indulgences and misunderstandings must be eradicated. For Theravadins including the king this is accomplished gradually through transformative self-enlightenment, rather than through familial, communal, governmental or therapeutic assistance.[11]

---

[9]A fully enlightened person who is not yet the Buddha of our time is called an Arahant. He/she has eradicated the ten hindrances to enlightenment: (1) belief in a permanent personality (ego), (2) doubt (destructive skepticism), (3) attachment to rites, rituals, and ceremonies, (4) attachment to sense desires, (5) ill-will and anger, (6) craving for existence in the form world (earth), (7) craving for existence in the Formless world (heavenly realms), (8) conceit, (9) restlessness, (10) ignorance.

[10]see Fromm *et al.* (1960).

[11]Eric Fromm contends that the enlightenment goal of Zen Buddhism (Chinese Chan Buddhism) is the same as "humanist" psychoanalysis: "The description of Zen's aim could be applied without change as a description of what psychoanalysis aspires to achieve;

These principles provide a moral compass for Thais, regardless of their spiritual attainments. Unlike the Judeo–Christian tradition they do not seek eternal relationships (love, romance, justice and glory) in this life, nor do they believe that state and international governance (including communism, socialism, and globalization) are satisfactory substitutes for enlightenment. Moreover, unlike the west their credo is not reinforced by guilt. Divine judgment and sin are secondary in shaping Theravadin conduct (operating mostly through cycles of rebirth), leaving shame by default as the principle ancillary mechanism for social control.

Thais of lesser understanding tend to act in accordance with group mores (folkways) that are quite indulgent from an enlightened Theravadin or western ethical perspective. People satisfice by going along with whatever unenlightened groups sanction, instead of seeking spiritual betterment, or utility optimizing. Duty is weak and self-indulgence strong. Despite popular approval of the Nobel Eightfold Path,[12] being energetic, aspiring, orderly, scrupulous, honest, considerate, dispassionate, selfless are often subsidiary for ordinary people. Many Thais are attracted to *la dolce vita*, tolerate huge income disparities, and are indifferent to enhancing long term communal material welfare. They are comfortable

insight into one's own nature, the achievement of freedom, happiness and love, liberation of energy, salvation from being insane or crippled" (see Fromm *et al.*, 1960, p. 122). The identity is weaker than he supposes because Zen priests do not aspire to be fully empowered, mentally "healthy", secular renaissance men and women. Moreover, the analogy cannot be applied even in a limited way to Theravada Buddhism which aims at nirvana, not ego empowering clarity. Fromm's vision is the antithesis of Theravada teachings. He seeks to fully actualize ego potential in everyday life, while Theravadins reject the goal as a delusion that preserves rather than destroys the ego, and therefore impedes progressive reincarnation, enlightenment and the attainment of nirvana. Psychoanalysis from a Theravadin perspective when it is effective is a palliative that precludes any ultimate cure unless combined with transcendent enlightenment. Zen Buddhism forms a middle ground because although it seeks transformative enlightenment, it is ambivalent about reincarnation, and deemphasizes the transcendental extinguishment of individual egos.

[12]Taboos and obligation are weak, but networking and group solidarity are important. The amorality and immorality of ordinary Thais are partly attributable to the Theravidin altitude toward permanence. Concepts like enduring love, loyalty and obligation to others imply permanent relationships that the doctrine disapproves. This subordination of social obligation to personal indulgence and incongruously to enlightenment is the key to understanding the divide between Japanese and Thai shame culture.

with the idea of a sumptuous earthly paradise for their king and other fortunate people,[13] content to take their own pleasure wherever they can. They work long hours at their own pace with little concern for upward mobility,[14] and tolerate poor working conditions, in a psychological space where Buddhist notions of futility and animist sensibilities compensate for material depravation.[15]

These satisficing attitudes have profound consequences in the private and public sectors.[16] Thailand has a democratic constitution (electoral balloting) and institutions, but its indulgent shame culture impairs their performance.[17] The people are not acculturated yet to true democratic self-governing,[18] and their representatives are often demagogic. There is balloting, but not popular sovereignty under the rule of law. Representatives use political office as a vehicle for personal gain, with scant concern for social welfare.[19]

---

[13]The golden temples and Buddhas of the Bangkok period 1768–1932 and paintings of the lavish life displayed on the walls of Wat Phra Kaew epitomize the image of regal opulence.

[14] Many Thais are acquisitive. They like western consumer goods and profit seek, but are unwilling to adopt western efficiency standards and therefore only incompletely maximize profits.

[15]Thailand is 94.6% Buddhist (2000 census), but the practice is syncretic combining Hindu and local divinities, as well as animist elements. Significantly, Thai Theravada imagery is devoid of the fierce, disciplinary manifestations of Buddhist deities common in Tibet and Japan.

[16]There is no obvious residue of an Indian-style cast system.

[17]Thailand has a shame culture. The guilt principle exists, but is secondary. This is probably due to the fact that Theravada Buddhists are supposed to use mental discipline as prescribed by the Eightfold path to govern their behavior so their souls can be extinguished in nirvana. They also are chastened by the Buddhist belief that sin affects their karma and reduces their position in the cycle of rebirth, but evil itself is not the issue. Thais are more concerned about avoiding pain, than feeling guilty about committing sins. This individualist approach to salvation, coupled with a world denying ethos that places little value on materialism makes Thai shame society less aroused and perfectionist than Japan's ichiban shame culture. Thais not only are less concerned about the "best", groups are very tolerant of deviant behavior outside their own immediate circles.

[18] see Rosefielde and Mills (2012).

[19] see Phongpaichit and Baker (1998) and Phongpaichit and Baker (2004).

Business departs similarly from the consumer sovereign ideal. Moral hazard and adverse selection abound, impairing competitiveness. Thailand also has made a virtue of permissiveness in the hospitality sector where a combination of Buddhist inspired friendly service (Thais describe Thailand as the land of smiles), and unenlightened pandering (sex industry) attracts tourists,[20] and outsourcers seeking a docile labor force, low wages and a pleasurable executive work environment. Thailand's other minorities: Chinese and Indians partly offset these deficiencies by adding dynamism in the financial, commercial and international trade sectors. This has been enough to support moderate growth with a dual economy,[21] but has not been sufficient to enable Thailand to outpace Japan, Confucian Asia, market communist China because Theravada Buddhist economies encourage incomplete profit and utility seeking, distain unseemly capital accumulation, and are a-competitive. Enlightened souls strive to produce as they believe they ought, with environmentally friendly technologies and humane labor conditions, not as market demand dictates, while the unenlightened fatalistically satisfice. Neither family nor group material obligations take precedence over enlightenment and/or passivity as they often do in Confuciansm influenced Asia, communalist Japan or the Judeo–Christian west. Buddha's wife Yasodhara for example did not lament her husband decision to abandon her and their son Rahula for a higher calling. She simply acknowledged the imperative of enlightenment, and emulated his decision by becoming Buddhism first nun at the age of 36.[22]

---

[20]Pandering includes all kinds of sexual services in multiple venues that has prompted some to describe the service sector as being prostitutized. For a fictionalized portrayal of Thai cultural contradictions see (Burdett, 2003).

[21]A growing minority of Thais are westernizing or wealthy, with the majority still ensconced in low income generating activities.

[22]Buddha, the historical Nepalese prince Siddhartha, born in Kapilavastu in 563 BC, married Yasodhara when he was approximately 26 and she was sixteen. They had a son Rahula. At the age of 29, Siddhartha abandoned his family to become an ascetic. Six years later he discovered the Middle Path and became enlightened. His wife became the first Buddhist nun shortly thereafter. The moral of this story for Theravadins is that the virtues of family, and familial obligations are subordinate to enlightenment. The attitude is consistent with the impermanence of egos, unlike for example, Catholic doctrine which twines married souls forever and makes abandonment a sin. The Thervadin outlook is not easily

Thailand's moderate economic growth and development over the past few decades therefore probably is mostly ascribable to non-religious factors, particularly the influence of energetic minorities, the throne and westernization. The king plays three distinct roles in the Thai system. First, the Royal family is the largest force in the economy. As early as 1910, the monarch's Privy Purse was the country's largest property owner, including one-third of central Bangkok. Thai kings combined their personal wealth with their administrative control of the state to assure the success of their commercial endeavors. During the years 1932–1936 when the present constitutional monarchy was established, the king's personal assets were separated from the Privy Purse Bureau and placed tax free in the Crown Property Bureau, professionally managed by the king's appointees. Although, the king is no longer the head of government, the crown often receives privileged treatment from the state enabling the Crown Property Bureau to operate effectively in the global economy, an institutional device analogous to similar forms of state support in South Korea (chaebols), communist China and Japan. The palace moreover has been an ideal joint venture partner. It has ownership stakes in the Siam Intercontinental, Erawan and Dusit Thani hotels. The CPB holds majority stakes in Siam Cement (the largest Thai industrial and petrochemical conglomerates), Christiani and Nielsen (one of the largest construction firms), Deves Corporation (a major telecommunications firm, through the CPB's holdings in Siam Commercial Bank). Other shareholdings include Honda Cars (Thailand), Y.K.K. Zipper (Thailand), Nanthawan (Obayshi), Thai Bridgestone, Minebea Electronics (Thailand), and Bangkok Aviation Fuel Service. According to Forbes, the market value of the CPB is approximately 36 billion dollars.[23]

Second, the monarch is a powerful stabilizing force in Thailand's fledgling democracy. The nation has had 17 charters and constitutions since 1932, partly as a consequence of numerous *coup d'etats*. Theravada

---

reconciled with modern feminism, which has birthed a novel casting Buddha as a male chauvinist cad who placed his own delusions above the needs of his family, and created a religion that rationalized his iniquities under the guise of universal impermanence. "How could the Buddha have such compassion for others, yet been so scared of intimacy, emotion and love?" (see Constans, 2009).

[23] see Sricharatchanya (1988, pp. 60–63), Ouyyanont (2007, 2008).

Buddhist sentiment has held the scale of violence in check, but the king's moral force also has played an important constructive role. Without it, direct foreign investment and outsourcing would have been reduced to a trickle.

Third, and a corollary of the second, the king has championed a Theravada Buddhist approach to development called the sufficiency economy, stressing the Middle Way including green development.[24] He urges self-restraint within the indulgent shame culture to facilitate modernization, while simultaneously putting spiritual ahead of material pursuits. Buddhist sufficiency is said to be a powerful tool for preventing economic crises,[25] and fastest is not best. Gradual modernization fosters stability and wellbeing. The rapid growth of *goods* which are really *bads* increases GDP in a statistical sense, but degrades welfare.

This stance, which has been formally incorporated in Thailand's ninth and tenth national and social development plans 2001–2006 and 2007–2011 is sincere. The crown generously supports numerous social projects.

The willingness of the king and the government to embrace modernization also is fundamental. Thailand maintains an open economy with a convertible exchange rate, and has positioned itself as the center of a commercial arc linking Tokyo with the Middle East via India. It not only draws direct foreign investment from the four corners of the global, but has built a business and bureaucratic middle class to support these activities and provide upscale services to various affluent communities. Although, the Theravada ethos is a-competitive, partial westernization,

---

[24] "After the economic crisis in 1997, His Majesty Bhumibol Adulyadej reiterated and expanded on the 'Sufficiency Economy' in remarks made in December 1997 and 1998. The philosophy points the way for recovery that will lead to a more resilient and sustainable economy, better able to meet the challenges arising from globalization and other changes". "The Sufficiency Economy' is a philosophy that stresses the middle path as the overriding principle for appropriate conduct by the populace at all levels. This applies to conduct at the level of the individual, families, and communities as well as to the choice of a balanced development strategy for the nation so as to westernize in line with the forces of globalization while shielding against inevitable excesses that arise". Available at http:wwww.rdpd.go.th/rdpd/EN/BRANDSITE/keywords.aspx.

[25] see Bhongmakapat (2012).

together with outsourcing is a fillip to competitive efficiency and a strong source of vitality.

Thailand's future thus is not being forged only in the cauldron of Theravada Buddhism and an indulgent shame culture. It is being shaped as well by the king's vision of the sufficiency economy seeking to blend spiritual values with westernization, in a comparatively open system. It is premature to judge whether this blending of east and west will be better than China's market communism, Taiwan's Confucian free enterprise, or Japanese communalism, but adaptive path dependence just might hold its own against the inclusive democratic free enterprise paradigm.

Buddhism and Wellbeing

Thai culture promotes material wellbeing and personal fulfillment, but is not fixated on living standards and GDP growth, appreciating that there is a tradeoff between individuals' mundane and spiritual welfare. As Thais see the matter there are rapidly diminishing returns to material consumption and secular personal development. The right approach consequently is to collectively optimize mundane and spiritual wellbeing, instead of relegating spiritual factors to afterthoughts. The Thai framework is doubly beneficial because it reduces mundane wants and diminishes psychological and spiritual discontent. Theravada Buddhism teaches that if people have "enough", which means having very little in accordance with its world denying orientation, they can still achieve spiritual enlightenment.[26] This is visibly manifest in the mildness and peacefulness of Thai society, despite the usual growing pains that accompany economic development, modernization and democratization. There is periodic political violence, but for the most part discontent and aggression are restrained.

The Thai cultural strategy for promoting wellbeing and alleviating anxiety is mostly attributable to Theravada Buddhism which provides every individual with the opportunity to attain enlightenment and thereby dissolve and merge his/her soul with the cosmic spirit. This mind

---

[26]Christian doctrine asserts much the same thing, but the religion is much more world affirming (oriented toward community action and service) than Theravada Buddhism.

management strategy has unique characteristics. Theravada Buddhists advocate virtuous behavior and disapprove of vice, but conscience is not primarily dedicated to eradicating sin. Its task is to internalize the Four Noble Truths and the Eightfold Path as a complete program for attaining nirvana. Theravada Buddhism teaches adepts to fix their attention exclusively on following the Eightfold Path. Each individual in this way will master his or her mind through [6] right effort, [7] right mindfulness, and [8] right concentration. People become increasingly serene as they achieve higher and higher forms of spiritual insight. Enoughness brings them fulfillment, contentment and bliss. It makes them "green", compassionate, merciful, and promotes a harmonious society, all as a prelude to extinguishment of their souls in nirvana.

Theravada Buddhists appreciate that inclusive democratic free enterprise also tries to improve people's wellbeing, but contend that secular solutions are only secondary paths. The only true highway to wellbeing, fulfillment and contentedness is the Middle Way.

Review

*Thailand is a Theravada Buddhist nation.

*Buddhism is a religion accepted in many different cultures, both shame and guilt alike.

*Buddhism's impact on economic behavior is not the same everywhere. Other factors, including shame and guilt control mechanisms co-determine its influence. Thai shame, and Chinese guilt based Buddhist societies have distinctly different characters.

*Shame cultural societies are especially susceptible to world denying when this is the collective goal because individuals do not have a higher set of socially approved principles to support their world affirming preferences.

*Theravada Buddhism and shame are separate and distinct factors shaping Thai productive behavior.

*Imperial authority is another potent influence. Theravada Buddhism is compatible with democracy, and Thailand has a democratic constitution.

However, this has not negated the king's authority. He is deeply revered and his pronouncements powerfully affect all aspects of Thai life.

*Thailand is an open society, receptive to aspects of western rationalist and humanist culture. Thais, like most other peoples do not fully embrace westernization. Instead, they select aspects that foster material prosperity (modernization), while rejecting western ego-centrism.

*Thailand has numerous economically important minorities, including Chinese Confucians, Indian Hindus, and Southeast Asian Muslims who filter the influences of Theravada Buddhism, shame and royal authority through their own subcultural prisms.

*Theravada Buddhism and shame driven behavior tilt Thai economy toward communalism. The king is an independent, centralizing force, while westernization fosters individual utility seeking.

*Thais satisfice, but do so in a Theravada Buddhist, shame cultural manner. They acquiesce according to a world denying logic focused on attaining spiritual enlightenment, rather than Confucian logic which compels members to subordinate themselves for the sake of familial harmony and prosperity.

*Most Thais view the attainment of selfless enlightenment as the true path.

*This requires a self-directed spiritual search that makes Thais more autonomous than they might otherwise be in authoritarian or communalist societies where conformity is the norm.

*Thais believe that ritual is inessential to the attainment of nirvana. They therefore place less importance on it than Confucians.

*Thais like the Japanese take cues from their communities, and are influenced by shame, but this does not impede their spiritual quest.

*Enlightenment is transformative from a Buddhist perspective. It frees souls from the cycle of reincarnation. This is the highest good, and therefore the only proper determinant of rational human conduct.

*The attitude profoundly affects Thai behavior, regardless of its metaphysical merit.

*The pursuit of material affluence from the Theravada viewpoint is misguided, even if its primary purpose is group welfare as in Japan.

*Mundane desires are perceived to be the cause of human suffering and impediments to spiritual progress.

*Material pursuits are justified only insofar as they facilitate spiritual progress.

*Theravada Buddhism provides detailed rules for engaging in material pursuits. They should be productive and green.

*People must engage in right occupations, design products as they should be. They should perform tasks competently, concentrate, utilize resources efficiently and exert themselves.

*Harmony and transcendence take precedence over riches. Other things equal, Thailand should underperform the material norms of their non-Buddhist competitors because they devote more time to spiritual pursuits.

*These ideas are codified in The Four Noble Truths, and The Eightfold Path.

*The first noble truth identifies the human predicament [perpetual earthly suffering (*dukkha*)]. The second noble truth is that illusory desire is the cause of human suffering.

*Theravada Buddhism claims that people do not have immutable selves, and therefore neoclassical utility maximizing is a delusion. Satisficing is much more sensible.

*The third noble truth is that salvation (*dukkha nirodha*) exists at the path's end, but not in this world. It is only found in nirvana; the extinguishment of the individual soul and its merger with the cosmic whole.

*The fourth noble truth is that freedom lies in following The Noble Eightfold Path, until the enlightened are freed from the cycle of rebirth.

*The Noble Eightfold Path (Middle Way) is divisible into three composites: wisdom, ethical conduct, and concentration.

*Wisdom requires (1) holding the right view (Buddhism), and (2) right intention (resisting temptation).

*Ethical conduct necessitates (3) right speech (truthfulness), (4) right action (shunning evil deeds), and (5) right occupations (eschewing criminal behavior). Enlightened beings refrain from harming others, and are compassionate.

*Concentration permits the wise and virtuous to implement their will through (6) right effort, (7) right mindfulness, and (8) right concentration.

*The Noble Eightfold Path facilitates enlightenment and makes human souls free.

*The process of Buddhist self-discovery is similar to humanist psychoanalysis, even though their respective metaphysics differ.

*Theravada Buddhists reject communist, social democratic and democratic free enterprise claims that heaven can be build on earth.

*Thai worry less about particular sins (guilt) than the shame of disregarding the Four Noble Truths, and the Noble Eightfold Path. Shame controls their daily behavior.

*The ethics of ordinary Thais are lax, compared with the Japanese. They are not energetic, aspiring, orderly, scrupulous, honest, considerate, dispassionate, or selfless. Many are attracted to "la Dolce vita", tolerate huge income disparities, and are indifferent to enhancing long term communal material welfare. They work long hours at their own pace with little concern for upward mobility, tolerating poor working conditions.

*Thais are not acculturated to being democratically self-governing, and their elected government is correspondingly unruly.

*Moral hazard and adverse selection are serious problems, and impair competitiveness. Outsourcers are attracted to Thailand because workers are readily exploited.

*The royal family is the most powerful force in the economy.

*The king's personal assets were separated from the state Privy Purse Bureau and placed tax free in the Crown Property Bureau, professionally managed by the king's appointees in 1936.

*This has created a chaebol like, state assisted institution that facilitates the operation of royal companies in the domestic and international economies.

*According to Forbes, the market value of the CPB is approximately 36 billion dollars.

*The king has been a stabilizing political and social influence, both facilitating outsourcing and direct foreign investment.

*The king is the nation's principal advocate of the "sufficiency economy", an environmentally friendly approach to economy compatible with the "Middle Way".

*He urges self-restraint within the indulgent shame culture to facilitate modernization, and counsels putting spiritual above material pursuits. Fastest is not best.

*The king's support for modernization is important, because otherwise Thais might be too inward looking.

*Although, the Theravada ethos is a-competitive, partial westernization, together with outsourcing is a fillip to competitive market efficiency and a strong source of dynamism.

Questions

1. Theravada Buddhism is embraced by most Thais, yet its precepts do not provide a complete guide to understanding economic behavior. Are religious values anywhere self-enforcing? Ponder and elaborate.
2. Two important ethical social enforcement mechanisms are shame and guilt. They are not mutually exclusive, but one or the other often predominates. Thailand has a shame culture. How might this influence its economic behavior in ways that the guilt mechanism would not?
3. Are all shame cultures alike? Compare Thailand's and Japan's shame enforced values governing their respective economic behavior.
4. What role does the king play in Thailand's economic system? How does this role differ from that of Japan's current emperor Akihito?

5. Is Thailand open, or closed to westernization? What aspects of westernization does it embrace? What aspects does it reject?

6. Some societies like Muslim Malaysia rely heavily on ethnic minorities such as overseas Chinese to invigorate commerce and industry. Does Theravada Buddhist Thailand display the same characteristic? What are the similarities? What are the differences? Hint: Consider the important role played by crown properties and business.

7. In what ways does Theravada Buddhism and shame tilt the Thai economy towards communalism?

8. Does Theravada Buddhism and shame encourage satisficing? Are Thai and Confucian satisficing the same? What are the key differences?

9. Most Thais view the attainment of selfless enlightenment as life's true path. Can you prove that this judgment is wrong? If so, do so. If not, discuss the comparative merit of the Theravada Buddhist and consumer sovereign democratic competitive approaches to ordering one's life. Why cannot you prove that nature is the only reality?

10. How does searching for the true path make Thais economically, politically and socially autonomous? Would social conformity be facilitated if Theravada Buddhism provided the full truth, and commanded everyone to obey?

11. Ritual is an aspect of Theravada Buddhism. It is a tool aiding each individual's quest for enlightenment, not a vehicle for inculcating values. Ritual for the later purpose (a central aspect of Confucianism), or any other is considered delusional. Which approach is more compatible with western rationalism? Why?

12. Why do Theravada Buddhists distinguish between enlightenment as insight, and a higher transformative phenomenon? What is the difference between insight and transformation here?

13. If Theravada Buddhists are right about transformative enlightenment, does this illuminate why they believe that seeking enlightenment is the highest form of rationality?

14. Western ethicist condemn greed, but encourage altruistic striving for the social good. Does this imply that Theravada Buddhists might consider altruism to be more laudable than enlightenment? Explain.

15. What happens to consumer sovereign democratic competitive theory if people emulate Theravada Buddhists and extinguish all material desires? Is there any place for materialism in Theravada Buddhist practice? Hint: Theravada Buddhists appreciate that the majority will remain unenlightened for many reincarnations and have established rules which enable people to gradually wean themselves from material cravings.
16. Is money, private property, or desire the root of all evil?
17. Why do Theravadans counsel people to be productive and green? Hint: If materialism were eradicated, the natural aspect of reality would be purified.
18. Theravadans believe that if people act economically as they ought, rather than as the market dictates, spiritual progress will be advanced. How is the Theravada Buddhist concept of desire connected to the idea that markets pollute the environment?
19. Could harmony and affluence be substitutes in neoclassical theory? Why did Marx think that they were complements?
20. What are The Four Noble Truths? List and describe.
21. Why is neoclassical utility theory compromised if people have mutable selves, and it is desirable to achieve states of non-self (*ananta*)? Explain.
22. Why is neoclassical utility theory irrelevant for people seeking *ananta* and nirvana?
23. If people have been aware of these deep value problems for millennia, why does neoclassical theory ignore them?
24. What are the eight components of The Noble Eightfold Path? Compare these precepts to the Ten Commandments and the Christian golden rule. Are any of these ethical concepts sufficiently detailed so that people know how to act properly in all circumstances? Explain.
25. How does the Freudian psychoanalytic agenda differ from the Theravada Buddhist procedure for discovering nirvana? Which approach is more exhaustive? Hint: Theravadins want to know the fundamental truths about all things. Freudians merely seek to learn what makes people demented.
26. Why do Theravada Buddhists consider Marxist Leninist utopianism rubbish?

27. Why do Theravada Buddhists favor shame discipline. Hint: Enlightenment is a process of discovering right conduct without priors. Guilt cultures assert and establish fixed categories of right and wrong that place boundaries on permissible spiritual search for enlightenment.
28. Thais are morally lax, yet devout. How does Theravada Buddhist preoccupation with enlightenment clarify this seeming contradiction?
29. Does the combination of Theravada Buddhism and Thai shame culture make people vulnerable to exploitation, and abet inequality? Explain.
30. Does the combination of Theravada Buddhism and Thai shame culture shed light on the volatility of Thailand's democracy? Hint: Do they prod Thais to be politically self-governing?
31. Does the combination of Theravada Buddhist world denying and shame culture exacerbate moral hazard and adverse selection?
32. Is Thailand's king merely a moral force, or does the royal family have immense economic clout?
33. What is the "sufficiency economy"? Does it embody the Theravada Buddhist spirit?

Exercises

Draw the Paretian ideal Edgeworth Bowley box (Fig. 1.1). Describe the impact of Thai principles on the length of the capital and labor vectors, the characteristics (for example work skills) of these factors, and the magnitudes (superscripts) of the isoquants. Where does Thai production occur in this space relative to the Pareto equilibrium E? Hint: Remember that the Pareto and Thai isoquant scalings differ (especially in the domestic sector where Theravada Buddhism and Thai shame culture restrict competition). Is there likely to be more than one wage-rental ratio at the Thai production point(s)? Explain. Hint: Thai utility seeking is strongly conditioned by local influences. Factors consequently are not universally allocated to best use, or in ways that competitively maximize individual worker utility. Is the associated distortion likely to be as great as under market communism? How does Thai satisficing affect monopsony power? How does it affect public programs and civic freedom? Whose preferences determine the demand for public goods and civic activities: state, business and Buddhist spiritual authorities, or Thai communities?

Relocate the Thai production point(s) in the Pareto production space (Fig. 1.2). Remember that satisficing reduces the isoquant values in Fig. 1.1. (Thai and Pareto production functions differ because Thai goods (qs) do not fully optimize individual consumer utility). Is the Thai production point(s) (characteristics adjusted to Pareto equivalent worth) likely to be weakly technically and economically efficient? Explain. Would your evaluation be more favorable to Thailand, if it is assumed that in the final analysis fully informed Thais conclude that the wellbeing they achieve through satisficing is greater than what can be expected from adhering to the neoclassical paradigm?

Draw the Paretian ideal Edgeworth Bowley product distribution box (Fig. 1.3). Will the Thai product distribution box be the same size? Elaborate. Remembering that factors do not earn the value of their generally competitive marginal products, will retail products be fairly distributed? Also given Thai market deficiencies, will retail distribution likely be technically and economically inefficient? Hint: Thai retailing is segmented with prices available in villages, or working class urban neighborhoods drastically lower than nearby upscale establishments. Explain. Are there likely to be multiple prices ruling in the Thai retail distribution space? Explain. Hint: Thais are not constrained by Japanese communalist sentiment to shun price discrimination.

Draw the consumer utility space (Fig. 1.4). Assume that one participant is of high social rank and the other a commoner. Locate the realized utility point *vis-à-vis* the Pareto E. Hint: The spectrum of remuneration in Thailand is exceedingly wide, probably on a par with market communism, and more inegalitarian than in tiger Confucian societies. Is Thai wellbeing lower both due to its productive deficiencies and inegalitarianism? Which is greater: Thai or market communist inegalitarianism? Elucidate the nuances. Is it likely that the wellbeing of high ranking Thais will surpass the Pareto ideal as in the case of their tigerland counterparts? Figure 1.4 can be construed to include Paretian government transfers. Could direct communal provision of services to the needy make Thais better off than their welfare state twins? Explain.

Draw the Thai Marshallian and Walrasian disequilibrium adjustment diagrams (Figs. 1.5 and 1.6), as well as the enterprise profit maximizing diagram (Fig. 1.7). Do Pareto efficient laws of supply and demand operate in Thailand? Hint: Are Thai domestic prices and wages set competitively in firms on a strictly individualistic basis? If not, explain why equilibria achieved, if any, are distorted?

Is Thai wellbeing closer to the Pareto ideal than to the standards of market communism, tiger Confucian markets, Japanese communalism, or North Korean command? How would you rank Thai Theravada Buddhist wellbeing compared with its Asian neighbors, and why?

PART IV

PAN-ASIAN SYSTEMS

Chapter 10

Asia's Futures

Diversity and Globalization

Asia's core economic systems differ fundamentally from American democratic free enterprise and the European Union's social democracy. They are based on kinship networks, communalism, Theravada Buddhism and communism which restrict or suppress democratic governance and unfettered market competition. This diversity conflicts with the western globalist vision which assumes that Asia's economies are transitioning to democratic free enterprise (the inclusive democratic competitive market standard). The west's faith is attributable to the hidden premise that if governments begin experimenting with balloting, and adopt markets of any kind, they will inevitably transition to democratic free enterprise.[1]

The belief is deeply felt, but implausible. It is not true that every rational person agrees, or should agree that the inclusive democratic competitive market standard is superlative.[2] Communists, Confucians, communalists and Buddhists all are confident that the future belongs to them. They prefer their economic systems and desire tomorrows on their own terms.[3] Some Asians want to preserve the pluralist status quo, others are musing about the possibilities for reform and pan-Asian systems building.

---

[1] see Fukuyama (1992).

[2] The belief that Asia will substitute democratic free enterprise for its systems cannot be disproven because every failure is viewed as a prelude to tomorrow's success, but this doesn't make the claim true.

[3] Karl Marx is quite explicit on this point in *Das Kapital*, Vol. 1. He and all his followers insist that communism will university supersede capitalism.

Coexistence

The attitudes of regional policymakers depend on numerous factors including population, economic trends, threat perceptions, ambitions and intraregional cooperative opportunities. Most leaders feel defensive, believing that they must accommodate to regional and global competitive pressures, or resist fundamental change, rather than proselytize their models.

North Korea's diehard Communist Party is wedded to the status quo. It might experiment anew with market communism at the fringes of the command system after Kim Jong-un consolidates power, but a clear break with communism seems light years away.

Japan is turning inward after two lost decades of subpar economic growth and declining regional influence. The Japanese appreciate what they have and desire to preserve it. They do not want to be *gaijin*, or alter their system even if they have to forego some wealth and power.

The Confucian tigers, Taiwan, Singapore and South Korea, encouraged by their superior economic performance are more self-confident, but recognize that they may have to liberalize familial networks further to retain their competitive edge in the global marketplace.

Thailand desires to protect its traditions and prosper by serving as an attractive platform for foreign outsourcers. It has some prospects for spreading its paradigm to Myanmar, Laos and Cambodia, but will not attract converts in Japan, Confucian Asia and market communist China.

Beijing is double-minded. On one hand, party leaders who trust the regime's statistics must conclude that market communism is the world's best system judged from the standpoint of sustainable long term growth. This emboldens them to press Confucian Asia, Japan and Thailand toward market communism (Beijing Consensus). On the other hand, party members who discount official growth claims (as they should), must worry about diminishing returns to modernization, and social discord. They are more concerned with finding ways to successfully reform market communism, or even abandon it altogether for a better economic system. This ambivalence makes China the region's wild card.

Whither China?

As previously discussed in Chapter 6, there are no solid grounds for presuming that China's market communist system is superior to any of its Asian or western competitors in the long run, or that Beijing's current "masters first, people second" version of market communism is sustainable. The prevailing system is anti-competitive, inegalitarian, "Legalist" and socially combustible. It is dependent on direct foreign investment, outsourcing, technology transfer, and flagging western and Japanese import demand. China's Communist Party recently decided to address these problems by replacing Deng's trade and foreign direct investment driven growth model. It announced that Beijing will stop subsidizing exports and protecting importables, shifting the resources released from the coastal provinces to rural China. This balanced development strategy could be beneficial, but will not be a panacea. It cannot eradicate the anti-competitive losses caused by Communist Party privilege granting, reduce income inequalities, increase civil liberties, defuse social resentment, or persuade the leadership to embrace inclusive democratic competitive free enterprise.

Xi Jinping as discussed in Chapter 6 has another option. He could curtail privilege-granting and share China's wealth more broadly, but there is very little concrete evidence to suggest that Communist party insiders will sacrifice their private interests for the people.

It can therefore be provisionally concluded that China's tomorrow is most likely to be more of the same. The Communist Party will continue lauding its "masters first, people second" brand of market communism, while those outside the magic circle will grow increasing disgruntled.

Pan-Asian Systems

Asia tomorrow, all things considered also should look much like today. Pesky North Korea aside, leaders across the region will try to preserve their systems and maintain at least the façade of cordiality by actively participating in cooperative regional economic organizations, including Asia-Pacific Economic Cooperation (APEC) and the Association of Southeast Asian

Nations (ASEAN).[4] The former is a forum of 21 Pacific Rim "Member Economies" seeking to promote free trade and economic cooperation throughout the Asia-Pacific Region. The latter is a geo-political and economic organization that has announced its intention to create an ASEAN Economic Community (AEC) by 2015. Some are calling for the creation of an East Asian Union (ASEAN PLUS FIVE) encompassing Japan, South Korea, Taiwan, China, North Korea, Indonesia, Malaysia, the Philippines, Singapore, Thailand, Brunei Vietnam, Laos, Cambodia, and Myanmar. Others endorse a China–Japan community headquartered in Okinawa.[5]

Neoclassical economic theory teaches that authentic free trade should improve the wellbeing of all participants, and intra-regional political coordination also could prove beneficial. Therefore, even if the representatives from the five core East and Southeast Asian economic systems joust for advantage in Pan-Asian cooperative institutions, there are no compelling grounds to anticipate harmful outcomes.

The same supposition, however does not apply when participants venture beyond cooperation and liberalization (Washington Consensus) to the formation of unified public and private governance regimes like the European Union (EU) because the five core East and Southeast Asian systems are mutually incompatible. The inclusive democratic competitive model cannot be Confucian, communal, Theravadin, market communist, or Stalinist. Japanese communalists cannot adopt the supremacy of Confucian kinship without foregoing the priority they accord to other groups. Theravadins cannot be Stalinists, so on and so forth.

All attempts to impose integrated regimes that gloss over the mutual exclusivity of Asia's core system among each other, and with democratic free enterprise are apt to have adverse consequences. The EU boasted that its supranational union would be harmonious, but instead finds itself in an

---

[4]ASEAN was established in 1967 and currently has ten members: Indonesia, Malaysia, the Philippines, Singapore, Thailand, Brunei, Myanmar, Cambodia, Laos and Vietnam. It has a population of six hundred million (more than the EU). ASEAN often meets with Japan, China and South Korea. These convocations are called ASEAN PLUS THREE. Taiwan is excluded as a gesture to China. North Korea, often called the hermit kingdom is treated as a rouge state. Available at www.asean.org/21083.pdg.

[5]see Morita and Chen (2012).

intractable crisis, as should have been easily foreseen.[6] Thus while Asia (North Korea aside) should continue prospering as its systems are currently configured, it runs of the danger of stumbling badly by overplaying its hand in the Pan-Asian "partnership" game. Cooperation, liberalization and openness are fine, as long as Asia avoids the "third rail"[7] by shunning efforts to make a single system out of five incompatible ones.

---

[6] see Razin and Rosefielde (2010, 2012).
[7] see Rosefielde *et al.* (2012).

Conclusion

There is no superlative economic system because neither perfect individualist competition, nor perfect planning assures that outcomes maximize wellbeing, fulfillment and contentment judged from various cultural, humanist, social, religious and ideological perspectives. Nonetheless, the merit of systems can be roughly gauged with indicators like per capita GDP, momentum, Gini coefficients, the United Nations Human Development Index, and the Legatum Index (see Chapter 1, note 25).

Contemporary Asia's Confucian, Japanese communal, Thai Theravada Buddhist and market communist systems perform relatively well on these measures. Japan, Taiwan, Singapore, Hong Kong and South Korea enjoy high standards of living. China, Vietnam, and the tigers are growing rapidly. Japan, Taiwan, Singapore, Hong Kong and South Korea also excel on the UN and Legatum indices. Hong Kong and Singapore have already surpassed the European Union's living standard and Taiwan may join this exclusive club soon.

Asia's core systems are performing surprising well on balance, adjusted for relative economic backwardness, judged with these conventional yardsticks, and may well be doing even better when humanistic and spiritual aspects of wellbeing, fulfillment and contentment are factored into the equation.

There are no compelling reasons for Taiwan, Singapore and Hong Kong to alter course, although they may choose to adopt the inclusive democratic competitive market model on other grounds. Japanese communalists may rethink their position if economic growth continues to languish. Market communists might decide to follow suit as China's and Vietnam's economies mature.

North Korean command communism appears to be Asia's only indisputable flop. While Kim Jong-un will surely reject this verdict, North Korea's leadership should seriously consider abandoning command central planning for something better.

These findings make it clear that patience is required in assessing systems merit on both theoretical and pragmatic grounds. It is easy to make cases for the inherent superiority of this or that system from various perspectives, but performance in the short, intermediate and long run seldom matches expectations. The prudent course is to closely monitor, model, assess and adapt.

Glossary

adverse selection
: inferior choices caused by the distorted incentives of coercive economic systems.

anatta
: Theravada Buddhist doctrine that the ego is a mutable agglomeration of experiences, not an eternal self, and hence is not-self. The soul should not be confused with a transient, self-delusive ego.

Arrow's Paradox (impossibility theorem)
: Mathematical proof that democratic balloting cannot provide representatives with a consistent community-wide ranking of alternatives. In other words, public provision of goods and services cannot satisfy demand as efficiently as competitive markets.

Asian values
: A term that came into vogue in the nineties suggesting that hard work, diligence, family piety, loyalty and benevolence were uniquely Asian values, inseparable from eastern authoritarianism.

autarky
: Closed economy with virtually no foreign trade.

autocracy
: State governance system with a single ruler (monarch). An autocrat may or may not be a dictator, hereditary ruler or totalitarian.

authoritarianism	Dictatorial behavior sanctioned by position. Autocrats are authoritarian state rulers.
Bao Cap	Vietnamese subsidy system providing low cost necessitates to the population during the terror-command communist period. Subsidies were gradually abolished in the subsequent Doi Moi (reform) phase.
Bergsonian social welfare function	A function aggregating individual utilities and relational variables used to generate social welfare indifference contours. Social welfare is optimized at the tangency of the Bergson W, and the utility possibilities frontier.
Bolshevik Party	The minority faction of the Marxist Russian Social Democratic Labor Party that seized state power under Vladimir Lenin's leadership November 7, 1917 and established a communist regime.
bounded rationality	A term acknowledging the limits of human rational choice making. People cannot search, process and maximize utility possibilities because they possess incomplete information, restricted cognitive and processing capabilities, and must decide in finite time intervals.
Bukharinite market communism	The Marxist spiritual father of Deng Xiaoping is Nikolai Bukharin who championed building Soviet communism on a market foundation during the mid 1920s. He was executed by Stalin in 1938 as an enemy of the people.
cardinality	In economics, a set of additive numbers representing homogeneous goods or utilities.
chaebols	A South Korean form of business conglomerate; family corporate groups filially connected with state patrons.

communalism	A system of governance based on commune (community) interest as opposed to individual self-betterment. The concept is akin to collectivism, where individuals use the group to advance their self-interest.
	Japanese communalism emphasizes consensus building as a device for identifying group interest.
communism	An ideal harmonious state where full abundance and the abolition of the exploitation of man by man is achieved by criminalizing private property, business and entrepreneurship, and liquidating the state as an instrument of authoritarian coercion. The concept is utopian because it cannot be proven that abolishing private property assures the predicted results.
comparative merit	The relative virtue of an economic system based on some weighted assessment of its net benefits.
computopia	A term coined by Egon Neuberger to suggest the possibility that computers might someday enable society to fulfill its dreams.
Confucianism	A system of family based state governance seeking harmony and prosperity achieved through filial loyal, piety, benevolence, trust and ritual devised by Kong Fuzi (551–479 BC). Every individual has an assigned role and duty which takes precedence over personal self-seeking.
culture	The written and informal rules that govern individual and collective utility (wellbeing) seeking, together with other aspects of human behavior.
Cultural Revolution	A "Great Proletarian Cultural Revolutionary" movement initiated by Mao in 1966 officially intended to subordinate technocratic to ideological

priorities, but with a hidden agenda of quelling political opposition.

daimyo — Territorial lords in feudal Japan under the tutelage of the Shogun.

democracy — Literally popular rule. As such it is compatible with majority balloting, consensus, and other procedures for ascertaining the people's will. In economics, popular determination of state programs, analogous to consumer sovereignty in the marketplace.

democratic free enterprise — In the west, popularly sovereign elected state governance combined with a laissez-faire private sector.

Doi Moi (Renewal) — Vietnam's socialist-oriented market economy reform program begun in 1986. Collectivization was gradually abandoned and private leasing business was encouraged first in the commodities sector and then more broadly.

dukkha (suffering) — One of the Four Buddhist Noble Truths. The claim that existence is suffering or more broadly disquietude.

dystopia — Anti-utopia, sometimes called cacatopia where everything is "perfectly" odious (hell).

economic efficiency — Degree to which the ideal basket of goods is produced, and/or consumed compared to productive or distributive potentials.

economic systems — Cultural, ethical, governance, institutional, property rights, legal and entitlement framework governing rational utility choice opportunities and decisions.

economies of scale	Variations in potential and efficiency associated with increasing or decreasing plant size in the production of a single good.
economies of scope	Variations in potential and efficiency associated with increasing or decreasing the size of distributive networks.
economies of trust	Variations in potential and efficiency associated with increasing or decreasing trust; that is confidence of being treated fairly and appreciated.
egalitarianism	Doctrine advocating that income and wealth be distributed equally to all members of society. Societies with narrow disparities of income and wealth are considered egalitarian. Societies with wide disparities are characterized as inegalitarian.
Eightfold Noble Path	Buddhist prescription for mitigating/solving the problem of *dukkha* (suffering), also called the Middle Way. It requires wisdom, right conduct and right concentration. The eight components are: right view, intention, speech, action, occupation, effort, mindfulness and concentration. These lead to right knowledge and liberation.
endogenous growth	Economic growth governed by diverse public policies in addition to the "natural" advances in science.
Enlightenment	In Buddhism, the belief that individuals can overcome suffering by following the eightfold path. When they fully acquire right knowledge, they are enlightened and liberated. This liberation is transformative, causing the soul of the enlightened being to merge with the cosmic spirit for all eternity surmounting paradox and mystery.

	In the west, the age (18th century) in which philosophers applied reason to discover the ideal possibilities of secular human action including democracy, free enterprise, and social organization.
exportables	The set of goods and services that are or could be exported under various plausible circumstances.
Euroschlerosis	A term linking high European unemployment and slow growth to hardening of the arteries. The pattern first emerged in the mid 1970s and persists today.
false consciousness	The existentialist psychoanalytic claim that most people have limited awareness causing them to conflate their clouded understanding with knowledge.
Falun Gong	A spiritual movement founded by Li Hongzhi in 1992 based on principles of *qigong*, Buddhism and Taoism. China's communist government banned it as a "cult" in 2000. Qi means "life force", and Falun Gong focuses on combining qi with moral rectitude.
family circle (*krugovaya poruka*)	Medieval Russian peasant tradition of mutual obligation and support regarding both tax burdens and group welfare. In Soviet and derivatively North Korean enterprise, it takes on the extended meaning of networks supporting members against the state by concealing capacities and swapping favors.
forced substitution	State or private restrictions compelling some to produce and/or consume sub-optimally.
Four Modernizations	Deng Xiaoping's reform policy goals adopted December 1978 mandating progress in agriculture, industry, national defense and science and technologies.

Four Nobel Truths

Buddhist credo asserting the four basic truths of life are: suffering/disquietude (*dukkha*); the cause of suffering (desire); possibility of overcoming suffering, and the path to its transcendence (Buddha's Eightfold Noble Path).

Gaige Kaifeng

Generic term for Deng Xiaoping's post-Maoist economic, social and foreign policy reforms literally translated as reform and openness. The four modernizations were its centerpiece. It is often referred to as socialism with Chinese characteristics.

Gini coefficient

A measure of statistical dispersion devised by Corrado Gini in 1912 commonly used to measure income or wealth inequality. It is based on the Lorenz curve, with low values indicating relative equality (Denmark 0.247) and high values relative inequality (Namibia 0.707). Most countries fall in a range between 0.24 and 0.36.

globalization

Claim that trade, direct foreign investment, capital flows, migration, transportation and communications are homogenizing the world's economies and societies. In neoclassical economics, the assertion that the globalization phenomenon will modernize and westernize the planet making it democratic, economically efficient, and civically empowered.

grass eating men

Japanese term for contemporary young men uninterested in power, advancement and women, preferring tranquility, fashion and a-sexual pursuits. They are also called herbivores.

Great Leap Forward

Radical Chinese reform strategy devised by Mao Tsetung 1958–1961, harnessing agro-industrial complexes and proletarian zeal for the cause of breakneck economic development. The program caused approximately 35 million premature deaths (killings).

guilt culture

Societies that use the concepts of sin and guilt as self-regulating individual disciplinary mechanisms (conscience). Behavior in guilt cultures is intrinsically right or wrong independent of group attitudes. This makes individuals autonomous.

Gulag

Glavnoe Upravlenie lspravitel'no Trudovykh Lagerei i Kolonii (Chief Directorate of Corrective Labor Camp Administration), a complex of World War I type Soviet concentration camps for imprisoning and "rehabilitating" criminals and enemies of the people through forced labor, initiated June 17, 1929.

harmonious society

In contemporary China, Hu Jintao's vision of the market communist future stressing harmony and prosperity with democracy, rule of law, equity, justice, sincerity, amity and vitality instead of development. The concept which echoes Confucianism, was written into the constitution in 2007 and 2008.

honne

Japanese word for truth (frankness) as distinct from conflict avoiding pleasantries.

household responsibility system

Deng Xiaoping's principle of permitting agrarian households to engage in some private activities in a collective environment, adopted in the late 1970s, and then extended to post-collectivized Chinese agriculture and industry.

humanism (concept of man)

In the western tradition, the idea that men and women have, should discover and actualize their virtuous potentials, instead of being straitjacketed in socially assigned roles.

ichiban	Best, Japanese principle of high quality production, even if extra expense reduces profit.
idea of the east	Diverse familial, communal, imperial and spiritual principles often involving satisficing that form the cultural core of Asian societies.
idea of the west	Essential aspects of western culture like humanism, enlightenment (reason), free enterprise, rule of law and civic empowerment shaping modern economic systems in the west.
imperialism	State governance system ruled without limitation by an emperor (often considered divine), whose edicts are the law. Past Asian empires tend to be viewed positively today while 19th century western imperial intrusions in the east are condemned.
importables	A set of goods and services that are or could be imported under a plausible set of circumstances.
indicative planning	Central plans serving as an aid to government regulation rather than coercive directives.
invisible hand	Adam Smith's concept that individual utility searching, and voluntary negotiated market transactions will enhance social welfare without state direction. The hand guiding these utility searches is invisible, unlike visible state directives.
just wages	Wages sufficient to provide a decent standard of living, even if more than the value of recipient marginal product. The concept is based on equity rather than efficiency considerations.
Keidanren	Japanese Federation of Economic Organizations founded in 1946 to promote big private business. It

was merged with the Nikkeiren (Japanese Federation of Employers) in 2002 to form the amalgamated Japanese Business Federation. Keidanren currently has 1,662 members in 1,343 companies, 130 industrial associations and 47 regional economic development organizations.

keitetsu

Network of Japanese companies with interlocking businesses and cross shareholding, usually coordinated by a "main" bank. The institution was created with the assistance of American occupational authorities as a surrogate for the zaibatsu (large companies pioneered by former feudal potentates during the post-feudal Meiji era).

killing fields

Large number of fields in Cambodia where the Khmer Rouge massacred enemies of the people. The killing fields are a symbol of Pol Pot's red holocaust (1975–79), which claimed about 2.1 million victims, roughly 25% of the population.

laissez-faire

18th century, anti-mercantilist slogan urging government to let business regulate itself.

laogai

Abbreviation for Laodong Gaizao ("reform through labor"), a misnomer for China's Gulag type penal forced labor system. Jung Chang and Jon Halliday estimate that there were 10 million *laogai* inmates on average during Mao Tsetung's reign.

laojiao

An administrative punishment introduced in 1957 involving forced labor in low security facilities. It is a mild version of *laogai*.

Legalism

A Chinese political philosophy that emerged during the period of the Warring States (475–221 BC) expounded by Han Fei Zi in the Book of Lord Shang during the Qin era. It takes the totalitarian position that the emperor is the law; that his edicts govern all behavior; that he should be inscrutable and is not bound by Confucian ethics.

lethal forced labor
Compulsory penal labor that causes prisoners to die prematurely.

liberalization
In economics, a broad term for government deregulation, and laissez-faire promotion.

Libermanism
Post-Stalin, Soviet economic reform movement aimed at creating a terror-free command communist economy through technocratic modernization, including the use of enterprise bonus incentives tied to accounting profits (profitability). The concept was pioneered by Evsei Liberman (1897–1981), a professor at Kharkov University, who became influential in the early 1960s.

Lockean social contract
A concept of democratic state governance devised by John Locke in his second treatise on government (1689) contending that people would be willing to surrender some of their natural liberties to acquire the benefits of political order arbitrated by impartial judges. The principle has been revived by John Rawls in his theory of justice.

lost decade (Japan)
A term used to describe Japan's stagnation 1991–2000 caused by the collapse of its asset bubble during the preceding decade. The initial lost decade has now become a lost two decades, with the economy performing worse than ever.

Marshallian automatic quantity adjustment mechanism
Increases and decreases in production driven by a rational desire to maximize utility whenever profit seeking is incomplete.

Marginalist concept devised by Alfred Marshall (1842–1924), stressing automatic output rather than price adjustments to alleviate excess disequilibrium demand.

main bank — In Japan, banks charged with coordinating the activities of individual keiretsu corporate clusters.

macroeconomic — Branch of economic theory concerned with the effects of money, interest, and aggregate effective demand on employment, production, price level stability and economic growth.

microeconomic theory — Branch of economic theory concerned with individual and collective rational choice in education, training, employment, factor allocation, production, investment, finance, distribution and transfers.

modernization — General term for the process of shifting from traditional to more advanced physical, managerial, administrative, supervisory and entrepreneurial technologies, without violating core cultures.

neoclassical economic theory — Theory that microeconomic behavior is best conceptualized as a rational individual utility search process where wellbeing is incrementally enhanced and choices made at the margin in education, training, employment, factor allocation, production, investment, entrepreneurship, finance, distribution and transfer. These principles can be rigorously expressed in mathematical terms as a "neo" classical reformulation of Adam Smith's invisible hand. Neoclassical economics is *positivistic* and can be applied to command planning as well as competitive markets. It need not be individually based, but this is the standard approach. Neoclassical thinking provides the foundation for concepts like Pareto optimality. These outcomes are derived positivistically, but have a normative aspect allowing theorists to claim that Paretian optimality is individualistically best.

neo-Confucianism   A term variously used to describe evolutionary developments in Confucian doctrine and ritual. The Song dynasty Chinese version mixed Taoist and Buddhist elements with family piety to give Confucianism a more spiritual orientation. The 15th century Joseon Korean manifestation stressed loyalty, family piety, benevolence and trust. There are also several modern schools, one led by Hsiung Shihli (1885–1968) integrating Buddhist elements emphasizing the heart/mind as the first principle of Confucianism, and another represented by Fung Yulan (1895–1990) incorporating western neo-realist philosophy to create Rationalist Confucianism.

New Life Movement   A movement initiated by Chiang Kaishek and his wife Soong Mayling in 1934 to counter communist ideology with an alternative social vision combining Confucianism, anti-capitalism, nationalism and authoritarianism. It was portrayed as furthering Sun Yatsen's people's livelihood program.

non-tradables   Set of goods and services produced domestically thought to be neither importables nor exportables under any plausible set of circumstances.

nirvana   In Buddhism, transcendent enlightenment, a state of total self and cosmic awareness and merging of the soul with the universe. There are numerous alternative characterizations of the same phenomenon, but in all cases nirvana is the highest accomplishment of the human spirit.

ordinality   In economics, natural numbers indicating orderings and ranks. They can be added, multiplied and exponentiated, however the operations do not yield results that are interpersonally comparable. Ordinality is sufficient to support all the principal positive inferences of neoclassical theory, but cannot produce useful measures of social utility and welfare.

outsourcing   Subcontracting to a third party. In contemporary economic discourse, the practice of foreigners supplying components to domestic firms, or producing domestic goods abroad, with the side effect of transferring technology. Host countries often find this to be an especially beneficial form of direct foreign investment. Separately, the term outsourcing is employed to characterize the semi privatization of government services, where traditional state services like the U.S. postal system are provided under contract by a private provider. The practice has benefits, but is also subject to rent-granting and other abuses.

palace *coup d'etat*   Violent seizure of state power by insiders.

Pareto optimality   Multiparty utility optimization and maximization where no party can negotiate a further exchange that makes one party better off, while leaving other parties worse off. The rule defines the terminal move in a multiparty utility enhancing search. When the principle is applied to society, it characterizes a social welfare best with Paretian attributes.

perestroika	Mikhail Gorbachev's program for radical economic leasing market reform, analogous to Deng Xiaoping's marketizing initiatives. Gorbachev tacitly endorsed spontaneously privatization and asset grabbing, but Deng's communist party was more disciplined, enabling China to avoid Soviet style economic collapse.
physical systems management	State economic management system conceived and implemented without prices and markets on an engineering basis. The principle provided the logical structure underpinning Soviet and Asian communist command economies.
planned chaos	Ludwig von Mises's characterization of the physical systems management practices behind the facade of rational command planning. He published a book titled *Planned Chaos* in 1947. Fredrich von Hayek shared similar views in his *Road to Serfdom*, 1944.
political economy	Originally the study of the interaction of institutional, legal and productive processes. Later, a moral perspective on economic systems. Today, the interplay of politics, classes, society, law and economics. The approach de-emphasizes rational choice, and highlights the broad class, societal and political factors shaping productive economic activity.
positivism	In economics, the identification of relationships (posits) linked with utility seeking suggesting cause and effect in education, training, employment, factor allocation, production, investment, finance, distribution and transfers, that do not require normative interpretation. Some argue that perfect correlation proves causality, but often

strong results can be obtained with multiple specifications. Advocates of the method consider this a minor blemish. In philosophy of science, positivism is considered a naive form of realism (see realism).

privilege-granting

Conferring usufruct rights, sinecures and tax-transfers to privilege-seekers.

privilege-seeking

Search for government benefices in the form of usufruct rights, sinecures, tax-transfers, and assets.

proletarian dictatorship

Bolshevik claim that it was the vanguard of the proletariat; that it had the right to speak for the proletariat, and establish an authoritarian regime to repress the people's enemies. The claim was unfalsifiable from the Bolshevik perspective because proletarians who dissented revealed themselves as the people's enemies.

realism

In the theory of economic science, claims that the cogency of theories of education, training, employment, factor allocation, production, investment, entrepreneurship, finance, distribution and transfers depends on the plausibility of causal specifications ascertained by comprehensively testing basic relationships, and their structural linkages. Realism has largely superseded positivism.

red directors

The head of a command economy firm, who receives plan directives, and sub-directs staff and employees. In principle, enterprise heads do not have any managerial discretion because all tasks are scientifically planned. However, in practice red directors formally and informally perform some managerial functions due to the "softness" of plan directives.

Red Guards	In China, a mass, mostly student movement orchestrated by Mao Tsetung to cow foes he claimed lacked revolutionary spirit (redness), and favored anti-communist technocracy. Red guards rampaged throughout China in 1966 and 1967 destroying more cultural assets than the Japanese had 1937–1945.
relativism	In normative economics, recognition that social welfare is a matter of perspective, rather than an absolute. Nonetheless, if norms are well specified, outcomes can be ordinarily ranked. (See Bergsonian social welfare function).
rule of law	In economics, the principle that constitutionally sanctioned contracts provide an inviolable basis assuring that obligations are fulfilled without state supervention (rule of men). The rule of law rule minimizes business risk, and injustice.
rule of men	In economics, the principle that rulers can do as they please undeterred by constitutions and contracts.
Sakoku	Tokugawa Iemitsu's policy of prohibiting Japanese contact with foreigners, except in a few designated ports. The policy was inaugurated in 1635 and lasted until the Convention of Kanagawa in 1858.
salaryman	Term for mid level Japanese corporate employee.
satisficing	Incomplete incremental utility (wellbeing) searching without attempting to compute the likely cost and benefits of additional exploration.
second best	Best constrained equilibrium given diverse institutional restrictions in an otherwise unfettered market regime. It is a positive rather than normative concept.

sensationism	In economic moral philosophy, the rejection of hedonism (sensation, and pleasure seeking) as an accurate description and appropriate base for utility (wellbeing) seeking.
shadow culture	Informal cultural rules governing illicit business, bureaucratic and private behavior.
shame culture	Societies that use the attitudes of authorities, including group consensus as a disciplinary mechanism instead of individual conscience, relying on absolute concepts of good and evil. Reliance on group and authority opinion reduces autonomy because people have no independent basis (right and wrong) for opposing group norms. Transgressors experience shame, rather than guilt because although they have not sinned, they have failed to conform. Japan, Thailand and to some extent South Korea are shame cultures.
social justice	The notion that competitive market outcomes often produce inequities and hardships that are unjust and require rectification. An economy is socially just when the poor and insecure are adequately protected regardless of their low material economic contribution to national income and wealth.
social welfare	The state of societal wellbeing codetermined by self-perceived individual utility and normative judgments about the social merit of economic outcomes. Although, the concept is clear, and alternative outcomes can be rationally appraised, welfare levels cannot be satisfactorily quantified.
soft directives	In command economy, plan directives are supposed to be complete and precise, leaving no room

for recipient discretion. Such directives are "hard". Directives that are incomplete, imprecise and leave room for managerial discretion are "soft".

sovereign	In economics, a term identifying individual(s) or group(s) whose preferences determine the structure of the system and its outcomes.
special economic zones (SEZ)	Zones where liberal commercial and investment laws are adopted to facilitate foreign trade and direct foreign investment while controlling foreign access to the country's interior. Deng Xiaoping introduced SEZs in Shenzhen, Xiamen and a few other port cities in the 1980s as part of his market communist reforms.
state owned enterprise (SOE)	In market communist Asia, enterprises entirely owned by the state (nation), initially restricted to implementing plan directives. They were subsequently permitted to participate in joint ventures with foreigners, and more recently in the sale of equity in the private marketplace. Many SOEs today are *equitized*, with outside equity stakes limited to 49%.
straitjacket society	Term coined by Masao Miyamoto condemning the rigidity of Japanese bureaucracy.
sufficiency economy	Theravada Buddhist inspired concept advocated by Thailand's king counseling people to restrain their material desires, pursue spiritual enlightenment, and live in harmony with the environment.
sunshine culture	Formal cultural rules governing virtuous business, bureaucratic and mundane private behavior.
taizidang	Princelings, affluent children of China's communist elites who have acquired their fortunes

through privilege-granting, privilege-seeking and privilege-controlling.

tatemae

The principle of making palatable public statements to avoid conflict or postpone dealing with the truth *honne*. Ingratiation is not primary.

Taylorism

Scientific enterprise efficiency management techniques devised by the American Fredrick Winslow Taylor in the 1880s, advocated by Vladimir Lenin.

technical efficiency

Degree to which any bundle of goods approximates its production potential, or the counterfactual equilibrium distribution frontier. Full equilibria are both technically and economically efficient.

technological progress

Productivity growth attributable to advances in technology.

Theravada Buddhism

The oldest surviving branch of Buddhism founded at the Third Buddhist Council around 250 BC. It is the predominant religion in Sri Lanka, Cambodia, Thailand, Laos, and Myanmar. Its primary tenets are the Four Noble Truths and the Eightfold Path.

tigers

Asian advanced industrial economies, the four little dragons are: Taiwan, South Korea, Singapore and Hong Kong said to have enjoyed miraculous growth because of their Confucian Asian values.

town village enterprises (TVE)

Market oriented public enterprises with private aspects operating under the supervision of towns and villages. Although, originally introduced in China by Mao Tsetung during the Great Leap Forward TVEs were transformed into market oriented institutions in 1978 by Deng Xiaoping. They mushroomed for nearly 20 years and then morphed into semi-private individual farms and businesses.

transition economies
Term presuming that post-communist reforms in Russia, central and eastern Europe, and Asia will propel them toward democratic free enterprise.

utility
In neoclassical economic theory, a psychological perception of usefulness (or from a hedonistic perspective, pleasure) that motivates rational economic choice making. The notion is deduced from people's ability to establish and rank preferences and is essential for the validity of the neoclassical vision.

Walrasian automatic price adjustment
Increases and decreases in prices (wages) driven by utility maximizing achieved through direct negotiation and auctions that establish allocative and inventory equilibrium in the labor and retail markets. The idea was first rigorously formulated by Leon Walras (1834–1910).

Weberian administration
Concept of rational public administration based on incorruptible performance of clearly defined administrative procedures devised by Max Weber, a German economist in *Economy and Society*, 1922.

welfare state
A system of state governance intended to advance national welfare. In contemporary usage, a free enterprise economic system with social democratic type income transfers and safety net, without an explicit socialist ideology.

wellbeing
A concept akin to utility that takes explicit account of non-hedonistic aspects of economic betterment, including ethics. Wellbeing involves a judgment about the composite effect of diverse utilitarian

experiences. Its connotation is more humanistic than the term welfare.

westernization   A process transforming traditional into western societies through cultural replacement. The cultural fundamentals of the west start with the notion that men and women should discover and actualize their individual potentials. They may take the consequences of their behavior on others into account, but resist unwarranted external pressure to accept assigned roles. Complete utility maximizing search is a corollary of full self-actualization. Also, westerners prize democracy and human empowerment. Cultures which subordinate these priorities cannot be western.

Sages and Rulers

Chiang Kaishek (1887–1975)

Supreme Leader of the Kuomintang after Sun Yatsen's death (1925), and ruler of Nationalist China 1928–1949; later President of the Republic of China (Taiwan) 1949–1975). His regime combined military dictatorship and nationalism with expressions of concern for social welfare. Private ownership and business were permitted, constrained by Confucian and socialist considerations.

Deng Xiaoping (1904–1997)

Paramount leader of China 1978–1997, but never held highest positions in the Communist Party or the state. Responsible for guiding China away from terror-command to stable market communism after Mao Tsetung's death. Deng succeeded where Gorbachev failed by maintaining discipline over insider asset seizing.

Gorbachev, Mikhail (1931–)

Last Soviet President, responsible for the economy's collapse and the USSR's disunion. He relied on Khrushchevian terrorless communism 1985 until 1987, and then switched to perestroika (radical economic reform). Leasing markets *arenda* were gradually introduced without disruption until insiders were given a green light to privatize state assets to themselves and hoard causing the economy to implode.

Emperor Hirohito (1901–1989)

Showa Emperor. He supported the Second Sino–Japanese War without qualms, but sanctioned war with America more reluctantly.

Hu Jintao (1942–)

Paramount leader of China since 2002 when he assumed the position of General Secretary of the Communist Party. He has pressed Deng Xiaoping pragmatic approach to constructing market communism with increasing sophistication under the banner of prosperity and a harmonious society. He was succeeded by Xi Jinping in 2012.

Hun Sen (1951–)

Prime Minister of Cambodia since 1979, key leader of the Cambodian People's Party since 1979, and former low level Khmer Rouge commander who participated in the Kampuchean holocaust. He collaborated with the Vietnamese to overthrow Pol Pot.

Khrushchev, Nikita (1894–1971)

First Secretary of the Communist Party of the Soviet Union 1953–1964; Chairman of the Council of Ministers 1958–1964. Substituted terror-free command communism for Stalin's terror-command. Tried to modernize while preserving the criminalization of private property, business and entrepreneurship. The experiment, considered an anathema by Mao and Kim Il sung, ended under Gorbachev in 1987.

Kim Il-sung (1912–1994)

Supreme Leader of North Korea (1948–1994), initially installed by Stalin in 1946 as head of Soviet occupied Korea. Kim was a captain in the Red Army and a long time Stalinist communist. He adopted Stalin's terror-command approach to governance, compatible with the ancient Legalist tradition.

Kim Jong-il (1941–2011)

Supreme Leader of North Korea, and General Secretary of the Workers' Party (Marxist–Leninist) since 2011. He is the second generation of the new Kim dynasty. He ruled in a despotic, Legalist manner.

Kim Jong-un (1983–)

Supreme Leader of North Korea, and General Secretary of the Workers' Party (Marxist–Leninist) since 1994. He is Kim Jong-un's illegitimate youngest son and the third generation of the Kim dynasty.

Kong Fuzi (Confucius 551–479 BC)

Chinese philosopher who sought to build beneficent imperial governance on extended family loyalty and virtue.

Lenin, Vladimir (1870–1924)

Russian communist leader; founder of the Bolshevik Party and Head of the Soviet State 1917–1924. Following Engels and Marx, he criminalized Russian private property, business and entrepreneurship, replacing it with command economy, and one party rule. He experimented with a limited form of market leasing communism (NEP), but it is still debated whether this was a tactic, or a preferred alternative to command-communism.

Mao Tsetung (1893–1976)

Founder of the People's Republic of China (1949) and Chairman of the Communist Party 1949–1976. Responsible for the Chinese variant of terror-command, the Great Leap Forward, and the Cultural Revolution.

Marx, Karl (1818–1883)

Utopian communist philosopher, whose dialectical materialism and market-driven, labor exploitation theory became the holy grail for 19th and

20th century working class/intelligentsia movements aimed at establishing socialist and communist economic systems.

Qin Shi Huang (259–210 BC)

First Emperor of Unified China (221 BC). Ruled in the Legalist command-despotic manner, and in this sense Mao's historical predecessor.

Stalin, Joseph (1878–1953)

General Secretary of the Soviet Union's Communist Party 1922–1953. Founder of terror-command communist governance (1929), adapted from Vladimir Lenin's War Communism.

Sun Yatsen (1866–1825)

Chinese revolutionary. First provisional President of China (post Ching dynasty) in 1912, and Father of the Nation. Founder of the Kuomintang. His philosophy was 19th century socialist romanticism stressing nationalism, democracy and social welfare, subject to a wide variety of expedient interpretations.

Bibliography

Aganbegyan, A (1989). *Inside Perestroika: The Future of the Soviet Economy.* New York: Harper and Row.

Akiyoshi, F and K Kobayashi (2008). Banking crisis and productivity of borrowing firms: Evidence from Japan. *REITI Discussion Paper.*

Amnesty International (2011). Irrefutable satellite evidence of prison camps in North Korea. April.

Aoki, M (2001). *Information, Corporate Governance and Institutional Diversity.* London: Oxford University Press.

Aoki, M (1988). *Information, Incentives and Bargaining in the Japanese Economy.* Oxford: Oxford University Press.

Aoki, M (2001). *Toward a Comparative Institutional Analysis.* Cambridge MA: MIT Press.

Aoki, M and R Dore (1994). *The Japanese Main Bank System.* Oxford: Clarendon Press.

Aoki, M, H-K Kim and M Okuno-Fujiwara (1996). *The Role of Government in East Asian Economic Development.* Oxford: Clarendon Press.

Aoki, M, J Gregory and H Miyajima (eds.) (2007). *Corporate Governance in Japan: Institutional Change and Organizational Diversity.* Oxford: Oxford University Press.

Arrow, K (1950). A difficulty in the concept of social welfare. *Journal of Political Economy*, 58(4), 328–346.

Arrow, K (1981). Optimal and voluntary income distribution. In *Economic Welfare and the Economics of Soviet Socialism*, S Rosefielde (ed.). Cambridge: Cambridge University Press.

Bate, R (2009). What is prosperity and how do we measure it? *AEI*, 27th October.

Bergson, A (1938). A reformulation of certain aspects of welfare economics. *Quarterly Journal of Economics*, 52(1).

Bergson, A (1954). On the concept of social welfare. *Quarterly Journal of Economics*, 68, 233–252.

Bergson, A (1966). *Essays in Normative Economics*. Cambrdige, MA: Harvard University Press.

Bergson, A (1967). Market socialism revisited. *Journal of Political Economy*, 75(4).

Bergson, A (1976). Social choice under representative government. *Journal of Public Economics*, 6(3).

Bhongmakapat, T (2012). Buddhist crisis prevention and management. In *Prevention and Crisis Management: Lessons for Asia from the 2008 Crisis*, S Rosefielde, M Kuboniwa and S Mizobata (eds.). Singapore: World Scientific Publishers.

Breslin, S (2011). China and the crisis: Global power, domestic caution and local initiative. *Contemporary Politics*, 17(2), 185–200.

Breslin, S (2011). The China model and the global crisis: From friedrich list to a Chinese mode of governance? *International Affairs*, 87(6), 1323–1343.

Brown, A (2009). *The Rise and Fall of Communism*. London: Bodley Head.

Buckley, C (2012). Briton killed after threat to expose Chinese leader's wife. *Yahoo!News,* 17 April.

Bukharin, N (1926). *Building Up Socialism*. London: Communist Party of Great Britain.

Burdett, J (2003). *Bangkok 8: A Novel.* New York: Alfred A. Knopf.

Chan, G H-S (2008). The development of social welfare policy in taiwan: Welfare debates between the left and the right. *Working Paper*, Doshisha University, Kyoto.

Chan, WT (1986). *Chu Hsi and Neo-Confucianism*. Honolulu: University of Hawaii Press.

Chang, J and Halliday, J (2005). *Mao: The Unknown Story, Jonathan Cape.* London: Jonathan Cape.

Chatterjee, SR and AR Nankervis (eds.) (2007). *Asian Management in Transition: Emerging Themes.* New York: Palgrave Macmillan.

Chien, TL and T Quang (2005). Human resource management practices in a transitional economy: A comparative study of enterprise ownership forms in Vietnam. *Asia Pacific Business Review*, 11(1).

Chin, A (2007). *The Authentic Confucius, A Life of Thought and Politics*. New York: Scribner.

Chol-Hwan, K and P Rigoulot (2001). *The Aquariums of Pyongyang*. Basic Books.

CIA (2009). *World Factbook*. Vietnam.

Collins, NT (2009). *Economic Reform and Employment Relations in Vietnam*. Abingdon: Routledge.

Confucius (2003). Confucius: Analects — with *Selections from Traditional Commentaries*. Indianapolis: Hackett.

Confucius. *The Great Learning*, quoted in Will Durant, The Story of Civilization, Vol. 1, Our Oriental Heritage.

Constans, G (2009). *Buddha's Wife*. San Francisco, CA: Robert Reed Publishers.

Cooke, FL (2005). *HRM, Work, and Employment in China*. London: Routledge.

Crisp, R (2006). *Reasons and the Good*. Oxford: Clarendon Press.

Dan Oh, K and R Hassig (2000). *North Korea Through the Looking Glass*. Washington, DC: Brookings Institution Press.

Descartes, R (1641). *Meditations on First Philosophy*.

Domar, E (1966). The soviet collective farm as a producer co-operative. *American Economic Review*.

Donne, J (1624). *Emergent Occasions*. Meditation 17.

Dorfman, R, P Samuleson and R Solow (1958). *Linear Programming and Economic Analysis*. New York: McGraw Hill.

Downs, C (1999). *Over the Line: North Korea's Negotiating Strategy*. Washington, DC: AEI Press.

Eberstadt, N (2009). China's family planning goes awry. *Far Eastern Economic Review*, 4th December.

Eberstadt, N (2009). What to read on North Korean politics. *Foreign Affairs*, 23rd October.

Erlich, A (1960). *The Soviet Industrialization Debate, 1924-28*. Cambridge MA: Harvard University Press.

Esping-Andersen, G (1999). *Social Foundations of Postindustrial Economies*. New York: Oxford University Press.

Etzioni, A (2010). Behavioral economics: A methodological note. *Journal of Economic Psychology*, 31.

Forsberg, A (2000). *America and the Japanese Miracle*. Chapel Hill: University of North Carolina Press.

Forsythe, M (2012). China's billionaire lawmakers make U.S. peers look like paupers. *Bloomberg News*, 27 February.

Freud, S (2002). *Civilization and its Discontents*. London: Penguin.

Fromm, E, DT Suzuki and R De Martino (1960). *Zen Buddhism and Psychoanalysis*. New York: Harper Colophon Books.

Fukuyama, F (1992). *The End of History and the Last Man Standing*. New York: Harper.

Fukuyama, F (1995). *Trust: The Social Virtues and the Creation of Prosperity*. New York: Free Press.

Fung, Y-L (1952–1953). *A History of Chinese Philosophy*. Princeton NJ: Princeton University Press.

Fureng, D (1986). China's price reform. *Cambridge Journal of Economics*, 10, 291–300.

Gainsborough, M (2007). From patronage politics to outcomes: Vietnam's communist party congress reconsidered. *Journal of Vietnamese Studies*, 2(1), 3–26.

Gandhi, J and A Przeworski (2006). Cooperation, Cooptation, and rebellion under dictatorships. *Economics and Politics*, 19(1), 1–26.

Gerschenkron, A (1962). *Economic Backwardness in Historical Perspective*. Cambridge Mass: Harvard University Press.

Gini, C (1921). Measurement of the inequality of incomes. *The Economic Journal*, 31.

Greenberg, G and M Haraway (1998). *Comparative Psychology: A Handbook*. London: Routledge.

Griffin, J (1986). *Well-being*. Oxford: Clarendon Press.

Gustafsson, B, L Shi and T Sicular (eds.) (2008). *Inequality and Public Policy in China*. New York: Cambridge University Press.

Haggard, S and M Noland (2007). *Famine in North Korea: Markets, Aid, and Reform*. New York: Columbia University Press.

Haggard, S and M Noland (2007). North Korea's external economic relations, Working Paper WP 07-7, Washington, DC: The Peterson Institute for International Economics, August.

Hare, P (2007). Industrial policy for North Korea — Lessons from transition. *International Journal of Korean Unification Studies*.

Harre, R (1972). *The Philosophy of Science*. London: Oxford University Press.

Harre, R and PF Secord (1975). *The Explanation of Social Behavior*. New York: Humanities Press.

Haybron, D (2008). *The Pursuit of Unhappiness*. Oxford: Clarendon Press.

Herbert, S (1956). Rational choice and the structure of the environment. *Psychological Review*, 63(2), 129–138.

Hobbes, T (1651). *The Leviathan, or the Matter, Form and Power of a Commonwealth, Ecclesiastical or Civil.* London, UK: Andrew Crooke.

Hsueh, R (2011). *China's Regulatory State: A New Strategy for Globalization.* Ithaca NY: Cornell University Press.

Huang, Y (2011). Rethinking the Beijing consensus, Asian Policy, No. 11.

Huchet, J-F and X Richet (2001). Between bureaucracy and market: Chinese industrial groups in search of new forms of corporate governance, Paper Presented at the American Economics Meetings, New Orleans, 6th January.

Huntington, S (1996). *The Clash of Civilizations and the Remaking of the World Order.* New York: Simon and Schuster.

Huntington, S (1996). The west: Unique, not universal. *Foreign Affairs*, 75(6).

Jae-Ku, C (2010). AFP. 18 March.

Japan's Samurai back in vogue (29 October 2009). *Economist.*

Jean, O (1992). Fiscal reform and the economic foundations of local state corporatism. *World Politics*, 45.

Jiang, L (2007). Can a hypocritically benevolent government go on for long? *Xin shiji*, March.

Johnson, C (1982). *MITI and the Japanese Miracle: The Growth of Industrial Policy, 1925–1975.* Stanford: Stanford University Press.

Kelley, L (2006). Confucianism in vietnam: A state of the field essay. *Journal of Vietnamese Studies*, 1(1), 314–371.

Kenneth, A (1963). *Social Choice and Individual Values*, 2nd Ed. New York: Wiley.

Kim, B-Y, Kim, SJ and K Lee (2007). Assessing the economic performance of North Korea, 1954–1989: Estimates and growth accounting analysis. *Journal of Comparative Economics*, 35(3), 564–582.

Kinzley, WD (1991). *Industrial Harmony in Modern Japan: The Invention of a Tradition.* London: Routledge.

Koo, H (2002). Civil society and democracy in South Korea. *The Good Society*, 11(2), 40–45.

Kraut, R (2007). *What is Good and Why.* Cambridge, MA: Harvard University Press.

Krugman, P (1994). The myth of Asia's miracle. *Foreign Affairs*, 73(6), 62–79.

Kuan, X (2004). How has the literature on Gini's index evolved in the past 80 years? *China Economic Quarterly*, 2.

Kudo, T and F Mieno (2007). Trade, foreign investment and Myanmar's economic development during the transition to an open economy. *Institute of Developing Economics Discussion Paper* No. 116.

Kung and Lin (2007). The decline of township-and-village enterprises in China's economic transition. *World Development*, 35(4).

Lan, J Y-C (2009). The politics of taiwanese welfare state transformation: Postindustrial pressures, regime shifts and social policy responses in the 1990s and beyond. Department of Public Policy and Management, I-Shou University Working Paper.

Landes, D (1999). *The Wealth and Poverty of Nations: Why Some are so Rich and Some so Poor*. New York: Norton.

Landes, D (2000). Culture makes almost all the difference. In *Culture Matters: How Values Shape Human Progress*, L Harrison and S Huntington (eds.). New York: Basic Books.

Landes, D (2000). Culture matters: How values shape human progress. In *Culture Makes Almost all the Difference*, L Harrison and S Huntington (eds.). New York: Basic Books.

Lange, O and FM Taylor (1938). *On the Economic Theory of Socialism*. Ann Arbor MI: University of Michigan Press.

Lankov, A (2007). *North of the DMZ: Essays on Daily Life in North Korea*. Jefferson, North Carolina: McFarland & Company.

Lee, H-S (2001). *North Korea: A Strange Socialist Fortress*. Westport, Connecticut, US: Praeger Publishers.

Lee, J (2009). Associated Press. 31 December.

Lenin, VI (1918). *Democracy The Proletarian Revolution and the Renegade Kautsky: Bourgeois and Proletarian Democracy*.

Liberman, EG (1971). *Economic Methods and the Effectiveness of Production*. White Plains, New York: International Arts and Sciences Publications.

Lipsey, R (2009). Some legacies of robbins an essay on the nature and significance of economic science, *Economica*, 76(1).

Lipsey, RG and K Lancaster (1957). The general theory of second best. *Review of Economic Studies*, 24(1), 1956–1957.

Locke, J (1641). *An Essay Concerning Human Understanding*.

Lorenz, E (1988). Neither friends nor strangers: Informal networks of subcontracting in French industry. In *Trust: Making and Breaking Cooperative Relations*, D Gambetta (ed.). New York: Blackwell.

Maddison, A (2003). *The World Economy: Historical Statistics*. Paris: OECD.

Mahbubani, K (2008). The case against the west. *Foreign Affairs*, 87(3).

McNally, C (2008). *China's Emergent Political Economy: Capitalism in the Dragon's Lair*. New York: Routledge.

Meade, J (1978). *The Just Economy*. London: George Allen and Unwin.

Michael, M (2009). *Orientalism and Islam: European Thinkers on Oriental Despotism in the Middle East and India*. New York: Cambridge University Press.

Miyamoto (1995). *Straitjacket Society: An Insider's Irreverent View of Bureaucratic Japan*. Tokyo: Kodansha International.

More, T (2002). *Utopia*, G Logan and R Adams (eds.). Cambridge: Cambridge University Press.

Morita, K and C Yun (2012). China-Japan cooperation. In *Prevention and Crisis Management: Lessons for Asia from the 2008 Crisis*, S Rosefielde, M Kuboniwa and S Mizobata (eds.). Singapore: World Scientific Publishers.

Myrdal, G (1968). *The Asian Drama: An Inquiry in the Poverty of Nations*, 3 Volumes. New York: Pantheon.

Nanto, DK and E Chanlett-Avery (2007). The North Korean economy: Overview and policy analysis. *CRS Report for Congress*, Congressional Research Service, Washington, DC.

Naughton, B (2007). *The Chinese Economy: Transitions and Growth*. Cambridge MA: MIT Press.

Neumann, JV and O Morgenstern (2007). *Theory of Games and Economic Behavior* (Commenorative Edition). New Jersey, USA: Princeton University Press.

Nietzsche, F (1954). *Thus spoke Zarathustra*. New York: Random House.

Nietzsche, F (1966). *Beyond Good and Evil: Prelude to a Philosophy of the Future* (Jenseits von Gut und Bose: Vorspiel einer Philosphie der Zunkunft). New York: Random House.

Nietzsche, F (1988). *Ecce. Homo: How One Becomes What One Is* (Ecce Homo: Wie man wird, was man ist).

North, D (1990). *Institutions, Institutional Change and Economic Performance*. Cambridge: Cambridge University Press.

North, D (1993). Economic performance through time. In *Nobel Prize Lecture*, The Nobel Foundation.

North, DC and R Thomas (1973). *The Rise of the Western World: A New Economic History*. Cambridge: Cambridge University Press.

Nozick, R (1974). *Anarchy, State and Utopia*. Oxford: Basil Blackwell.

Nussbaum, M and Sen, A (eds.) (1993). *The Quality of Life*. Oxford: Clarendon Press.

OECD (2008). Growing unequal: Income distribution and poverty in OECD countries. Country Note: Japan.

Ouyyanont, P (2007). How Thailand's royals manage to own all the good stuff. *Asia Sentinel*, 2nd March.

Ouyyanont, P (2008). The crown property bureau in Thailand and the crisis of 1997. *Journal of Contemporary Asia*, 28(1).

Pareto, V (1906). *Manuel of Political Economy*.

Paul, G and K Zhou (2009). How China won and Russia lost. *Hoover Institution Policy Journal*.

Paus, E, P Prime and J Western (2009). *Global Giant: Is China Changing the Rules of the Game?* Basingstoke: Palgrave Macmillan.

Peng, I (2004). Postindustrial pressures, political regime shifts and social policy in Japan and South Korea. *Journal of East Asian Studies*, 4(3).

Phongpaichit, P and C Baker (1998). *Thailand's Boom and Bust*. Chiang Mai: Silkworm Books.

Phongpaichit, P and C Baker (2004). *Thaksin: The Business of Politics in Thailand*. Chiang Mai: Silkworm Press.

Promta, S (2007). Morality, body and mind. *The Chulalongkorn Journal of Buddhist Studies*, 6(1).

Quinn-Judge, S (2006). Vietnam's bumpy road to reform. *Current History*.

Ramo, J (2004). The Beijing consensus. *Foreign Policy Centre*, May.

Razin, A and S Rosefielde (2010). Global financial crisis 2008 and beyond: A rude awakening. *Israel Economic Review*, 8(2).

Razin, A and S Rosefielde (2012). What really ails the Eurozone?: Faulty supranational architecture, *Contemporary Economics*, 4.

Razin, A and S Rosefielde (2012). A tale of a politically-failing single-currency area, *Israel Economic Review*, 10(1).

Rigoulot, P (1999). Crimes, terror and secrecy in North Korea. In *The Black Book of Communism*, S Courtois, *et al.* (eds.), Cambridge: Harvard University Press.

Romer, P (1990). Endogenous technological change. *Journal of Political Economy*, 98(5), S71–S102.

Rosefielde, S (1970). Economic theory in the excluded middle between positivism and rationalism. *Atlantic Economic Journal*, 4.

Rosefielde, S (1979). Post positivist scientific method and the appraisal of nonmarket economic behavior. *Quarterly Journal of Ideology*.

Rosefielde, S (2005). Russia: An abnormal country. *The European Journal of Comparative Economics*, 2(1), 3–16.

Rosefielde, S (2007). The illusion of westernization in Russia and China. *Comparative Economic Studies*, 49, 495–513.

Rosefielde, S (2007). *The Russian Economy from Lenin to Putin*. Oxford: Blackwell.

Rosefielde, S (2010). *Red Holocaust*. London: Routledge.

Rosefielde, S (2010). *Russia's Aborted Transition: 7,000 Days and Counting,"* Mezhdunarodnaya konferetsiya, Institutsional'naya ekonomika: razvitie, predpodavannie, prilozheniya, 17–18, Noyabrya 2009, Moskva, conference volume.

Rosefielde, S (2012). The impossibility of russian economic reform: Waiting for godot. In *Russian Reform*, S Blank (ed.). U.S. Army War College.

Rosefielde, S and DQ Mills (2013). *Democracy and its Elected Enemies: Political Capture and America's Economic Decline*. Cambridge: Cambridge University Press.

Rosefielde, S and RW Pfouts (1986). The firm in Illyria: Market syndicalism revisited. *Journal of Comparative Economics*, 10(2).

Rosefielde, S and RW Pfouts (1988). Economic optimization and technical efficiency in soviet enterprises jointly regulated by plans and incentives. *European Economic Review*, 32(6).

Rosefielde, S and S Hedlund (2009). *Russia Since 1980*. Cambridge: Cambridge University Press.

Rosefielde, S, J-R Chen and M Hakogi (2012). Asian union. In *Prevention and Crisis Management: Lessons for Asia from the 2008 Crisis*, S Rosefielde, M Kuboniwa and S Mizobata (eds.). Singapore: World Scientific Publishers.

Rosefielde, S, S Mizobata and M Kuboniwa (2011). *Two Asias: The Emerging Postcrisis Divide*. Singapore: World Scientific.

Rozman, G (ed.) (1991). *The East Asian Region: Confucian Heritage and its Modern Adaption*. Princeton NJ: Princeton University Press.

Samuelson, P (ed.) (1966). Optimal compacts for redistribution. In *Collected Scientific Papers*, Vol. 4, Chapter 257. Cambridge: MIT Press.

Samuelson, P. Reaffirming the existence of a reasonable bergson-samuelson social welfare function. *Economica*, 44.

Sandel, M (1998). *Democracy's Discontent: America in Search of a Public Philosophy*. Cambridge MA: Belknap Press of Harvard University Press.

Sandel, M (1998). *Liberty and the Limitations of Justice*. Cambridge: Cambridge University Press.

Sandel, M (2009). *Justice: What is the Right Thing to Do?* New York: Farrar, Straus and Giroux.

Scalapino, R and L Chang-Sik (1972). *Communism in Korea*, Vols. I and II. Berkeley, California: University of California Press.

Schroeder, G (1979). Soviet economy on a treadmill of reform. In *Soviet Economy in a Time of Change*, Vol. 1, pp. 312–40. Washington, DC: US Congress, Joint Economic Committee.

Schumpeter, J (1942). *Capitalism, Socialism and Democracy*. New York: Harper.

Sen, A (1977). *Rational Fools: A Critique of the Behavioral Foundations of Economic Theory*. Princeton, New Jersey: Princeton University Press.

Shirk, S (1993). *The Political Logic of Economic Reform in China*. Berkeley: University of California.

Shleifer, A (2005). *A Normal Country: Russia After Communism*. Cambridge: Harvard University Press.

Shleifer, A and D Treisman (2004). A normal country. *Foreign Affairs*, 84(2), March/April.

Shram, P (1969). *The Development of Chinese Agriculture, 1950–59*. Champaign, Illinois: University of Illinois Press.

Solow, R (1956). A contribution to the theory of economic growth. *Quarterly Journal of Economics*, 70(1).

Solow, R (1957). Technological change and the aggregate production function. *Review of Economics and Statistics*, 3(3).

Sricharatchanya, P (1988). *The Jewels of the Crown*.

Stokes, M (1997). *Apology of Socrates*. Warminster: Aris and Phillips.

Sugden, R (2009). Can economics be founded on indisputable facts of experience. *Economica*, 76(1).

Tawney, RH (1920). *The Sickness of the Acquisitive Society*. New York: Harcourt, Brace and Company.

Tselichtchev, I (2012). *China versus the West: The Global Power Shift of the 21st Century*. Singapore: John Wiley & Sons.

Tselichtchev, I and P Debroux (2009). *Asia's Turning Point: An Introduction to Asia's Dynamic Economies at the Dawn of the New Century*. Singapore: John Wiley and Sons.

Vu, K (2009). Economic reform and growth performance: China and Vietnam in comparison. *China: An International Journal*, 7(2).

Weber, M (1947). *The Theory of Social and Economic Organization*. New York: The Free Press.

Williamson, J (1993). Development and the Washington consensus. *World Development*, 21, 1239–1336.

Williamson, J (2012). Is the Beijing consensus now dominant? *Asian Policy*, No. 13, January.

Wong, CPW (1988). Interpreting rural industrial growth in the post-mao period. *Modern China* 14(1).

Woo, WT (2007). The real challenges to China's high growth: Institutions, poverty, inequality, environment and fiscal balance. *Comparative Economic Studies*, 49.

World Bank (2007). *World Development Indicators*. Washington DC: World Bank.

World Bank (2012). *China 2030: Building a Modern, Harmonious, and Creative High-Income Society*.

Wright, A (1961). *Confucianism and Chinese Civilization*. Stanford: Stanford University Press.

Xu, G (2011). State-owned enterprises in China: How big are they? *World Bank Blog*, 19 January.

Zhou, H (2010). Empirical research on China's capital flight: A China case study. Honors Thesis, Peking University.

Index